Managing organisations in 1992

The single European market will have a profound impact on our thinking about the structure of our industries and the nature of European competition. Its effects will be felt among both consumers and those concerned with running competitive businesses. *Managing Organisations in 1992* contributes to our understanding of management theory and practice and identifies some implications of the single market across a range of strategic and operational concerns.

The volume is divided into three sections: I. International Business and 1992; II. Corporate Performance and Management Control; III. Decision-making and Implementation. Chapters cover a range of industries, from financial services to microcomputers and machine tools. Key issues of concern to practising managers and academics alike are addressed: such as strategic and financial management, technological collaboration, international competitiveness, international marketing and corporate performance.

Managing Organisations in 1992 presents insights from some of the UK's leading academics in the field of management into a wide range of issues crucial to European organisations post 1992. It will appeal to all those involved in the theory and practice of management and in particular those seeking to grasp the implications that the single market provisions will have for managers.

Managing organisations in 1992

Strategic responses

Edited by
Peter Barrar
and Cary L. Cooper

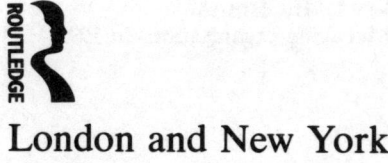

London and New York

First published in 1992
by Routledge
11 New Fetter Lane, London EC4P 4EE

Simultaneously published in the USA and Canada
by Routledge
a division of Routledge, Chapman and Hall, Inc.
29 West 35th Street, New York, NY 10001

Typeset in Times Roman by
Falcon Typographic Art Ltd, Edinburgh & London
Printed in Great Britain by
Mackays of Chatham PLC, Chatham, Kent

British Library Cataloguing in Publication Data
Managing organisations in 1992: strategic responses.
  I. Barrar, Peter II. Cooper, Cary L. (Cary Lynn),
  1940–
  658.4

Library of Congress Cataloging in Publication Data
Managing organisations in 1992: strategic responses/edited by
  Peter Barrar and Cary L. Cooper.
  p. cm.
  Based on papers presented at the third national conference of the
  British Academy of Management, held Sept. 1989 at Manchester
  Business School.
  Includes bibliographic references and index.
  1. Industrial management – Great Britain – Congresses.
  2. Management – Great Britain – Congresses. 3. European
  Economic Community – Great Britain – Congresses.
  4. Europe 1992 – Congresses.
  I. Barrar, Peter, 1946–. II. Cooper, Cary L. III. British
  Academy of Management. IV. Title: Managing organisations in 1992.
  HD70.G7M33   1992
  658.4'012—dc20   91–21541   CIP
ISBN 0–415–06662–X

Contents

Part II Corporate performance and management control

Part III Decision-making and implementation

Figures

Tables

Contributors

Beverly Alimo-Metcalfe is Senior Lecturer in Occupational Psychology at The Nuffield Institute for Health Service Studies, University of Leeds.

Peter J. Buckley is Professor of Managerial Economics at the University of Bradford Management Centre.

Val Brophy is at The Management School, Imperial College, University of London.

Sandra Dawson is Professor of Organisational Behaviour at The Management School, Imperial College, University of London.

Stewart Dunlop is at the Fraser of Allander Institute, University of Strathclyde.

Peter Grinyer is at the University of St Andrews & University of St Andrews Management Institute.

Mairi Gudim is at the Department of Economics and Management, Paisley College.

Neil Hood is Professor of Business Policy, Department of Marketing, University of Strathclyde.

Stephen G. Longden is Lecturer in Finance and Accounting at the Aston Business School, Aston University.

Peter McKiernan is Senior Lecturer in Marketing and Strategic Management at the Warwick Business School, University of Warwick.

Robert van der Meer is at the Strathclyde Business School, University of Strathclyde.

Susan Miller is at the Organizational Analysis Research Unit, University of Bradford Management Centre.

C. L. Pass is at the University of Bradford Management Centre.

Kate Prescott is at the University of Bradford Management Centre.

Gerard Puccio is at the Center for Studies in Creativity, State University College at Buffalo.

Tudor Rickards is Senior Lecturer in Creativity at the Manchester Business School, University of Manchester.

Claire Shearman is at the Information Technology Institute, University of Salford.

Marilyn A. Stone is at the Heriot–Watt Business School, Department of Business Organisation, Heriot-Watt University, Edinburgh.

Barbara Townley is Associate Professor in the Department of Organisational Analysis, Faculty of Business, University of Alberta, Edmonton, Canada.

Barry Witcher is Research Programme Director of the Durham University Business School.

Roy Wilkie is at the Department of Human Resource Management, University of Strathclyde.

Stephen Young is a Professor of Marketing and Director of Strathclyde International Business Unit, Department of Marketing, University of Strathclyde.

Preface

For organisations throughout the European Community, '1992' heralds the establishment of a single internal market. The objective of the European Council is, to have achieved by 1992, 'an area without internal frontiers in which the free movement of goods, persons, services and capital is ensured'.

Three particular categories of non-tariff barriers to achieving this objective will be largely abolished by the single market. These are: (1) the physical barriers to free movement imposed at national frontiers by customs formalities and controls, (2) the fiscal barriers caused by differing rates of indirect taxation between member countries, and (3) the technical barriers caused by differing national standards, certification procedures and regulations. These largely relate to health and safety provisions and consumer protection. Also, the barriers created by differing public sector and governmental procurement policies favouring national suppliers.

The effects of removing these barriers has been estimated by the European Commission to be substantial. An increase in the total GDP of the community of between 4 per cent and 5 per cent within eight years, reductions in transportation and administration costs, the removal of anti-competitive tendering policies and the opening-up of larger markets to scale benefits, in particular, by the removal of technical barriers. Thus, the benefits of increased competition will flow through to consumers throughout the Community.

However, these benefits will not be equally shared within the Community. The effects of increased competition will lead to increased markets and opportunities for some organisations and, inevitably, to loss of markets for others. There will be a redistribution of markets and employment between competitors within industry sectors. The structure and location of industries will change with new alliances, exits and new entrants as firms strive for greater operational efficiencies and benefits of scale. Hence, for individual organisations there are tremendous opportunities presented by the single market – but, the 'downside' is that there are also significant threats in the event of an inability on the part of managers to respond effectively to the conditions created by the removal of barriers within the market.

A number of the more significant issues arising from this new economic order are addressed in this book. Three main themes have been chosen within which to reflect some of the concerns of managers preparing for the single market. The themes are:

1 International business and 1992
2 Corporate performance and management control
3 Decision-making and implementation

These themes were pursued at the third national conference of the British Academy of Management in September 1989 at Manchester Business School. Over forty papers were presented describing theoretical work and applied research carried out by academics from throughout the UK.

Following this event, a number of the leading academics were invited to submit chapters for this book based on the work they had presented to the conference. The chapters have been grouped under the above themes within each of three sections.

The first section is concerned with international competition and the implications of the single market. In Chapter 1, results from a research study into aspects of competitiveness within the financial services sector are discussed. Measures of competitiveness are identified as falling within three main factors: competitive performance, competitive potential and management process. These factors are discussed within the context of a sector facing considerable change as a result of the single market provisions. In Chapter 2, the strategic responses of multinational machine tool companies are considered both within a global context and within the single European market. The dominance of the Japanese and their involvement as local producers within Europe provides valuable insights into the evolution of this global industry. Chapter 3 discusses the development of the microcomputer industry and the strategy and performance of IBM as the dominant player. The authors use a theoretical framework to provide insights into IBM's strategy and that of the industry. Chapter 4 specifically addresses the position of Spain as it prepares for full membership of the European Economic Community in 1992 and the marketing implications for Scottish industry and the potential for increased exports for a number of product sectors. Chapter 5 tackles the issue of technological collaboration within Europe, arguing that the opportunities and incentives are considerable and may well be a significant determinant in the evolution of European businesses. The first section concludes with a review, in Chapter 6, of a 'new type of marketing', based on Total Quality Management (TQM). The author argues that this approach may well be particularly suited to the single European market post-1992.

The second section is concerned with issues relating to corporate performance and management control. In Chapter 7, the authors review a wide literature on corporate recovery and report on a study using case data within which they examine the characteristics and conditions facing companies at different stages in the prospect for recovery. Chapter 8 reports on a comparative study of performance evaluation in currency risk management. The study found that in a majority of the twenty-three cases considered, some form of performance evaluation was carried out – albeit of a relatively basic standard. Chapter 9 is concerned with analysing the performance of management planning systems and an approach is developed which, it is argued, provides a form of ex post analysis appropriate to the uncertainties facing management in the growing internationalisation of European businesses. Chapter 10 is the fourth in which issues of performance evaluation are considered, but at the level of the individual in performance appraisal. In an insightful discussion on the role of performance appraisal and the metaphorical use of the 'gaze' as an instrument of management control, the author argues its implications for individual behaviour, labour process and organisational change. Chapter 11 considers the role of assessment/appraisal with respect to the career opportunities of women. In so doing, the author provides further insight into the issues developed in the previous chapter. It is argued that human resource policies need to address the real potential for gender bias in assessment. This is required if the barriers to women's career development are to be removed, with many implications for the ability of organisations to successfully meet the considerable pace of change confronting them with the coming of the single market. The final chapter in this section, Chapter 12, considers issues of regulation and control in health and safety at work. In the European context, issues of harmonisation of reporting, common policies and the need for comparative statistics are clearly identified as an enormous task in the ongoing development of organisational/managerial capability for self-regulation and control.

The third section is on decision-making and implementation and comprises three chapters covering a broad range of issues. Chapter

13 presents a model of problem-solving based on three stages or dimensions: problem finding, idea finding and implementation. The model has been tested on groups of MBA's engaged on realistic tasks involving the above three stages. The authors suggest that individual stylistic differences may be significant in their effect on group dynamics. In a European context, it is further suggested that multicultural projects may well present potential for conflict through misunderstandings of cognitive style differences. The problem of getting decisions enacted through successful implementation is addressed in Chapter 14, in which an empirical study is described of decision implementation in a number of British organisations. Factors affecting success or failure in implementation are suggested and the added cultural attributes in cross-national post-decision processes are identified as potentially significant. Finally, in Chapter 15, a thought-provoking article considers the nature of decisions and decision-making and the dearth of moral philosophy in their deliberation and re-evaluation.

We have been fortunate to be able to gather papers of such high quality for this book. Our contributors have responded patiently to our editorial requests and have produced chapters which will appeal to both academics and practitioners alike. The chapters cover a diverse range of issues and we hope that readers will benefit from the information and insights gained whilst tackling the challenges presented by the emerging single European market.

Peter Barrar
Cary L. Cooper

Part I

International business and 1992

1 Measures of international competitiveness

Empirical findings from British banks, building societies and insurance companies[1]

Peter J. Buckley, C. L. Pass and Kate Prescott

THE CONCEPT OF INTERNATIONAL COMPETITIVENESS: A RESUME

This chapter is the third in a series of articles addressing the problem of establishing a framework for measuring the international competitiveness of firms. The first paper 'Measures of international competitiveness: A critical survey' (Buckley *et al.* 1988) presented a review of recent literature on competitiveness, much of which concerns itself with single measures which purport to be surrogates for competitiveness. A cursory examination of the various surrogates provides a complex array of possible approaches varying widely in scope (that is, measures of performance, measures of factors providing future competitive potential and qualitative measures of managerial factors leading to competitive success) and level of analysis (that is, country, industry, firm and product level). By taking the relative scope of the measures as the central theme, measures were categorised into three groups:

COMPETITIVE PERFORMANCE
COMPETITIVE POTENTIAL
MANAGEMENT PROCESS

By categorising the measures in this way it becomes apparent that the '3 Ps' describe different stages in a dynamic competitive process. Potential measures describe the inputs into the operation, performance measures the outcome of the operation and process measures the management of the operation. Thus, the paper concludes that competitiveness cannot be considered to be a static concept, but an on-going process. The interrelationship between the various measures is demonstrated in Figure 1.1.

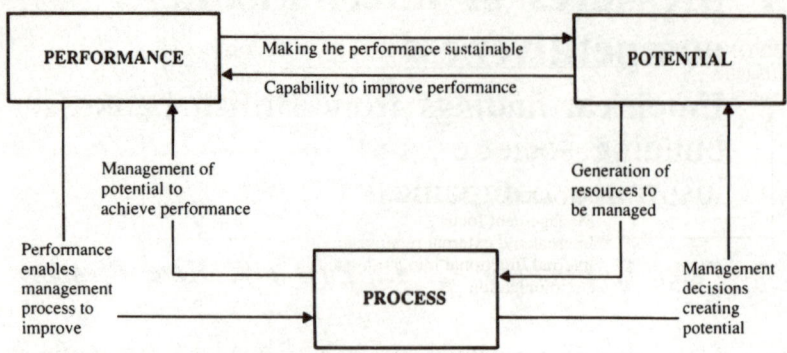

Figure 1.1 Aspects of competitiveness

Figure 1.1 presents the 'empty box' theoretical view applicable to all levels of analysis (country, industry, firm and product) designed to encompass all forms of foreign activity (exporting, licensing and other contractual arrangements and foreign direct investment – including joint ventures). The second paper in the series 'Measures of international competitiveness: Empirical findings' (Buckley *et al.* 1990) addresses the problem of filling these empty boxes at the level of the firm. Using a sample of firms from five manufacturing industries (glass, industrial gases, pharmaceuticals, scientific instruments and paint) the measures of competitiveness most frequently used by managers in their assessment of foreign operations were drawn together to fill the boxes. The results of the survey are presented in Figure 1.2.

It was evident from this analysis that profitability and market share were widely cited by firms across all five industry sectors, and were thus seen as applicable at a national level. Potential measures, whilst not showing a high degree of general applicability, showed a high degree of uniformity within the different industry sectors/industry groups. These may be regarded, therefore, as characterising competitiveness at an industry level. Conversely, management process indicators tend to be firm-specific, dependent on the historical development and character of the individual organisation.

MEASURES OF INTERNATIONAL COMPETITIVENESS: THE CASE OF FINANCIAL SERVICES

A separate treatment was deemed necessary for financial services as a result of certain specific features which characterise services from

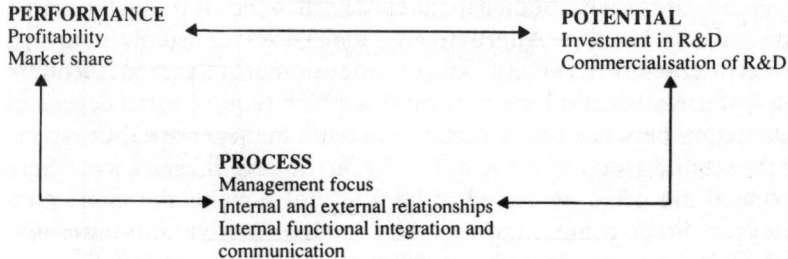

Figure 1.2 Aspects of competitiveness: results from the manufacturing sector

goods. Boddewyn *et al.* (1986) classify services according to their international tradeability, based on the extent to which the service is embodied in physical goods and the degree of inseparability in provision of the service:

1 service commodities, which are distinct from their production process are tradeable across national boundaries and thus exportable;
2 where production cannot be separated from consumption a foreign presence is necessary;
3 where services comprise a mix of distinct commodities and location-bound service elements, some location substitution is possible.

There are two distinct elements implicit in this classification which suggests that trade and investment patterns for services differ from those associated with goods. First, where production and consumption cannot be separated, and some form of foreign presence is necessary, decisions on foreign market servicing are pre-determined and thus the firm's pursuit of competitiveness is constrained within certain modes of market servicing. Second, the inseparability of production and consumption often involves a strong personal element in the supply of the service which brings management of personnel into the forefront of managing the competitive process. By analysing the financial services sector separately from manufacturing firms it is possible to assess whether these factors impact on the measures of competitiveness used by managers within the banking, building society and insurance sectors.

The financial service sector is also a useful medium for assessing measures of competitiveness in service industries as the wide array of products and services offered within this sector traverse the three groupings provided by Boddewyn and co-workers. Credit card sales quite clearly fall into the first grouping, wherein the services offered by credit cards are embodied in the card itself, which is tradeable across international borders. Alternatively, financial advice usually involves a direct interaction between producer and customer and current accounts, deposit accounts and loan applications which require some degree of interaction between the customer and bank manager are thus typical of the second group of services. Finally, in the case of insurance, where products are often perceived to be sold, not bought, the interaction involves direct contact between sales representative and customer, although the actual contract can be supplied by a central unit.

MANAGEMENT RESPONSES

This section presents a discussion, by industry group, of the key process, performance and potential measures used by the companies interviewed. The sample includes six banks (including all four clearing banks), eight building societies and ten insurance companies. The difference in sample size across the various sectors mirrors the relative degree of concentration of the three different sectors. The building societies, whilst in the early stages of internationalisation, were able to provide information concerning the way in which they plan to manage the competitive process of their international expansion. Responses were confined to issues of European expansion (rather than international expansion as was the case for manufacturing firms), due to the fact that building societies are not permitted to operate outside Europe. This provides a standardised set of target countries considered by the sample of companies.

Banks

De-regulation of financial markets in the UK has resulted in a blurring of the traditional boundaries between banks, building societies and insurance companies. Banks, which were once the bastions of current accounts, deposit accounts, unsecured loans and more recently, credit cards have, in recent years, ventured into the mortgage and insurance markets. The result is that many are now more akin to 'financial supermarkets' than specialist providers of a restricted array of financial services. This trend has resulted in increasing competition in many financial markets and a reassessment by many banks of their overall objectives and future business horizons. A recent survey in *The Economist* on international banking (1990) suggests that the new highly competitive market place faced by many banks has made them more aware of the need to be efficient, streamlined profitable organisations with a broader view of potential expansionary paths encompassing international markets. These assertions can be tested by assessing the measures currently being used to assess competitiveness at an international level.

Performance

Return on capital and return on equity were the most commonly cited performance indicators mentioned by all six banks in the sample. The banks are aware that in order to justify investment in foreign operations they have to be confident that capital could not have earned greater returns elsewhere. As their whole business revolves around money management and investment for gain, the culture of banking organisations can potentially act as a barrier to international expansion in that short-term gains may be hard to achieve and investment consequently difficult to justify. This culture is particularly evident in two institutions who have made a conscious decision not to expand internationally in retail financial services at the present time (although they are developing their international corporate banking division). Two banks went on to justify this measure in terms of maximising returns to shareholders. Three banks indicated that profitability was an important measure, one firm highlighting that the time to profitability is a key consideration in their market servicing decisions, another asserting that profitability is becoming increasingly important as competition intensifies. The latter firm indicated that cost cutting is an important element in maximising profits, as is 'developing interfaces between products'. This theme was iterated by the third firm that mentioned profitability which is concerned with 'profitability of customer relationships', that is, the maximisation of the potential available within their customer base – achieved through cross-selling. Thus there is clearly some belief that the 'financial supermarket' can provide an important source of profits.

There was some evidence that these measures are not used indiscriminately. One firm indicated that measures depend on the form of market servicing, it being impossible to assess joint ventures in the same way as wholly-owned operations. This stems from the different objectives set for such operations. Another organisation stressed the fact that some operations are merely judged on the perceived future potential which helps to support a progressive, long-term commitment to internationalisation.

Unlike the manufacturing sector, market share was not adduced to be an important measure of competitive performance. It was mentioned by only one firm in the sample, which indicated that market share and profitability are more to do with marketing projections than performance measures.

Potential

A wide array of competitive advantages were identified. Two banks highlighted continual innovation as a source of competitive advantage. Whilst accepting that new innovations can be copied rapidly and relatively cheaply, by continually introducing new products they believe that they can always keep one step ahead of their competition. To some extent it is believed that this is easier to achieve in certain European markets than it is in the UK, due to the fact that markets such as Spain, Italy and Portugal are less developed than the sophisticated UK market, and thus the scope for introducing new, and relatively innovative products is greater. Another firm also highlighted the relative sophistication of the UK market as a source of competitive advantage. As the UK market is more developed than many other European markets, they have already dealt with a lot of the new expansions now taking place across Europe and are thus better prepared to manage them. However, they recognise that by trying to deal with the issues in the same way as in the UK they could overlook important issues. Consequently they are prepared to adapt their approach to local market conditions.

One bank stressed customer service as their major advantage, and in this respect they have dedicated themselves to a total quality management approach. They believe that because it is so pragmatic it allows the firm to improve its bottom line. They concern themselves with the price of quality and the price of non-conformance. As 'quality' is difficult to measure, they spend time identifying consumer needs and wants and then develop products and systems to satisfy these needs. They also believe that they have a good central delivery system for their card services enhanced by their total quality management initiative.

Another firm mentioned their clearly focussed strategy as a source of advantage, identifying areas in which they can excel and make money and thus generate returns to their shareholders. One smaller institution views its size as allowing better lines of communication than a lot of its larger competitors and a more personalised service to their customers. Other potential indicators, each mentioned by one firm, include size and stature, flexibility, good indigenous management, low cost production, a good image and a good network throughout Europe. It is interesting that only one firm felt their European network was an advantage considering that all managers highlighted distribution networks and a well established customer base as being the key competitive advantages in Europe.

One bank felt that there is very little to differentiate between the clearing banks. Although branding might provide some advantage, and the way they sell and deliver differs to some extent, neither have resulted in growth above and beyond the other clearers.

Process

Process indicators fall into four clear groups. First, three firms view good indigenous management, and autonomy of operation of their foreign subsidiaries as giving their organisation strength. Within this group, one firm stressed that their reluctance to impose a blueprint for management on their foreign subsidiaries has given the foreign operation the freedom to manage within the constraints of their own local environment. A second firm believes that major benefits accrue from a collective desire to achieve, which will succeed if British and foreign managers work together, all personnel making a contribution to the overall business. The final firm sees employing 'key personnel' with good contacts in the local market as providing the most advantages.

Second, there are two firms who regard training as the key potential indicator, and are currently investing large amounts in training staff – particularly retraining 'back-room staff for front-room duties'. As technology supersedes personnel in administrative roles, many institutions are refocussing training on how to sell and how to deal with customers. This approach enhances the drive for cross-selling as more contact time between staff and customers in the bank branches provides the opportunity to sell a range of products to existing customers.

Third, one firm believes their focussed approach is the best way to proceed. As firms cannot be all things to all people, by focussing on activities where they display strengths they can concentrate resources and management time on areas of business where they are confident that they can make returns and achieve performance targets. Finally, one firm believes that developing good technological systems to move money, and process applications quickly is an important part of facilitating the business. However, in this respect, they believe that many banks are on an equal footing, and although it does not provide much of an advantage, it is a prerequisite of competitive performance.

Building societies

Like the banks, the building societies have recently extended outside their traditional spheres of business – mortgage finance – into areas more traditionally associated with banking and insurance companies. Many have also integrated backwards into the estate agency sector in order to capture business at an early stage in the house purchase chain. Associated services, such as removals, transit insurance and property insurance have also been explored and developed by some institutions keen to cross-sell services to 'captive' housebuyers.

Unlike the banks, however, building societies have only recently been given permission to extend their selling activities into European markets. Many are therefore at an early stage of development and much of what follows is therefore speculative, based on research of European markets, rather than experience in particular countries.

Performance

Among the building societies, more emphasis is placed on profitability than was the case in the banking sector. Six out of the eight sampled firms mentioned profitability as a key indicator. There was also some evidence to suggest that the societies take a longer-term view of expansion. One firm indicated that they accept that initially they have to accept losses, but look to a return to profits in three years, or in some instances, five years. They also recognise that there are loss-leader benefits to be earned. A second firm emphasised that they measure 'long-term profitability' rather than immediate return on their assets. A further firm stressed that at the end of the day what they are trying to assess is how hard their assets are working for the company.

Only two organisations mentioned return on capital. One enumerated their target for new projects as 25 per cent ROCE within the first couple of years. The other suggested that once a new business venture begins to generate profits, then they measure ROC performance.

Other indicators which were mentioned include the extent to which the new venture enhances corporate image and the amount to which it consumes management effort and the opportunities for generating scale and scope economies by linking activities.

Market share was mentioned by two organisations as being of critical importance in the UK market, although in their European developments they expect that it will be a less meaningful indicator in the short term when activities are small-scale. One manager suggested that, in isolation, market share measures would not provide much information on performance. A move from 0.3 to 0.4 per cent would only be considered good if return on assets continued to be favourable.

Potential

Again, a wide variety of competitive advantage indicators were provided by interviewees. Three firms mentioned the efficiency of their money management as offering potential advantages and enhancing profitability. Efficient wholesale funding operations provide a solid financial base which is expected to support future expansion and development. One firm, however, noted that their good capital ratios makes them more attractive to predators, particularly foreign firms seeking to enter the UK market. A second source of potential emanates from the relative sophistication of UK building society products over European equivalents. The sophistication of endowment mortgages – which allows customers to borrow up to 100 per cent – and the wide choice of products were mentioned by four societies. This was particularly stressed in relation to Southern Europe, whose markets are not perceived to be well advanced. Linked with this, two societies suggested that UK building societies have a good pan-European reputation, being regarded as experts in the field of mortgage finance. For these firms, playing on their corporate name is proposed as a way of promoting quality.

Other indicators include size and security (yielding a good credit rating), customer service and product knowledge.

Four of the eight building societies clearly feel that they have potential advantages which can readily and successfully be exploited in European markets. Two of these stressed that although they do not consider themselves advantaged over UK competitors, they are confident that they have superior products compared to many European companies, are leaner and more efficient. The remaining four societies see greater potential, in the short term, in developing their national activities by extending their regional coverage, rather than planning European expansion.

Process

There is general consensus among the building societies that their lack of international experience serves as a major disadvantage in

extending their operations into Europe. Recruitment of personnel with experience in overseas markets is consequently a critical objective for all firms wishing to set up activities overseas.
One manager indicated that they can (a) buy in staff with experience, (b) train staff to deal with such operations, or (c) hire indigenous managers with relevant expertise. Two firms, however, fear
that overcoming the problem of lack of experience will not be
so easily achieved. As the culture of the organisation is domes-
tically oriented, it will take a lot of time to open up the minds
and outlook of managers to accept and actively pursue European
expansion.

One firm highlighted the disciplinary mix among its top executives
as providing a well balanced management team able to develop the
business in all key areas of activity.

Insurance companies

The insurance industry across Europe has witnessed a great increase in
competitive pressure over the last few years, partly as a result of the
de-regulation of financial markets and partly as a result of increasing
affluence of European consumers which has enticed many firms to
expand into neighbouring markets. This has put pressure on many of
the smaller institutions and resulted in a certain degree of concentration within the industry as firms have sought merger opportunities in
order to protect their interests. Another trend is the development of
close ties between many insurance companies and banking institutions
across Europe, in an effort to expand customer networks through the
established branch systems of the leading banking institutions. This
latter trend is continuing apace in the UK insurance market, and in
the strategies being followed by UK players to extend their activities
into Europe.

Performance

Profitability was mentioned by nine out of the ten insurance companies in the survey but never as a sole indicator of performance.
In most instances the measure is used in conjunction with investment income and fund performance. There were three instances
where firms recognise that short-term profits have to be traded for
long-term gains. Here the focus was sustained sales growth over
the short term which is expected to yield satisfactory profits in the
longer term. In an effort to achieve profit targets, only two firms

highlighted a cost-minimising strategy. In all other instances increased sales performance was the main thrust of improved performance – achieved through increased productivity of salesmen, regional expansion and geographic diversification. The only firm which did not mention profitability and fund performance, a small specialist motor insurer, was merely concerned with sustained growth of their overseas operation.

Return on capital was only mentioned by two firms and market share by one organisation.

Potential

Product innovation/creativity was mentioned by five of the ten organisations. Three of these, however, recognise that their products are not unique and can be easily replicated by competitors. One firm went on to stress, therefore, that it is not so much the development of new products which is the key to competitive success, but rather the rapid introduction of these products into the market and managing their portfolio to generate maximum gains from innovative products. Their success in this area is enhanced by a wide geographical network. This latter point was mentioned by three firms, who believe that experience in several international markets gives them scope to offer European packages. This, however, is more beneficial to their corporate business than at a retail level. Along with the innovativeness of products, one firm believes the quality of its products enables it to take advantage of earning a high proportion of sales through independent agents who readily promote their products on their merit. This is, however, difficult to replicate in many European markets where independent agent networks are less developed. The firm is, therefore, actively encouraging independent agents to set up in Spain in order that they can by-pass the tied system between banks and insurance companies. Another firm believes that their strength lies in the differential focus of their products which means that they do not become involved in potentially damaging price cutting strategies. In order to maximise the benefits they have spent a lot on retraining staff towards a customer orientation. Working through agents, however, prevents them from taking this stance abroad.

Efficient money management was adduced to be a major source of competitive advantage by four out of the ten insurance companies. Other advantages mentioned include the strength of indigenous managers in underwriting, the quality of the salesforce (being of graduate calibre which is rare in many European markets), small size which allows for flexibility and greater receptivity to customer needs, and in-depth knowledge of a specific market segment.

Process

There is an apparent divergence of opinion regarding the benefits and pitfalls of autonomous management of overseas operations. Four firms believe that it is a positive approach, allowing the personnel invested with knowledge of the market – competitors and customers – a free hand to plan and develop the business in close proximity to the market. Two organisations, conversely, fear that *too much* autonomy is given to subsidiary companies and foreign operating units, greater benefits being earned from closer integration of foreign operations and domestic business. One manager stressed this point by asserting that strength comes from interdependence, and scale economies can be achieved by centralising certain functions rather than the present system of duplicating activities in various locations. However, he recognises that the present system of autonomous management offers the benefit of greater results accountability, as the operating companies have no-one to hide behind. In conclusion, he suggests that a balance needs to be struck between those operations which can be most efficiently managed centrally, and those that need to remain autonomous.

One firm highlighted the importance of constantly reviewing methods of distribution – seeking new ways of delivering products and by-passing the often highly competitive structures in existence in many foreign markets. Two further firms pointed to their focus on core strengths as generating a strong business culture and clear direction for future growth. Other factors include minimising costs, remaining independent, being small and thus having fewer layers of bureaucracy, and staff training and development.

All firms reiterated the importance of money management and investment decisions, critical to the financial security of the organisation and future growth potential.

KEY FINDINGS: THE EMPTY BOXES FILLED

Through the twenty-four interviews conducted with British banks, building societies and insurance companies it was possible to highlight the various factors managers consider to be important indicators of their competitiveness. In almost every case it was possible to categorise the findings under the identified headings – performance, potential and process.

Performance

Profitability is the most widely used indicator across the whole sample, being of particular importance in the building society and insurance sectors. Despite the assertions of *The Economist's* report on international banking (1990) that banks are becoming less concerned with return on capital and more aware of the need to manage for profit, the underlying ethos of banks appears to be making this transition difficult. As the bank's business is centred on investment for gain, investing in foreign operations can be hard to justify in the short term, where capital could have been used more profitably elsewhere. To some extent, therefore, this is impeding European expansion, particularly as the overbanked nature of much of Europe suggests that the time to profitability will be slow, the generation of a customer base taking considerable time in highly competitive markets. Many of the banks which are expanding their retail activities in Europe are therefore concerned with methods of market servicing which allow rapid returns to be made (that is, joint ventures), or are adding retail activities to facilities which were originally established to support the internationalisation of their domestic corporate customers, maximising returns from existing capital assets overseas.

The banks are not, however, the only sector concerned with investment performance. Whilst nine out of the ten insurance companies mentioned profitability, this was never cited as a single indicator, and in most cases was mentioned in conjunction with investment income and fund performance. In this sector, however, the two indicators appear to be less interlinked, and while both profitability and fund performance are deemed a prerequisite of competitiveness, several firms are prepared to accept short-term losses in profitability for long-term gains.

Conversely, many building societies cited profitability as the only measure. Again, there was evidence that companies are prepared to take a long-term view of opportunities, initially accepting losses as long as long-term growth opportunities are apparent.

Unlike the manufacturing sector, market share is not considered to be an important performance indicator in international markets. Although two building societies indicated that it is important to their domestic activities, due to the small-scale activities in Europe, the indicator is not particularly useful.

Potential

A wide array of potential indicators were cited by the sampled firms. The innovativeness of products and their relative sophistication were frequently mentioned by organisations in all sectors. However, there is an understanding that innovations are easy to replicate by competitors, and although there are some lead-time advantages, these are not sustainable in the long term. 'Sophistication' refers to the fact that UK products are assumed to be more advanced than those offered in many European countries.

The liberal nature of the UK retail financial service market, particularly in the last few years, has meant a high degree of competition, out of which organisations have developed a wide array of highly differentiated products, tailored to the needs of consumers in all market segments. This process is assumed to stand UK producers in good stead to introduce new products into European markets which have been heavily regulated, and consequently dominated by price competition. Certain managers, however, while highlighting such potential, were careful not to overstate the benefits. They are aware that the introduction of new products needs to be done gradually and initially it is important to gain consumer confidence by offering products which are familiar.

Money management was adduced to be an important indicator in the building society and insurance sectors although, interestingly, not by bank executives. Those firms mentioning this factor view it as an essential part of securing a firm business foundation to sustain the future potential of the organisation.

Amongst the banks and insurance companies there was some evidence that the existence of a European network is an advantage. It is worth noting here that many building societies highlighted the fact that, as newcomers to Europe, the lack of a distribution network is a major disadvantage. As much of Europe is overbanked/overbranched in all areas of financial services, generating a customer base from scratch is considered by many institutions to be prohibitively expensive in terms of the time to profitability and the costs of persuading customers away from indigenous producers. Access to existing distribution networks through joint ventures is therefore considered by many firms with no presence overseas as the most attractive option, and in some cases, the only option.

Some of the smaller firms within the sample, whilst recognising that their size can be a disadvantage in terms of financial muscle, credit ratings and the size of their customer base, compensate for these disadvantages by stressing their flexibility, lack of bureaucracy and good internal communication flows and receptivity to customer needs.

Process

Within the ambit of management process indicators a lot of emphasis was placed in all sectors on recruitment, staff training and development. Again, the building societies believe that the lack of European experience among their staff puts them at a disadvantage *vis-à-vis* many of their competitors. Furthermore, while recruitment of key staff, training and employment of foreign managers can minimise the problems to some extent, the nationally oriented business cultures of many of the societies is expected to hamper the smooth European expansion of activities. The divergence of opinion regarding the benefits and pitfalls of giving autonomous control to foreign operations raises the issue of foreign market knowledge. The banks and insurance companies who view autonomy as offering clear advantages do so in the belief that foreign managers are better able to plan and control operations as a result of their first-hand knowledge of the market. Attempting to manage foreign operations along English lines is consciously avoided in recognition of the fact that all markets are different and require adaptation, not only of products, but also business practices and approach. Those insurance companies believing that foreign activities should be more closely integrated with domestic operations stress the economic benefits of avoiding duplication of activities in various locations.

There is also evidence of conflicting attitudes towards product diversification (establishing financial supermarkets) and focussed strategies wherein firms concentrate on their core strengths. This may be partly attributable to the size of the sampled firms, the smaller firms, recognising that they cannot be all things to all people, concentrate their resources in areas of activity where they most clearly have potential competitive advantages. The larger firms, who can often diversify through acquisition, where the package includes personnel experienced in the new business discipline, have more scope to incorporate a wide range of products in their portfolio. Alternatively, the same broad mix of products can be achieved by both large and small firms by synergistic joint ventures or the establishment of tied arrangements. However, within this approach, the smaller firms recognise that they may potentially become takeover targets in the future.

SUMMARY

Although several factors were identified under each heading within the three industry sectors, it is possible to extract the major findings to fill the empty boxes and provide an overall picture which characterises the financial services industry. Returning to the empty boxes of Figure 1.1, it is possible to summarise the findings as follows:

1 Competitive *performance* : Profitability and investment perfor-
                                    mance
2 Competitive *potential* :   Product innovation/sophistication
                                    Money management
                                    European network
3 Management *process* :   Recruitment and training of staff
                                    Division of control
                                    Diversification vs. Focus

Clearly, then, the results from the financial service sector (summarised in Figure 1.3) differ from the findings for the manufacturing sector. Although profitability remains a key issue, the importance of money management replaces market share in the case of *Performance* indicators. This reflects the financial as opposed to market orientation of financial service firms. Product innovation, whilst akin to R&D and commercialisation of R&D in the *Potential* indicators of manufacturing firms, provides less scope for sustainable competitive advantage in the financial sector because of the ease with which products can be replicated and the infeasibility of patenting such new developments. Consequently, further measures are needed which show evidence of sustainable advantages. Hence the importance placed on money management, which provides a firm economic foundation for future development, and a European network through which new business can be generated and new innovative products introduced rapidly to a wide customer base. Whilst management focus appears of equal importance to manufacturing and financial service firms, *Process* indicators in financial services place more emphasis on personnel issues than is the case in the manufacturing sector. The division of control between operating units and head office mentioned by some manufacturing managers, is viewed as being more critical in financial services because it is difficult to divide these factors from the personnel issues on which so much importance is placed.

Overall, whereas in the manufacturing sector performance measures appeared to be universally applicable, potential measures specific to particular sectors and process indicators firm-specific, this kind of

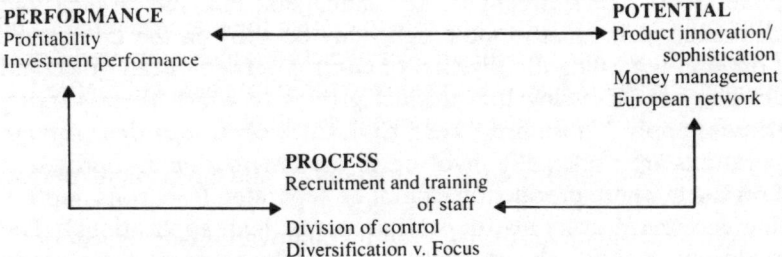

Figure 1.3 Aspects of competitiveness: results

distinction is not apparent in the financial service sector. This may be partly due to the blurring of traditional boundaries between the three sectors which has occurred in response to the de-regulation of financial markets. As firms are now offering a wide range of products across the traditional business sectors, the diversity of measures identified in each sector may result from the diversity of products being offered.

Some of these differences may be explained in terms of the features which characterise services from goods. First, in terms of indicators of competitive potential, the weight placed on European networks may be partly attributable to the inseparability of production and consumption. As firms require a market presence to offer many of the products within their portfolio, great emphasis is placed on gaining access to distribution networks. The short time horizons of several organisations, imposed through their strong financial orientation, prevents greenfield options being considered. As a customer base takes a long time to establish, and thus a return to profitability cannot be made rapidly, there is strong preference for joint ventures within all three sectors. The key motivation for such consideration is gaining access to indigenous firms' distribution networks and customer base allowing rapid market penetration and immediate profits. Managers in all sectors stressed that distribution is the key competitive advantage in the delivery of a wide selection of financial products. There was great consensus that the lack of a distribution network, and the problems of initiating joint ventures with appropriate indigenous organisations, acts as a barrier to competitiveness in European markets. Great emphasis is therefore placed on the careful selection of potential partners and relationship management over time.

Second, the importance of personnel issues in the assessment of the management process may be explained by the strong personal element in the provision of some financial services. This not only applies to the recruitment of key managers, but also branch and sales personnel. Finally, some light may be shed on the divergence of opinion regarding the division of control between head office and subsidiary by assessing the product groups to which these varying attitudes apply. Those firms keen to devolve control to their foreign operations are principally involved in the distribution and provision of products where production cannot be separated from consumption (that is, current accounts, deposit accounts: loan applications). The organisations thus rely on suppliers' knowledge of customers and market conditions derived from their first-hand knowledge of the market. Alternatively, those firms seeking to centralise control over certain activities in order to offer advantages of scale economies, were insurance companies wherein direct contact between supplier and customer involves sales representatives, but the processing of applications and supply of contracts can be handled centrally. As the insurance product comprises a mix of location-bound service elements (the sales effort) and commodities (the contract) control over the separate elements of the supply process can be divided between host country and head office.

NOTE

1 This paper results from a study of the internationalisation of UK financial services firms financed by Beddows and Company. It forms part of a three year project at the University of Bradford Management Centre – 'The Foreign Market Servicing Strategies and Competitiveness of British Firms', sponsored by the Economic and Social Research Council (ESRC) in the Competitiveness and Regeneration of British Industry Programme (Grant No. F:20250027).

REFERENCES

Boddewyn, J. J., Halbrich, Marsha Baldwin and Perry, A. C. (1986) 'Service multinationals: Conceptualization, measurement and theory', *Journal of International Business Studies* 16 (3), 41–57.
Buckley, Peter J., Pass, C. L., and Prescott, Kate (1988) 'Measures of international competitiveness: A critical survey', *Journal of Marketing Management* 4 (2), Winter, 175–200.
Buckley, Peter J., Pass, C. L., and Prescott, Kate (1990) 'Measures of international competitiveness: Empirical findings from British manufacturing companies', *Journal of Marketing Management* 6 (1), Summer, 1–14.
The Economist (1990) 'A survey of international banking', 25 March.

2 The strategic responses of multinationals in the machine tool industry

Stephen Young, Stewart Dunlop and Neil Hood

BACKGROUND AND EVOLUTION

An efficient machine tool (MT) sector is of vital strategic importance to any economy which aims to maintain a vibrant industrial base. And, although the contribution of MTs to manufacturing value added in the major industrial economies is fairly small – *ca*.2 per cent (O'Brien 1987), they have appropriately been dubbed as the 'spider in the industrial web'. This has been true in the past and will continue to be so in the future, since modern machine tools (hardware and increasingly software) will be core components in the 'factory of the future'. As a reflection of a series of interrelated factors – chiefly applications of electronics-based technologies, slowly declining demand and the rise of Japan – considerable structural upheaval has taken place in the industry worldwide. Evidence of the latter is seen in large-scale job shedding, numerous mergers and acquisitions and management buy-outs in Europe and America especially, in what is still basically a sector dominated by smaller and medium-sized enterprises. Fundamental policy reappraisals are thus taking place in most organisations with a focus on international business strategy. The purpose of this chapter is to illustrate the nature and diversity of this strategic change, highlighting the influence of one particular environmental shock, namely the creation of the Single European Market (SEM). The evidence is drawn from a personal interview survey of foreign- and UK-owned machine tool companies operating in Britain, undertaken in 1989 and 1990.[1]

The machine tool industry environment

The advent of electronics and computer numerical control (CNC) in the 1970s totally changed the environmental characteristics of the

MT industry and competitive advantage factors. With CNC came a change in technological trajectories (Rendeiro 1988), with manufacturers continually having to update their models in order to offer state-of-the-art. New machine tool concepts appeared, particularly the highly flexible multi-purpose machine tools known as machining centres. These tools, moreover, had applications in some of the fastest growing industries of the world, such as instrument engineering and office machinery. Economies of scale and scope were of increasing importance (Collis 1988) and lower levels of vertical integration began to be in evidence (Rendeiro 1985). Finally, declines in demand were recorded as a consequence of substantially increased MT productivity on the back of CNC as well as changes in parts design and the introduction of new materials. Japan was both a cause of and the most efficient exploiter of such developments, and its share of world production and exports rose substantially, causing major problems for the fragmented industries in Europe and the USA.

A number of the industry characteristics which emerged from the 1970s will continue through the 1990s. Given the benefits provided to machine tool users by CNC tooling, the certainty is that the industry will progress to the development and installation of more advanced manufacturing systems; and much has been made of the 'factory of the future', automated and integrated from procurement through to dispatch via computer integrated manufacturing (CIM). However, diffusion is proving slower than expected and the likelihood is of 'iterative automation' beginning with flexible cells before moving to flexible manufacturing systems let alone CIM, and an emphasis on compatibility and connectability. The development of systems business adds a new dimension to industry evolution, since the successful suppliers will take turnkey responsibility for an entire project incorporating a package of machine tools, production engineering expertise and computer hardware and software.

There is fairly general agreement that the successful systems suppliers will be large firms; but other than that, blurring industry boundaries mean great uncertainties as to the successful competitors of the future, as between machine tool enterprises, electronics and computer companies, software houses and computer consultancies. For the smaller machine tool makers, joint ventures and cooperation agreements may represent a route into systems business; otherwise such companies are likely to be drawn into intense competition for the generally declining markets for stand-alone machines.

In line with changing industry/environmental characteristics, competitive advantage factors have also changed. One of the latter which is particularly significant in the context of international business strategy is marketing, sales and service. In the pre-CNC era sales were conventionally made via agents and distributors, and service networks were not required, since servicing requirements for a machine tool after installation were minimal (Collis 1988). Marketing and distribution gradually increased in importance after the early days of Japanese penetration of CNC tools and by the 1980s had become extremely important. One article in a trade journal (Rohan 1984) talked of: 'Company-run regional technical centers . . . bringing increasingly complex control technology nearer to customers and their place of business . . . replacing sales offices or distributors'. Selling factory automation is further changing both marketing methods and the customer/supplier interface: in regard to the former, for example, increased attention is being paid to divisional or corporate advertising emphasising total product line and corporate capabilities; while the seller/customer relationship is of necessity becoming ever closer. Yet it is questionable how far many companies have recognised the importance of these downstream activities in competitive advantage, especially in dealings outside the home market.

International business in machine tools and foreign involvement in UK industry

International trade in machine tools has historically been very significant, with exports representing around half of total production in Italy, France and UK, and 60 per cent or more in the case of Germany. Among the major Western producers, the USA is distinctive in having a much lower export/production share – in the 15–25 per cent range during the 1980s. The strong trade performance is a reflection of the nature of the industry: there are many ways of segmenting the machine tool market and of differentiating products through customisation; having identified a niche in the home market, even small producers might be able to sell into similar niche markets abroad.

Japanese performance, again export-based, was based on a very different concept, namely, that of a scale-intensive, product standardisation strategy. Japanese companies invested heavily in modular design, having first identified a broad set of market needs internationally. The Japanese were rarely willing to depart from the standard set of flexible designs, and would only do so if an important geographical market was in the early stages of penetration. CNC capabilities which offered significant cost and flexibility advantages to customers enabled the Japanese to overcome the desire of users to have products which were customised to their own individual needs. Thus Japanese strategy in small machine tools was volume-based, characterised by a long-term commitment to increasing market share on a global basis; and in many senses was similar to the strategies employed by Japanese producers of consumer goods. The outcome was a rise in Japan's share of world trade from 13 per cent at the start of the 1980s to nearly 20 per cent at the end of the decade, despite the existence of voluntary export restraints with the USA and EC.

On the basis of extensive trade flows among nations, the machine tool industry was 'international' even before the arrival of the Japanese, along a spectrum ranging from 'domestic' to 'international', 'multinational' and 'global'.[2] It could not be typified as multinational (let alone global) since there were few companies with a spread of manufacturing facilities around the world or even of sales subsidiaries. For the larger North American enterprises, for instance, production facilities in the USA and UK would be a likely pattern for any multinational manufacturer; but licensing overseas would be more common, as a reflection of the limited market potential for niche producers. Moreover, strategies for international markets were of a multi-domestic variety, with product offerings being substantially tailored to the needs of customers in different countries (Porter 1986). In this respect the Japanese were again unique, for their volume strategies designed to cater for a broad target market, required globalisation (albeit still export-based).

The shake-out of the Western machine tool industry in the face of Japan's three strategic thrusts – small CNC machine tools, volume and cost, and globalisation – can be illustrated very strikingly by the UK situation. The index of UK machine tool industry employment (1985=100) fell from 133 in the third quarter of 1981 to 95 in the fourth quarter of 1986 (MTTA 1989). Foreign multinational companies (MNEs) located in the UK were not immune from this shake-out: the number of foreign-owned machine tool firms shrank from 33 in 1981 to 16 in 1988 by divestments, sell-offs and management buy-outs, with employment declining from 7,120 to 2,165 over the same period (Young and Dunlop 1990). Interestingly, at the start of the 1980s the foreign-owned share of the machine tool industry in the UK was well above that for manufacturing industry as a whole. This confirms the attractiveness of the UK as a location for (especially US) MNEs, in an industry where multinational activity in general is low (O'Brien 1987). While not the subject of this chapter, greenfield entry by these MNEs was relatively infrequent, with acquisition of UK licensees being probably the single most common entry route.

In summary, the Western machine tool industry at the beginning of the 1990s was characterised by a considerable degree of volatility, as companies sought an effective response to the Japanese in the areas of product policy, generic strategy and international business strategy; within an environment of declining demand, shifts in industry economics favouring the large firm and blurring industry boundaries with the development of systems business.

1992 AND THE MACHINE TOOL INDUSTRY

The Single European Market adds yet another environmental dimension for machine tool producers, although several studies have suggested that the market liberalisation programme is unlikely to have a major impact in this sector. Pelkmans and Winters (1988) found that there were few impediments to trade within the European Community (EC) on account of public monopoly, national aid or nationalistic procurement in machine tools, and indeed the long-standing tradition of exporting in the industry appears to confirm that there are few artificial or economic barriers to trade. The evidence of the Cecchini Report (1988) also found (somewhat contrary to the work of Scibberas and Payne 1985) that scale economies were not a particularly important feature of the industry. And so there would appear to be few advantages from plant rationalisation policies designed to leverage scale advantages. Cecchini did suggest, however, that there might be some gains from increased cooperation within the industry, particularly to complete product ranges by exchange/specialisation with other companies and to develop more advanced CNC or CIM capabilities. There would appear to be some scope for increased sharing of product development in Europe because even the largest companies seem too small to underwrite the costs involved in developing the 'factory of the future' systems described above, and this is perhaps one reason behind some of the joint ventures which are in place in the industry (*Machinery* 1988).

The major area where 1992 is likely to have an impact in machine tools is in developing common standards. Currently, the EC industry faces three major barriers in this area (*The Engineer* 1988):

1 health and safety regulations;
2 quasi-legal standards, most often those used as a reference in technical regulations; and

Table 2.1 Summary of multinational strategies

	Case 1 Accumulative conglomerate	Case 2 Regional rationaliser	Case 3 Focus factory phoenix	Case 4 Cautious challenger	Case 5 International invader
Focus of activities[a]	Multi-domestic/ regional	Multi-domestic	Multi-domestic formerly; potentially global at present	Regional/global	Global
Generic strategy	Niche	Niche	Cost (potential)	Differentiation	Cost/ Differentiation
Basis of competitive advantage	Engineering craft skills Unique product in niche areas	Engineering craft skills Reputation Quality	Current competitive advantage based on reputation, ability to handle difficult projects, engineering craft skills Future competitive advantage relating to cost reduction, volume production, world class manufacture, out-sourcing	Design and specification plus training, engineering support and after-sales service to customer	Leading edge manufacturing systems; engineering support development/ manufacturing/ marketing interrelationships; market definition and marketing strategy

1992 Opportunity or threat	Opportunity or threat depending upon response	Little effect	Little effect	Little effect	Little effect (but management of political environment important)
Future prospects	Uncertain	Uncertain	Potential for success	Best-placed to compete with Japanese	Expanding market share in Europe
Categorisation of subsidiary strategy according to other typologies in literature	Miniature replica – innovator/product specialist[b]	Miniature replica	Product specialist	Marketing satellite plus	Miniature replica
	Contributor[c]	Implementer	Strategic leader/ contributor	Implementer	Implementer

[a] After Porter (1986).
[b] Based on the typology in White and Poynter (1984).
[c] Based on the typology in Bartlett and Ghoshal (1986).
Source: Authors, derived from interview data.

3 testing and certification procedures.

The situation in Europe is thought to have improved since 1983, when all national regulations were required to be notified to the relevant standards body (CEN) in mechanical engineering, but there are still in existence a host of regulations covering the above issues. The net effect of the removal of these will be to ease importing from present production facilities, although there is no evidence at present that they constitute a major barrier to trade. Taking this issue alone, the effect of the SEM will be a reduction in local engineering performed to deal with diverse regulations and, therefore, a limited reduction in local content. However, as will be argued later, the need for improved communication and liaison with customers over systems will necessitate a stronger local presence.

The more important issue in any event concerns external relations issues and the response of non-EC companies (especially Japanese producers) which are concerned about selling into Europe after 1992. In machine tools, protectionist barriers have already been raised, with voluntary restraint agreements restricting the number of Japanese CNC lathes and machining centres entering the Community market (*The Engineer* 1987). As will be shown, a number of greenfield investments and acquisitions have been made by Japanese producers in the EC since 1987. Concerning established MNEs in the Community, limited restructuring in MTs could follow, were the major customers in, for example, the automobile industry to centralise production on a European basis.

ILLUSTRATIONS OF MULTINATIONAL STRATEGIES

In a sector characterised by such structural volatility, it is not easy to discern long-term strategies, but a number of illustrations of multinational responses (with a particular emphasis on responses to the Single Market) are presented below. The cases are summarised in Table 2.1.

Case 1 – Accumulative conglomerate

Illustrative of this category is an American corporation (part of a venture capital group), which has identified opportunities to create a global machine tool group from low cost acquisitions of family-owned and failing businesses. Its planned generic strategy can be characterised as the pursuit of a series of global niches from its established operations and acquisitions so far limited to the USA and the UK. Operations in the two centres are being rationalised so as to manufacture separate product ranges for world markets, with marketing responsibility for all products being split geographically (the UK taking Europe, Middle East and India).

The recency and continuing nature of the company's development in machine tools means that a group identity and group synergies have not yet been exploited. Indeed weaknesses are recognised in slippage of market profile with ownership changes and poorer service to customers. With a significant reliance on bought-in components and a small customer base, the UK company feels squeezed between powerful buyers and suppliers. Strategy for the SEM is to involve rebuilding market share, since, despite its role, only 15 per cent of UK company sales are made in Continental Europe. The first task is considered to be the sale of reference machines in the various countries to provide a base from which to launch a sustained effort in the EC. Sales offices in Germany and France are essentially spares and service operations, with sales taking place through agents elsewhere. Building the sales companies and extending distribution through improved agency arrangements and mutual marketing agreements is the challenge for 1992; whilst at the same time defending the UK market base. In Italy the company had planned an acquisition to facilitate market penetration, but negotiations fell through, and this was changed into a reciprocal marketing deal.

Time is not on the side of a company pursuing this type of strategy, with the efforts of continual reorganisation and restructuring diverting attention from key strategic tasks, with potentially debilitating effects. Much depends on the funds the parent corporation is prepared to commit and the time-scale over which it is looking for profit returns: certainly very substantial investment is needed in manufacturing technology, new product development and marketing.

Case 2 – Regional rationaliser

The multinationals in the regional rationaliser category had much in common with the accumulative conglomerate above, except that the emphasis was on restructuring existing operations rather than acquisition-based restructuring. For one company in this group, quasi-autonomy at a European level was being replaced by a more centralised approach, directed from the USA, with the aim of creating a genuinely multinational business. The role of the UK subsidiary was that of a manufacturer of part of the overall corporate product line for Europe. Sales in the rest of the world, excluding the USA, for this range are allocated to American or UK subsidiaries on the basis of price quotations to distributors. It was admitted that this had led to problems, with distributors playing one group company off against another. The MNE has a substantial market share, albeit within a small, highly specialised niche, and problems have been experienced in obtaining the volume necessary to ensure profitability; the fact that the markets for its large machine tools lie in the declining heavy engineering sector will not make this task any easier for the future. The corporation as a whole is substantially vertically integrated, and, indeed, among the sample of firms studied, only this multinational and the 'international invader' produced numerical controllers in-house, and, uniquely, the former supplied its own castings.

As part of the strategy of multinationalism, the SEM is providing the impetus for the group as a whole to attack the Continental European market in a more sustained and concerted way than hitherto. During 1987 and 1988 no machines at all were sold on the Continent, and during the 1980s as a whole the average was about one machine per year out of total annual sales of 22 machines approximately. At date of interview the company had virtually no representation in Germany, and none in France after a disastrous experience during the last decade which saw five distributorships come and go. Evaluations taking place at present may lead to the establishment of a European salesforce. Aside from distribution, standards are the major item to be tackled, and, on a slightly wider plane the offering of a 'Euro-product'. The latter will mean offering machine tools with, for example, Siemens as opposed to in-house controllers.

Some interesting observations were made about the requirements for success in Continental Europe. It was recognised that the company would have to provide (a) capabilities in the language of the customer, (b) an ability to negotiate in the terms they were used to, and (c) a level of service up to that expected from a national supplier, as well as being competitive in terms of price, delivery, etc.

Reflecting the state of the industry, the corporation discussed in this 'regional rationaliser' category was acquired and subsequently divested by a US conglomerate, and now finds itself as a dedicated machine tool group. The question is perhaps how long it will remain in this category, and indeed whether there is a future within an end-game scenario for facilities both in the USA and the UK.

Case 3 – Focus factory phoenix

Unusually in the machine tool industry, this US company developed a wide spread of facilities around the world, after its first overseas factory was set up in Britain in 1934. As with all the 'first-comers' (long-established MNEs in Europe) (Young *et al.* 1991), substantial rationalisation has been in evidence in this company, employment in the UK, for example, having fallen by over one-third in the five years to 1988 as part of a worldwide restructuring programme. The corporation has embarked upon a low cost, volume-based strategy revolving around world-class manufacturing, essentially replicating the Japanese. This is being implemented through independent focus factories with full profit and loss responsibility for each major machine tool product category and world market mandates.[3] A centralised organisation with vertically integrated facilities is being replaced by decentralisation and much lower levels of vertical integration (bought-in items represent as much as 75 per cent of final product value in the UK operation).

With the strategy only being announced in 1988, new manufacturing and product policies are still at the early stages of implementation in the UK. New manufacturing practices and technologies are being introduced in pursuit of 'manufacturing-based competitive advantage' (Hayes and Wheelwright, 1984). A multiplicity of low volume products are being phased out ('getting away from letting engineers design products') in pursuit of product standardisation and volume manufacture.

Single European Market issues were regarded as primarily to do with standards and regulations, especially in the areas of quality and safety. As the company was already well-established in Continental Europe, with direct sales into France, Germany and Italy and agents elsewhere, questions of developing marketing and distribution were not a problem. The major change, regarded as inevitable even without 1992, was the further rationalisation of competitors and therefore the volatility of competition and competitive practices.

Still burdened with excess space and recognising that 'if we started again it wouldn't be from here', there is substantial commitment throughout the corporation to succeed as a big player within the machine tool industry. It is not clear, however, how far the more autonomous focus factory concept will facilitate competitiveness *vis-à-vis* Japan. The view is that since the focus factories have their own area of specialisation, each is better able to keep close to the market and the customer. But success is going to depend heavily also on group support, which at present appears to be being reduced.

Case 4 – Cautious challenger

The West German machine tool industry has historically been one of the strongest in the world, and the companies have followed a fairly common and cautious export-based approach in their internationalisation. Typical of this is one welding and cutting equipment producer which had a sales presence in the UK since the 1930s, before setting up its own sales and service subsidiary in 1960. After cutting back sharply in the 1970s in the face of Far Eastern competition, the firm evolved to small-scale assembly operations in Britain in 1987. But an SEM-related study on the possibilities for larger-scale decentralisation of assembly was initiated at the end of the 1980s by a new executive coming into the machine tool company from another group enterprise. The UK company was optimistic that it would gain this assembly franchise against competition from group companies in France and Austria. Initial savings of 23 per cent on German costs were estimated, and with learning curve benefits after assembly commenced, total savings of around 30 per cent were predicted. These differences in costs were essentially derived from direct wages and fringe benefits which were 100 per cent higher in Germany (wage rates alone 35–45 per cent higher).

As with other German enterprises, the cautious challenger is moving very slowly to offshore activity, partly a reflection of tradition, partly of resistance from German unions, and prospects for production as opposed to assembly outside Germany seem remote. The exception concerns instances where foreign subsidiaries identify market gaps for new tools not produced by the parent, in which case authority to design and manufacture may be granted to the affiliate (one such case existed in the sample). What is more likely perhaps is a different type of foreign direct investment evolution, namely towards the formation of sales, engineering & consultancy subsidiaries overseas to facilitate the 'human skills customisation' which will generate competitive advantage in the era of growing systems business. Interestingly, therefore, cautious German MNEs have the advantage over the Americans of not being burdened with redundant manufacturing capacity in politically sensitive foreign locations, while having the flexibility to exploit the opportunities of the 1990s.

Case 5 – International invader

In a quite different situation again is the international invader, entering Europe with an established market base and able to plan optimally in terms of site location, build a state-of-the-art factory and focus upon the European market as a whole (in the case concerned, 85 per cent of the Japanese company's sales were made in Continental Europe). The company philosophy is to produce core machines capable of a variety of uses, with a range of options to meet market requirements globally (derogatorily but inaccurately termed 'peas-in-a-pod' strategy by another multinational). Key elements of competitive advantage include world class manufacturing, utilising FMS and CIM systems internally; in-house control or supply of key technologies (e.g. numerical controllers); and the emphasis upon a broad rather than narrow market segment giving scale advantages and the possibility of rapid upgrading of process technology.

It was argued by the company that the decision to produce in the UK was taken against a backcloth of corporate strategy emphasising manufacture within the main market areas. The UK was selected because of language, and because the company president liked the idea of building in the home of the industrial revolution. The actual site was chosen to be close to the company's sales office and demonstration area established some years previously. Presumably financial assistance was a factor also, as £5.2 million aid was received under the FMS grant scheme. It was argued that protectionism was not a factor in the decision to establish a manufacturing facility in Europe as the decision had been made before protectionism had become a major issue in machine tools.

The UK company is one of a number of 'miniature replica' assembly facilities (White and Poynter 1984) around the world, serving regional markets with part of the parent corporation's complete product range.[4] The principle underlying this is the well-established one that it is easier to sell where manufacture takes place.

Planned with Europe (if not the SEM) in mind, it is hardly surprising that there are no major issues surrounding 1992. In a company with an extremely well-established manufacturing base in Europe, the main impact of 1992 was seen in terms of ease of movement of goods across national boundaries. It has to be said, however, that the company recognised problems on the political front (complaints from European competitors concerning low levels of local content and failure to transfer technology) and this may be viewed as a 1992-related issue.

The shock-waves surrounding the European entry of this Japanese producer cannot be overstated. The company, in terms of performance, is in a different league to most other domestic or multinational machine tool enterprises in Europe. In 1988, for instance, turnover per employee was well over double the average for all machine tool MNEs in Britain; fixed assets per employee were eight times as great as the average. And a competitor pointed out that the Japanese MNE's sales targets were equivalent to the entire European machine tool sales in the particular segment in which they were operating. Despite the strong statement of the deputy managing director when interviewed that this machine tool maker would not build another factory in Europe, it has now been announced that a components manufacturing facility will be set-up in France, with perhaps another to follow in Germany at a later date.

While this entry decision is the most prominent, several other Japanese firms either acquired or increased equity stakes in European machine tool enterprises from 1987 onwards and there have been at least two greenfield entrants in the components' field. Most of these direct investments have taken place in Continental Europe rather than the UK. Despite the protestations of the international invader, it seems likely that protectionist pressures proved important in that investment decision and crucial in those made subsequently. From the firm perspective, many Japanese machine tool companies are cash rich; local production in Europe not only circumvents VRAs but offsets some of the effects of the strong yen and the companies are confident of their competitive edge given their export performance over the years.

DISCUSSION

The case illustrations (summarised in Table 2.1) largely confirm the 'big issues' for firms which were discussed at the beginning of this chapter. It is difficult to avoid the conclusion that the key issues revolve around Japan vs the rest of the world, and that the SEM is a less important environmental variable than other industry-related factors. In relation to the former, the American (and to a lesser extent Continental European) MNEs operating in Britain suffer the same 'competitiveness gap' as indigenous British MT producers, as highlighted in a recent paper from the Industrial Bank of Japan (1989) (Figure 2.1). The superiority of Japan in mass

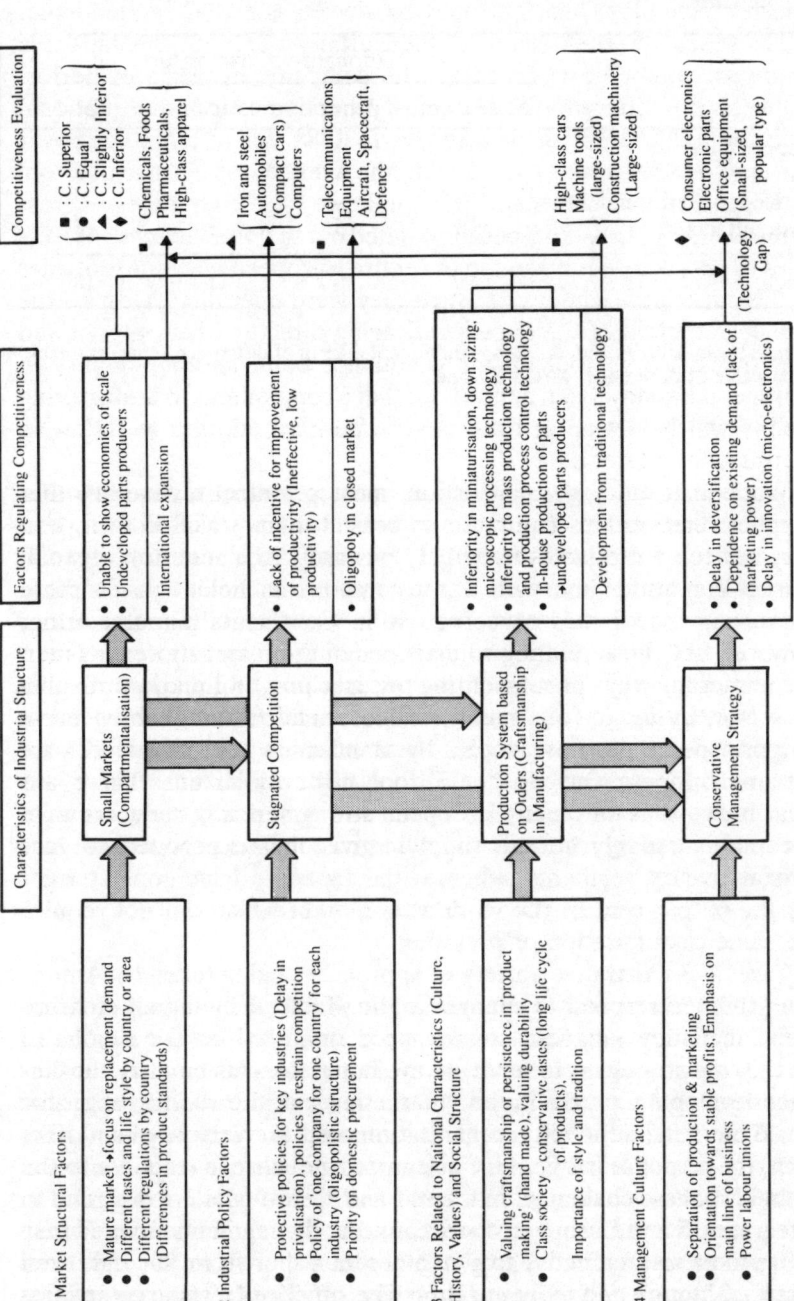

Figure 2.1 Why EC industries are strong in 'producing by order' and are weak in 'mass production'. (From Industrial Bank of Japan, 1989: Chart 3.)

Table 2.2: Sample foreign-owned companies' attitudes to SEM 1992 (number of companies)

	Nationality of ownership			
	N.America	*Europe*	*Japan*	*Total*
Opportunity	1	–	–	1
Threat	–	–	–	–
Both opportunity and threat	2	–	–	2
Little effect[a]	8	6	1	15
Total	11	6	1	18

[a] Typical comments included: 'damp squib', 'not a scrap of difference', 'parent unable to conceive of differences within Europe'.

Source: Interview data.

production technology, production process control technology and supplier relationships (in-house or bought-in) are well known, and very difficult for others to combat, especially in a situation of weak market conditions and with a history of retrenchment. Even more interesting than issues concerned with world class manufacturing, however, are those relating to market definition and strategy. There are numerous ways of segmenting the machine tool market: it splits by sector, by usage (e.g. metal cutting, metal forming), by general purpose/special purpose tools, by stand-alone as compared with systems business and by heavy tools/light tools, etc. There are clear indications that many European and American producers have become excessively niched, supplying customised products to very narrow market segments, whereas the Japanese have gone straight for the 60 per cent of the worldwide market which did not require the same customisation or precision.

Cases 1–3 illustrate a variety of approaches being taken by American MNEs to respond to changes in the world machine tool environment, including Japanese dominance in small NC machine tools. In Case 3, the strategy is to replicate the Japanese, with country subsidiaries developing, producing and marketing specific product ranges for world markets: although reorganisation costs are very large and risks high, the response is a genuine attempt to globalise in response to the global Japanese challenge. In Cases 1 and 2, strategies are designed to integrate US and European operations, but the segments covered may prove to be too restrictive to give other than short-term success, even if rationalisation and reorganisation pays off. The German companies

Table 2.3 Planned responses to SEM 1992 (number of responses[a])

| | Nationality of ownership | | | |
	N. America	Europe	Japan	Total
Develop Euro-product	1	–	–	1
Major marketing effort in Continental Europe	2	–	–	2
Replace agents/distributors with sales companies	3	–	–	3
Form alliances with Continental European companies	3	1	–	4
General awareness activity	4	2	–	6
Manufacture/assembly in Continental Europe	–	1	–	1
None	1	3	1	5
Total	14	7	1	22

[a] Number of responses are greater than number of companies.

Source: Interview data.

studied appeared to be better placed to respond to the demand characteristics of the 1990s with their international supply strategies providing greater flexibility. Commitment to product differentiation, moreover, meant less likelihood of being driven into niche markets by Far Eastern competition.

As regards 1992, the argument developed elsewhere (Young *et al.* 1991) that the 'latecomers' (as compared with the 'first-comers') will be the major beneficiaries of the Single Market applies in machine tools as in other sectors. The Japanese case (Case 5) shows how new greenfield entry has facilitated the development of yet another layer of competitive advantage. Despite the increased competition from this source and the fact that sales by sample North American companies into Continental Europe averaged only 15 per cent of their total sales in 1988, the SEM was still seen as having little effect (Table 2.2).

As a consequence of playing down the impact of 1992, planned responses are disturbingly limited as Table 2.3 suggests. The general theme is one of trying to increase market penetration in Continental Europe, by a variety of means. It seems that many foreign MNEs in the UK lost Continental European markets during the problems of the 1970s and 1980s, and a number are at the stage of completing strategic and manufacturing reorganisation before making efforts to re-enter the Continental market. A German company in the sample responded to this view by suggesting that if some MNEs were only now thinking of trying to build a significant presence, they were far too late already. Particular concern in Table 2.3 attaches to the limited commitment to replacing agency and distributorship agreements by more direct selling arrangements including the support of resident sales engineers, as competitive advantage has systematically shifted downstream. Similarly the limited planned activity in cross-frontier alliances and cooperations is both surprising and alarming. It is difficult to avoid the conclusion that many American and European companies are still only 'playing' and have not really recognised the fundamentals of the industry and the changes which have and will continue to take place.

NOTES

1 The study on 'Foreign subsidiary roles and British competitiveness' was funded by the ESRC. Eighteen overseas-owned machine tool companies in the UK were interviewed, together with twelve UK-owned firms. The aims of the research overall were to develop a framework for classifying the roles and strategies of foreign subsidiaries; to explore the consequences of corporate strategies and strategic change for UK competitiveness; and to derive policy conclusions relating to industrial and corporate policies.

2 Defined as follows: domestic – competition is chiefly between domestic producers; international – competition is trade-based; multinational – MNEs compete with each other from dispersed manufacturing facilities, but there is no coordinated, integrated approach to international strategy; global – companies plan and implement coordinated strategies for world-wide markets irrespective of the method of supplying these markets.

3 The concept of the 'focus factory' is similar to that of 'lead subsidiary', 'centre of excellence' and 'world product mandates'. See Bartlett and Ghoshal (1986).

4 The 'miniature replica' is one of a typology of multinational subsidiaries defined as follows (White and Poynter 1984):

Marketing satellite:	marketing subsidiaries.
Miniature replica:	a smaller-scale version of the parent company.
Rationalised manufacturer:	a producer of a particular set of component parts or intermediate products for incorporation elsewhere into final goods.
Product specialist:	development, manufacturing and marketing responsibility for a limited product line for regional or global markets. See also 'focus factory' (Note 3).

Strategic independent: subsidiary is permitted independence to develop lines of business for overseas markets.

REFERENCES

Bartlett, C. A. and Ghoshal, S. (1986) 'Tap your subsidiaries for global reach', *Harvard Business Review*, November/December, pp. 87–94.

Cecchini, P. *et al.* (1988), *The European Challenge 1992 – The Benefits of a Single Market*, Aldershot, Hants, Wildwood House.

Collis, D. J. (1988) 'The machine tool industry and industrial policy 1955–82', Harvard Business School Case Study 9–388–117.

The Engineer (1987) 15 October.

The Engineer (1988) 28 April, p. 18.

Hayes, R. H. and Wheelwright, S. C. (1984) *Retaining Our Competitive Edge: Competing Through Manufacturing*, New York, John Wiley.

Industrial Bank of Japan (1989) 'EC 1992 and Japanese Corporations', *IBJ Review*, 8, 12 July.

Machinery (1988) 7 October.

The Machine Tool Technologies Association (MTTA) (1989) *Machine Tool Statistics 1989*, London, MTTA.

O'Brien, P. (1987) 'Machine tools: Growing internationalisation in a small firm industry', *Multinational Business* 4, 23–34.

Pelkmans, J. and Winters, A. (1988) *Europe's Domestic Market, Chatham House Papers 43*, London, RIIA/Routledge.

Porter, M. E. (ed.) (1986) *Competition in Global Industries*, Boston, Harvard Business School Press.

Rendeiro, J. O. (1985) 'How the Japanese came to dominate the machine tool industry', *Long Range Planning* 18(3), 62–7.

Rendeiro, J. O. (1988) 'Technical change and vertical disintegration in global competition: Lessons from machine tools', in N. Hood and J.-E. Vahlne (eds) *Strategies in Global Competition*, London, Croom Helm.

Rohan, T. M. (1984) 'Tool-builders reach out', *Industry Week*, 20 August.

Scibberas, E. and Payne, B. D. (1985) *The Machine Tool Industry*, London, Technical Change Centre.

White, R. E. and Poynter, T. A. (1984) 'Strategies for foreign-owned subsidiaries in Canada', *Business Quarterly*, Summer.

Young, S. and Dunlop, S. (1990) 'Dimensions of multinational activity in the UK machine tool industry', Strathclyde International Business Unit Working Paper 90/1, University of Strathclyde.

Young, S., McDermott, M. and Dunlop, S. (1991), 'Non-EC multinationals and the single market challenge', in B. Bürgenmeier and J.-L. Mucchielli (eds), *Multinationals and Europe* 1992, London, Routledge.

3 Competitive strategy in the market for microcomputers

Strategy and performance of the dominant firm

Robert van der Meer and Mairi Gudim

INTRODUCTION: SEGMENTATION

The most commonly distinguished segments in the computer or information systems (IS) industry are mainframe computers, minicomputers, microcomputers, peripherals, software, maintenance and other services, and data communications (Figure 3.1).[1] The International Business Machines (IBM) Corporation has typically held a dominant position in almost all of these segments (Figure 3.2).

This chapter will analyse IBM's competitive strategy in the market for microcomputers. To guide the analysis, the chapter will propose a theoretical framework and, based on an analysis of IBM's competitive strategy in the mainframe computer market in the 1960s, it will formulate a number of specific hypotheses relating to the

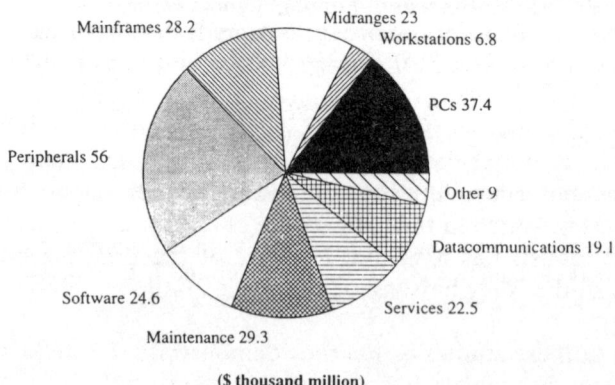

($ thousand million)

Figure 3.1 Segments in the information systems industry, 1989. (From *Datamation*, June 1990.)

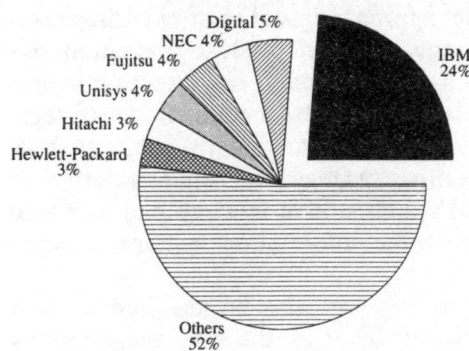

Figure 3.2 Major companies in the information systems industry, 1989. (From *Datamation*, June 1990.)

competitive strategy of the dominant firm in an industry subject to rapid technological change. After reviewing its current strategy and performance in the microcomputer market, IBM's new corporate strategy for the 1990s will finally be addressed.

THEORETICAL FRAMEWORK

The information systems industry has been analysed before by a variety of authors. There follows a brief review of the methodology behind some of these studies, pointing out advantages and drawbacks.

Several studies of the information systems industry have been carried out by economists (see, for example, Shaw and Sutton 1976; McAdams 1982; Brook 1986). These have tended to be based on the Structure–Conduct–Performance (SCP) model of industrial economics. The SCP model shows how the structure of an industry influences the conduct (including the competitive strategies) of the firms in that industry, which in turn affects the performance of these firms and of the industry as a whole. Because of the time period covered in these studies they have tended to focus on the mainframe computer market.

An advantage of these studies is that they demonstrate that IBM's competitive strategy has always been based on its perception of the structure of the information systems industry in terms of the barriers to new entrants, the rivalry among existing competitors, the threat of substitute products, etc. The studies show how IBM has managed to defend its dominant position *vis-à-vis* its competitors in the mainframe computer market.

But adopting the 'economic' approach has at least two disadvantages. First, by its very nature this approach tends to overemphasise the role of the dominant firm as a price leader; less attention is thus paid to the other important elements of IBM's competitive strategy. Second, this approach encourages a predominantly static analysis of the dominant firm's competitive strategy: the studies referred to above do not show how IBM's competitive strategy had a crucial effect on how the structure of the information systems industry developed over time.

The information systems industry can also be analysed using a strategic management framework, such as the one suggested by Porter (see, for example, Quinn *et al.* 1988, cases 1–7 and III–5). Porter (1980, 1985) combines concepts from the fields of business policy and industrial economics in order to demonstrate how a firm's strategic options are constrained by the view that the firm takes of its external environment, in particular the competitive situation that the firm faces in its industry. He argues that there are two basic types of sustainable competitive advantage that a firm can possess: low cost or differentiation; and all competitive strategies can be reduced to three generic strategies, namely cost leadership, differentiation and focus. According to Porter, each of the generic strategies involves a fundamentally different route to competitive advantage: a firm that engages in each generic strategy but fails to achieve any of them is 'stuck in the middle' and will achieve no competitive advantage at all.

Porter's generic strategies may be linked to the industry life cycle concept – a concept that has a clear analogy with the product life cycle – in order to analyse the relationships between the stage of industry development and the strategic positions of individual firms within the industry. According to a view held by many authors, the emergent and growth phases of the industry life cycle are characterised by product innovation and differentiation, whereas standardisation, both in product and in process design, is the most important feature of the mature stage of industry development (see, for example, Porter 1980, figure 8.2). On the basis of this view it is often argued that the dominant firm within the industry, acting as the market leader, should follow a competitive strategy which conforms to the current stage of industry development as follows: in the emergent and growth phases of the industry life cycle the dominant firm should use either a differentiation or a cost leadership strategy in order to 'keep ahead of the field'; whereas in the mature phase, when price competition is likely to be severe, the dominant firm ought to concentrate on a strategy based on cost leadership and the raising of barriers to entry (see, for example, Johnson and Scholes 1988, figures 7.3 and 7.4).

A different view is taken by Gilbert and Strebel (1988), who develop Porter's basic framework by arguing that:

1 'Competitive moves exploit the possible sources of competitive advantages in the industry. Their degree of effectiveness evolves with the industry life cycle and is influenced by the moves of other competitors.'
2 'Successful strategies rely on a sequence of competitive moves. There are only a few such successful sequences corresponding to different industry situations.'

Using the microcomputer market as an example, Gilbert and Strebel contend that the transition from the emergent to the growth phase of the industry life cycle is marked by standardisation and a shift to competitive advantages based on low delivered cost through process and distribution efficiency. They also contend that the mature phase of the industry life cycle is characterised by 'rejuvenation' – that is, a shift to product differentiation and innovation – in addition to cost reduction and process efficiency; in the mature stage of the industry development, firms must base their competitive advantages on both low delivered cost and high perceived value through differentiation. This implies that Gilbert and Strebel, in common with a number of other authors, reject Porter's assertion that the pursuit of more than one competitive advantage at the same time will necessarily lead to none being achieved at all.

According to Gilbert and Strebel, successful strategies generally consist of a planned sequence of strategic moves from one position to another, at the right stage of industry development; such successful strategies are termed 'outpacing' strategies. They distinguish between two different outpacing strategies:

1 A 'pre-emptive' strategy should be implemented by a market leader in order to actively shift the industry life cycle from the emergent phase to the growth phase. It consists of a high-perceived-value move by establishing a product standard, followed by a low-delivered-cost move by investing in process improvements as soon as the standard is accepted by the market.
2 A 'pro-active' strategy is often implemented by an industry follower after the industry transition to maturity in order to escape the stalemate of lower growth and destructive price wars. It involves

building a low-delivered-cost position from which to launch a high-perceived-value move by focussing on selected market segments.

The theoretical framework developed by Gilbert and Strebel implies that the relationship between the stage of industry development and the competitive strategy of the dominant firm in the industry is two-way: if successful, the implementation of a new competitive strategy by the dominant firm will move the industry life cycle from one phase to the next. Also, Gilbert and Strebel give some indication as to which sequence of competitive moves by the dominant firm is likely to be effective at any particular stage of industry development.

Before investigating whether, and to what extent, the Gilbert and Strebel framework can be used to analyse IBM's current competitive strategy in the market for microcomputers, we shall examine the extent to which this framework is useful for an analysis of IBM's competitive strategy in the market for mainframe computers in the 1960s. As a result of this latter analysis, we intend to demonstrate that recent developments in the market for microcomputers have been foreshadowed by past developments in the information systems industry as a whole.

IBM'S COMPETITIVE STRATEGY IN THE MAINFRAME COMPUTER MARKET IN THE 1960s

As the economic studies referred to above demonstrate, the level of concentration in the mainframe computer market has always been very high. Since its emergence, this market segment has been dominated by IBM; the latter's competitors have typically held much lower market shares. This high level of concentration results mainly from very high barriers to entry into this market segment. These barriers take a number of different forms:

1 High economies of scale: as a firm's output increases, the average costs (per unit of output) of research, production, marketing, maintenance and other services fall rapidly.
2 A high degree of product differentiation, caused mainly by the software required to make the hardware run not being portable among systems produced by different manufacturers, or even among the systems produced by the same manufacturer. As a result, once a user has committed himself to a particular manufacturer's computer system, the costs involved in switching to a different system are typically very high – this is known as 'software lock-in'.
3 High absolute cost barriers, including the cost of the capital needed

to gain and then maintain market share. These absolute cost barriers used to be reinforced by IBM's practice of leasing rather than selling its computers, thereby increasing the amount of capital required by a new entrant into the market. Capital requirements were also raised by IBM's policy of only providing complete systems including hardware, software, maintenance and other services – a practice known as 'bundling'.[2] The effects of the learning curve – which predicts that average production costs will fall as more units of a particular high-technology product are produced over time, thus giving an absolute cost advantage to established firms over new entrants – have only been important in raising cost barriers insofar as IBM has developed proprietary product designs and process technologies.

There have been other factors facilitating IBM's dominance in the mainframe computer market, such as the absence of buyer power on the part of IBM's customers. Quite often buyers lacked the necessary technical expertise to make informed decisions, and therefore relied on IBM to choose the most appropriate package for them. Because of the superiority of computer data-processing systems over manually operated systems, substitute products were not acceptable. In consequence, buyers' price sensitivity tended to be low: in order to get a computer system that they perceived as satifying their business needs, users were quite willing to pay a premium price to a supplier with a reputation for quality.

As is obvious from statements from Thomas Watson Jr. – the son of IBM's founder, and the man who was himself in charge of IBM between 1956 and 1971 – IBM's overall business strategy has been over the years to gain and subsequently maintain a dominant market share in every growth segment of the information systems industry, and to contest vigorously every significant new entry into the industry by rival manufacturers (quoted in DeLamarter 1986: 56). In the process, IBM has always been willing to sacrifice short-term profits, if necessary. To understand fully how this policy was implemented in the mainframe computer market in the 1960s, we must consider the historical development of this market segment, using the industry life cycle concept.

We can divide the life cycle of the mainframe computer market into three phases, namely:

First phase (1951–64)   – emergence
Second phase (1964–70)   – growth
Third phase (1970 onwards) – maturity

In the first phase, IBM's achievement of dominance in the emergent computer industry was based on its dominant position in the adjacent market for accounting machines based on punch card technology, rather than on any technological superiority over its rivals. IBM competed with other computer manufacturers offering complete data-processing systems which continuously threatened to erode its market share, by using a 'fast follower' technological strategy – that is, a strategy based on the adoption of proven innovations of others. (With some notable exceptions, such as the development of the System/360 family of mainframe computers and the introduction of the IBM PC discussed below, this has remained IBM's favoured technological strategy.)

IBM responded to these competitive threats to its dominant position by implementing a pre-emptive strategy, thereby shifting the mainframe computer market into the second phase of its life cycle: in 1964 IBM introduced the System/360 family of mainframe computers which was designed to knock out the existing competition. The main principle on which the computers in this system were based was that of standardisation: the different components of the system were designed to work in almost any combination with each other. The System/360 family was quickly established as the dominant design for mainframe computers (Tushman and Anderson, 1986). Its introduction further stimulated the rapid development of the market already occurring because of a positive 'network externality' (Chow, 1967): as more and more organisations own computers, more and better software is written, and more people are trained in the use of the new technology; therefore, the value to the buyer of having a computer increases. The greater the degree of standardisation in computer design, the more important this network externality is likely to be.

Through the development of the System/360 family IBM became, for a limited, but crucial period, the technological leader and consequently gained an important first-mover advantage: because of learning curve effects and the greatly increased economies of scale derived from the standardisation inherent in the design of the System/360 family, IBM was the first manufacturer of mainframe computer systems to be able to move to a position based on low cost. By thus establishing cost leadership IBM successfully contained the threat to its market share from its old rivals – the technological 'pioneers' in the mainframe computer market. Also, because the introduction of the System/360 family significantly increased the minimum efficient scale of production and the amount of capital required to enter the market with a complete mainframe computer system, entry barriers for firms wishing to produce their own proprietary systems were raised even further.[3]

During the growth phase of the mainframe computer market IBM faced a range of competitive threats. For instance, the Control Data Corporation (CDC) threatened IBM's position of technological leadership by launching its technically superior 6600 model; this challenge was eventually beaten off by IBM using its superior strength in product marketing. On the other hand, the Digital Equipment Corporation (DEC) attempted to avoid direct competition with IBM in the mainframe computer market by targeting the newly created market segment of minicomputers. However, once IBM had secured its position as market leader in the mainframe computer market from threats by technologically innovative firms offering their own proprietary systems, the most serious threat to its long-term profitability stemmed from the entry into the information systems industry by a new group of manufacturers adopting the industry standards that IBM had established.

The introduction of the hardware and software standards on which the System/360 family was based significantly reduced the degree of product differentiation in the market. Therefore, entry barriers were lowered for a group of independent manufacturers who took advantage of the simple and stable interfaces among the various components of the System/360 family, to adopt focus strategies, based on low cost or differentiation or both, by targeting both system components on which IBM earned particularly high profits (such as add-on memory) and peripheral devices (such as disk and tape drives). By acting initially as technological fast followers these so-called plug-compatible-manufacturers (PCMs) benefited from positive externalities associated with IBM's technological and market leadership: they offered owners of IBM mainframe computers fully compatible system components and peripherals of a superior design and/or of a lower price than the ones supplied by IBM itself. Because IBM derived a large part of its total profits from the sale of system components and peripherals, the growth in the PCMs' share of the sales of these items posed a long-term threat to IBM's profitability.

IBM enjoyed significant first-mover advantages, both in terms of cost and, in particular, in terms of product marketing, over the PCMs. Initially, therefore, IBM was able to assume the role of price leader: by predicting the sales of its smaller competitors at different levels of the IBM-imposed market price, IBM could select the price levels that would maximise its own profits. But a pricing policy based on price leadership in markets subject to rapid technological change will, ultimately, be successful only if it is backed up by continuing technological leadership. Because IBM was unable to maintain its technological leadership over the PCMs, IBM's cost and marketing advantages diminished over time: the PCMs were able to undercut the high prices that IBM charged to its customers and still earn themselves large profits. Despite IBM's switching to a limit-pricing policy – designed to set prices at levels that ensured high profits for itself, while simultaneously limiting the expansion of existing rivals and the entry of potential new competitors – IBM's share of total industry sales of system components and peripherals was steadily eroded in the late 1960s.

As the mainframe market moved into the third phase of its life cycle, the only way that IBM could avoid the possibility of future destructive price wars with the PCMs was to implement a pro-active strategy: in 1970 IBM launched the new System/370 family of mainframe computers which was designed to re-establish a high degree of product differentiation in both the market for mainframe computers and the adjacent market segment of peripherals. In particular, the System/370 family was planned to make it much more difficult for independent manufacturers to make system components and peripheral devices that were fully compatible with the components and devices on which IBM charged its high profit mark-ups. In consequence, compatibility among the products from rival manufacturers of system components and peripherals declined, but there was also a serious diminution in compatibility among the elements of IBM's own product range.

The introduction of the System/370 family might be described as a high-perceived-value move in the sense that, in the eyes of users, it set the range of IBM products clearly apart from the range of products offered by IBM's competitors. Since its entry into the computer industry, IBM had attempted to pursue a policy of price discrimination: it would charge high prices, based on the IBM concept of 'functional pricing' – which involves setting a price according to the increase in function or performance as seen by the customer, not according to the actual delivered cost of that function – in those (sub-)segments of the market where it faced little or no competition, and lower prices in those (sub-)segments where it did have to contend with effective (existing or potential) competition. The decrease in product differentiation caused by the introduction of the System/360 family made this policy less easy to implement; conversely, the launch of the System/370 family would enable IBM to use this policy to great effect again.

Although the launch of the System/370 family reaffirmed IBM's dominance in the markets for mainframe computers and peripherals, this dominance was not based on continuing technological leadership by IBM in these market segments. As predicted by the relevant economic and organisational theory – summarised by Mueller (1988) – innovations are to be expected from newcomers rather than from established firms for a number of reasons. First, from an economic perspective, the net profits from a successful product innovation are lower for the established firm than for a newcomer, because the former must take account of the effect of the innovation on the profits that it is earning on its existing range of products. Second, from an organisational perspective, a large, rigidly structured firm may suffer from problems of control loss and information distortion; and it may not be able to offer its managers the necessary incentives to undertake the enormous risks surrounding major innovations.

In the development and introduction of the System/360 family IBM was less affected by the economic problem, because its installed base of computers was still relatively small, and managed to overcome the organisational problems. But by the time the System/370 family was launched IBM suffered from most of the problems of large size: its installed base of mainframe computer hardware and software was now very large; the innovative designer Gene Amdahl ('the father of the System/360') left the company because

> IBM was too concerned with protecting its present price and cost structure to bring out products that could provide users with better performance for lower prices. New technology was available to build such machines, but the company was locked into its skewed pricing scheme to such a degree that it could not act without adversely affecting revenues and profits.
>
> (DeLamarter 1986: 220–1).

After 1970 IBM reverted to a fast follower technological strategy in the mainframe computer market; in consequence, its record of product innovation in this market segment has not been impressive since.

However, the large installed base of mainframe computer hardware and software that IBM had built up in the 1960s also gave it a crucial advantage over its rivals: it firmly established IBM as the 'arbiter of technical standards' (Shaw and Sutton 1976: 102), in the view of both users and many competitors in the mainframe computer market and its adjacent market segments (peripherals, software, maintenance). With the launch of the System/370 family IBM began to exploit this competitive advantage fully: it retained its position as market leader by keeping total control of the operating environment, both in hardware and in software terms, on which most of the industry's products were dependent. IBM could introduce changes in technical standards at short notice and without reference to its competitors, so that to users the latter firms always appeared to be lagging behind. (For instance, IBM could change the interfaces between the various components of its mainframe computer systems and withhold critical information about these changes from its rivals. Until these competitors had solved the technical problems caused thereby, IBM was able to limit users' choices to its own high-priced products and earn monopoly profits.) On the other hand, because the majority of users were unwilling to deviate from the industry standards as defined by IBM, for IBM's rivals to follow differentiation strategies of their own and introduce potentially successful innovations was very risky, both to themselves and to those who bought their products, unless and until these innovations were adopted by IBM for its own product range.

Despite the fact that after 1970 a new company, Amdahl Corporation, entered the mainframe market, selling complete computer systems that were designed to be fully compatible with IBM's own systems, IBM's competitive advantage in the mainframe computer market has proved to be enduring: in the 1970s and 1980s IBM's market share and profitability in this market segment have consistently been very high. Only in the last few years has IBM faced another serious threat in the market for mainframe computers, namely from Japanese manufacturers. In 1989, however, IBM still held more than 40 per cent of the market for mainframe computers (*Datamation* 1990).

Based on our analysis of IBM's competitive strategy in the mainframe computer market in the 1960s, we can formulate a number of specific hypotheses to guide our analysis of the market for microcomputers:

1 In an industry subject to rapid technological change, and in which there is a dominant firm, the establishment of, and control over, industry-wide technical standards is an essential factor in both the development of the industry and the competitive strategy of the dominant firm.
2 Technical standards may be established by the dominant firm through the implementation of a pre-emptive strategy; the establishment of these standards will stimulate industry growth because of a positive network externality.
3 Unless the technical standards are controlled by the dominant

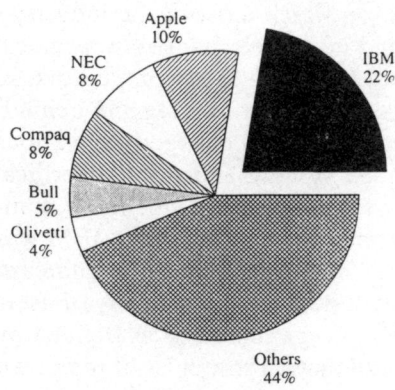

Figure 3.3 Major companies in the microcomputer market, 1989. (From *Datamation*, June 1990.)

firm from the outset, they will reduce the degree of product differentiation between the firms in the industry and, eventually, encourage new entry.
4 If the dominant firm loses its technological leadership over the new entrants, it will attempt to gain control over the technical standards through the implementation of a pro-active strategy; if successful, this strategy will increase the degree of product differentiation and enable the dominant firm to maintain its market leadership.

Note that in our analysis the concept of a pro-active strategy is applied in a manner that is quite different from the one originally suggested by Gilbert and Strebel: rather than being implemented by an industry follower focussing on selected market segments, we suggest that a pro-active strategy will be used by the dominant firm in order to maintain its market leadership in a range of segments.

IBM'S COMPETITIVE STRATEGY IN THE MICROCOMPUTER MARKET

Barriers to entry into the microcomputer market are much lower than is the case for the market for mainframe computers for a number of reasons:

1 Although it is hard to get accurate information on economies of scale in the various stages of producing and marketing micro-computer systems, we may safely assume that these economies

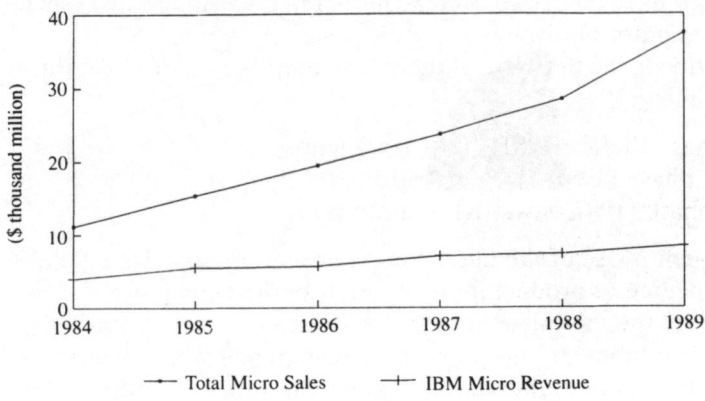

Figure 3.4 The microcomputer market. (From *Datamation*, 1985–90.)

of scale are much smaller than in the market for mainframe
computers: in the microcomputer market average costs (per unit of
output) of research, production and maintenance are comparatively
modest, and manufacturers can rely on an established network
of dealers rather than having to set up their own distribution
channels.

2 The degree of product differentiation in the microcomputer market has tended to be comparatively low: since 1981 almost all
microcomputers sold for business purposes have used a microprocessor chip (the Intel 80×86 family and, to a lesser extent, the
Motorola 68000 series) and an operating system (mainly Microsoft
DOS) sold on the open market by independent suppliers.

3 Because leasing microcomputers has been virtually absent, and
bundling microcomputer hardware, software, maintenance and
other services together in one package has been relatively unimportant in marketing terms, the cost of the capital required to
enter the microcomputer market has not been a major barrier.
Furthermore, many of the new entrants into this market segment
have largely avoided adverse learning curve effects by adopting well-established non-propietary product designs and process
technologies.

Also, as buyers of microcomputer systems have become better
informed, they have come to regard the particular brand of hardware as less important than its ability or otherwise to run the

desired (independently-supplied) applications software. In consequence, they have tended to become more price sensitive with respect to microcomputer hardware.

We can divide the life cycle of the microcomputer market into three phases, namely:

First phase (before 1981)   – emergence
Second phase (1981–7)   – growth
Third phase (1987 onwards)   – maturity

The emergent phase of the microcomputer market was characterised by a high degree of product innovation. The microcomputer systems developed by the various manufacturers were completely incompatible with each other. In this phase microcomputers were regarded as being the domain of enthusiasts and game players. However, despite the lack of compatibility between different systems, and despite serious business applications being few and far between, sales grew rapidly.

In line with its overall business policy of gaining and subsequently maintaining a dominant market share in every growth segment of the information systems industry, IBM entered the microcomputer market in 1981. It established a 'special operating unit' called Entry Systems with complete responsibility for designing, manufacturing and marketing the IBM Personal Computer (PC). Rather than relying on system components designed and manufactured by IBM itself, and carefully guarding the design of the overall microcomputer system, the Entry Systems unit used bought-in components (such as the Intel 8088 microprocessor chip) from independent suppliers in an 'open architecture' design with standard interfaces, the specification of which was made freely available. Furthermore, the Entry Systems unit commissioned the independent software house Microsoft to develop an operating system (called MS/PC DOS) which was also made publicly available and which rapidly generated a large amount of applications software.

Many authors (for example, Kotler 1986: 607–8) have argued that in its development of the IBM PC the Entry Systems unit deviated from the competitive strategy that IBM used in the mainframe computer market at that time; this strategy involved using only proprietary technology both in the hardware and software elements of its mainframe computer systems. However, that argument is misleading if it ignores the relationship between a firm's competitive strategy in a particular market segment and the stage of development of that market segment. Whereas in 1981 the mainframe computer market had been in its mature phase for some time, the microcomputer market was only just emerging. In line with our second hypothesis, the development of the IBM PC, which established a product standard for microcomputers, was a competitive (high-perceived-value) move analogous to the development of the System/360 family of mainframe computers in 1964. With the launch of the IBM PC in 1981, IBM implemented a pre-emptive strategy and thereby shifted the microcomputer market into the second phase of its life cycle.

At the beginning of the 1980s new software applications packages had been developed, such as spreadsheets (VisiCalc, for instance) and word-processing packages (WordStar, for instance) which were ideally suited for use on a microcomputer. As the popularity of these packages grew among business users, the need for a microcomputer system which could run these packages with the minimum amount of fuss became ever stronger: the IBM PC with its MS/PC DOS operating system suited this role to perfection. The IBM PC proved an enormous commercial success and was quickly established as the dominant design for microcomputers. As predicted by our second hypothesis, the hardware and software standards introduced by the IBM PC combined with the positive network externality already mentioned in our analysis of the market for mainframe computers greatly stimulated customer demand: after 1981 there was an explosive growth in the sales of microcomputer systems, in which growth IBM had a major share. Between 1981 and 1984 IBM captured more than a third of the market for microcomputers.

Through the development of its PC, IBM became the technological leader in the microcomputer market. Because it was the first company to benefit fully from economies of scale in the manufacturing and marketing of microcomputers, IBM also achieved cost leadership. The manufacturers that used to dominate the microcomputer market with their own proprietary systems before 1981 (the technological pioneers in the microcomputer market, such as Acorn, Apple, Commodore, etc.) got into serious difficulties after IBM's entry into this market segment. Their problems were mainly caused by the fact that, although capital requirements in the microcomputer market are lower than in the mainframe computer market, the cost of developing one's own proprietary system is nevertheless very high. The deadly combination of a long design stage and the short product life that is caused by rapidly advancing microcomputer technology means that the only way in which a firm that wants to produce non-IBM-compatible systems can maintain its market share is by consistently producing 'winners' (that is, commercially successful products)

(Schofield 1985). As soon as one of these manufacturers produced a microcomputer system that did not sell well (something that was almost bound to happen at some time), the capital required for the development of the next-generation product range was lacking. Of the manufacturers of non-IBM-compatible systems only Apple Computer Inc. managed to maintain a significant market presence; eventually, this company switched to a focus strategy based on differentiation with its technologically innovative Apple Macintosh range.

Because the open architecture of the IBM PC made any attempt by IBM at product differentiation extremely difficult, the main threat to IBM's position as market leader came from the entry into the microcomputer market of a new group of independent manufacturers adopting the hardware and software standards that IBM had set – in agreement with our third hypothesis. These latter manufacturers acted initially as technological fast followers in order to benefit from positive externalities associated with IBM's technological and market leadership: they offered IBM-compatible microcomputers ('IBM clones') of a superior design and/or a lower price than the original IBM products. Not only were the economies of scale gained by IBM in the production and marketing of its IBM PC range shared, to some extent, by the clone manufacturers, but, more importantly, the latter firms avoided the high development costs normally associated with the industry and could quickly follow any product innovations introduced by IBM. Although IBM revamped its product range a number of times, first – in 1983 – with the PC XT and then – in 1984 – with the PC AT based on the Intel 80286 microprocessor chip, all these product innovations were based on the open architecture design of the original IBM PC and were followed ever more rapidly by IBM's new rivals. From 1985 onwards, even the high degree of brand loyalty enjoyed by IBM was not enough to stop the phenomenal growth in the market share of the manufacturers of IBM clones.

At the start of the growth phase of the microcomputer market IBM exploited its first-mover advantages over the clone manufacturers by establishing itself as the price leader. However, this position was increasingly hard to maintain as IBM's initial cost and marketing advantages were eroded. Most of the clone manufacturers concentrated the production of their computers in low-wage countries in the Far East and used established dealer networks to reduce distribution costs. Also, as IBM was unable to maintain its technological leadership, some of the clone manufacturers targeted technologically innovative products at certain highly profitable market niches – for example, Compaq in the case of portable computers. Because the clone manufacturers were able to undercut the prices set by IBM and IBM's customers were less and less willing to pay premium prices just to have the IBM label on their microcomputers, the inconsistency between IBM's twin aims of high profit margins and large market share became more and more obvious.

After 1985 IBM made some attempt to retain its share of the microcomputer market by reducing the high profit margins on its products in a switch to a limit-pricing policy; but it was clear that a rigorous pursuit of such a policy would be ultimately self-defeating. IBM lacked a significant cost advantage over the clone manufacturers and was unable to differentiate its products to a sufficient degree from the clones – both factors implying lower barriers to entry into the microcomputer market. Therefore, any future price increase necessary to restore IBM's profitability would soon be followed by a renewed erosion of its market share. As predicted by our fourth hypothesis, as the microcomputer market moved into its mature phase and sales no longer grew at an exponential rate, IBM realised that it could only maintain its market leadership by the implementation of a new competitive strategy: it had to implement a pro-active strategy in order to reintroduce a significant degree of product differentiation.

In April 1987 IBM launched its entirely new Personal System/2 (PS/2) range of microcomputers. By incorporating proprietary technology into both the hardware and the software side of the PS/2 range, IBM made a radical departure from the principles on which its original PC was based. On the hardware side, IBM abandoned the open architecture design of the IBM PC and replaced the PC AT expansion bus, which was (and has remained) the industry standard, by the so-called Micro Channel Architecture (MCA) expansion bus, of which the technical design is patent-protected. In the period immediately following the introduction of the PS/2 range IBM began to enforce its microcomputer patents by charging hefty licence fees to those of its competitors wanting to incorporate its proprietary technology into their own products.[4] On the software side, IBM introduced a completely new operating system called OS/2 (developed jointly by IBM and Microsoft) which, unlike the industry standard MS/PC DOS operating system, is under IBM's control and forms part of its proprietary Systems Applications Architecture (SAA) concept. (The SAA concept is the common framework for developing and using applications software across IBM's entire range of computer hardware, from mainframe computers all the way down to microcomputers.)

The launch of the PS/2 range was clearly intended to be a high-perceived-value move on IBM's part: by differentiating its own products from the ones offered by its competitors in the microcomputer market, IBM planned to move away from limit-pricing and towards a policy of price discrimination, based, perhaps, on its traditional concept of functional pricing. The basis for this product differentiation was technological, not so much in the sense of IBM regaining its position of technological leadership in the microcomputer market – in the view of many technical experts the technology incorporated in the PS/2 range with its OS/2 operating system was neither radically new nor (much) superior to the existing technology – but in the sense of IBM being able to exploit its position of arbiter of technical standards in this market segment. With the introduction of its PC in 1981, IBM had set technical standards based on 'open systems' – an open system enables users to choose among the hardware and applications software of many different suppliers; in contrast, with the launch of the PS/2 range in 1987, IBM attempted to use its dominant position, in terms of its installed base of microcomputer systems, to replace these open systems with systems based on its own proprietary technology over which it had complete control.

The implementation of a pro-active strategy in order to gain control over technical standards had given IBM a decisive competitive advantage in the mainframe market in the 1970s – in the sense that it enabled IBM to maintain both a dominant market share and high level of profitability. We shall now consider whether this type of strategy has been as successful in the market for microcomputers.

IBM'S CURRENT PERFORMANCE IN THE MICROCOMPUTER MARKET

On the hardware side of the new PS/2 range, the introduction of the proprietary MCA expansion bus has not been a success, so far. The vast majority of microcomputers now in use (that is, at the end of 1990) still contain the old-style PC AT expansion bus, with which the new MCA expansion bus is mechanically and electrically incompatible. Unfortunately for IBM, this situation is unlikely to change in the near future: microcomputers with the MCA bus only account for about a quarter of current sales by value – which is close to IBM's own market share.[5] The reluctance of both users and IBM's competitors to abandon the current industry standard and commit themselves to the MCA bus has been strengthened considerably by the fact that in September 1988 a number of manufacturers including

Compaq, Olivetti, Tandy and Zenith formed a consortium to develop a new expansion bus, the so-called Extended Industry Standard Architecture (EISA) bus, which is based on and compatible with the PC AT bus. Since its introduction in early 1990, a considerable number of manufacturers have incorporated this EISA expansion bus in their latest microcomputers based on the Intel 80486 microprocessor chip. In response, IBM is promoting greater acceptance of the MCA bus by appearing to soften its stance on licensing agreements and promising to share its development intentions with its rivals.

As regards the new operating system OS/2, some compatibility with the current industry standard operating system MS/PC DOS has been built in, in the sense that applications software written for MS/PC DOS can run under OS/2, but cannot use any of its advanced features.[6] Nevertheless, three years after its introduction OS/2 has a disappointingly low take-up: despite its offering multi-tasking facilities, which enable a user to run more than one program at the same time, most users still run popular business applications packages, such as Lotus 1–2–3, dBase, WordPerfect, etc., under MS/PC DOS. In 1990, the latter operating system's leading position was further strengthened when Microsoft launched a very popular version of Windows, the multi-tasking graphical user interface for microcomputers running MS/PC DOS, thereby negating many of the alleged advantages of OS/2. Currently it appears that, for some time to come, MS/PC DOS will remain the standard operating system for stand-alone microcomputers.

When considered as an operating system for microcomputers linked in a local area network or, more generally, as part of the operating environment for multi-user distributed computing, OS/2 is in direct competition with the UNIX operating system which, arguably, is becoming the industry standard for these applications (*Datamation* 1990: 185). UNIX is an open system which first became popular with scientific users; over the last few years it has been gaining increasing acceptance for business applications.[7] Already, UNIX is the most popular operating system for workstations (which are akin to top of the range microcomputers), and its range of applications is widening considerably to include 'desktop' microcomputers (middle of the range microcomputers) on the one hand, and minicomputers on the other hand.[8]

So far, IBM's attempt to introduce new technical standards based on its proprietary MCA expansion bus and OS/2 operating system into the microcomputer market, has not succeeded. Not only have

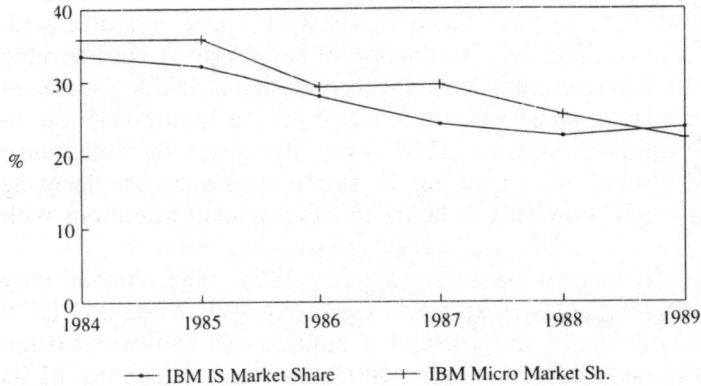

Figure 3.5 IBM's share of the microcomputer market. (From *Datamation*, 1985–90.)

the existing ('open') standards based on the PC AT bus and MS/PC DOS survived, but, even more ominously, their eventual replacements are likely to be based on the EISA bus and UNIX, neither of which are under IBM's control. In the microcomputer market, therefore, IBM's implementation of a pro-active strategy has not given it a decisive competitive advantage: since the launch of the PS/2 range, IBM's share of the microcomputer market has continued to decline rapidly. In 1989 IBM held just over 22 per cent of the microcomputer market, down from more than 35 per cent in 1985; there is little evidence that this decline in market share has been accompanied by a compensating rise in profitability (Figure 3.5). (Although IBM did abandon its limit-pricing policy after the launch of the PS/2 range and raised its profit margins on microcomputers from the low levels seen in 1986.)

During its growth phase, the focus strategies of smaller manufacturers such as Compaq were already beginning to create a number of sub-segments in the market for microcomputers; this process has accelerated in the current, mature phase, so that we can now distinguish between 'pocket-sized' PCs, 'notebooks', 'portables', 'desktops' and PC 'fileservers'. On the other hand, coincident with the microcomputer market entering its mature phase – and, to a certain extent, as a result of it – there has been a growing emphasis in the information systems industry on connectability (or 'connectivity' in industry jargon): the ability of different elements in a corporate information network to communicate and cooperate with each other.

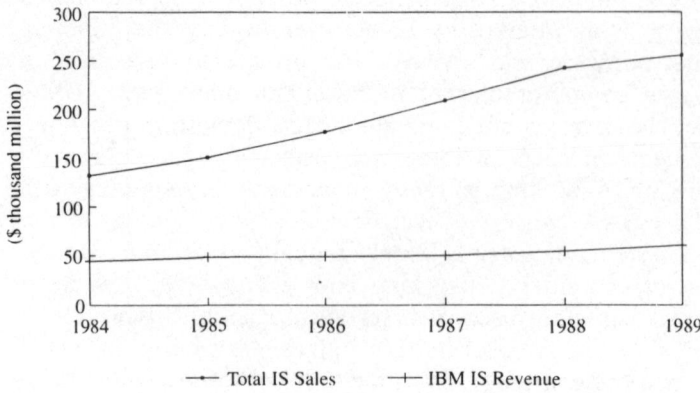

Figure 3.6 The information systems market. (From *Datamation*, 1985–90.)

This is providing a powerful stimulus towards re-integrating segments of the information systems industry which were previously widely separated, such as mainframe and microcomputers. Whereas in the 1980s, the microcomputer market could be viewed in isolation, this will be no longer possible in the 1990s: especially for IBM, which is the market leader in almost all of the many segments of the information systems industry, its future success in the microcomputer market will depend heavily on its future success in the industry as a whole.

IBM'S CORPORATE STRATEGY FOR THE 1990s (Figures 3.6 and 3.7)

In the late 1980s, IBM formulated a new corporate strategy for the 1990s under the direction of John Akers, its chief executive: to use its SAA concept to re-establish itself as the provider of complete information systems including hardware, software, data communications and consulting services (*Datamation* 1989: 26–49). Advertising itself as being – through SAA – in the best position to define its customers' business interests in the area of information management, IBM would like to be considered as the natural choice for the manager of the integrated computer environment: IBM wants to provide the design, specification, implementation, maintenance and ongoing management of its customers' information system resources. (As has been noted already, the OS/2 operating system developed for

IBM's PS/2 range of microcomputers is promoted as an (essential) building block in the SAA concept.) One possible interpretation of this strategy is as an attempt by IBM to reintroduce the bundling of hardware, software and services that proved so successful in the mainframe computer market in the 1950s and 1960s. IBM's stated policy, however, is not to preclude rival firms from providing specific elements of such an integrated package – particularly on the software side – as long as these elements are compatible with its proprietary SAA concept. Given that the future growth of the information systems industry is widely thought to be concentrated in the area of computer networking and 'client-server' systems,[9] in which areas commonly accepted technical standards have yet to be established, there is another, more plausible, interpretation of IBM's new corporate strategy: to gain control of technical standards for corporate network management, and thus to gain an enduring competitive advantage across all the main segments of the information systems industry.

However, IBM's competitive strategy in this respect faces serious opposition, not just from almost all the other computer manufacturers, but also, crucially, from powerful user groups, such as the US and UK governments and the European Commission, who are backing the so-called Open Systems Interconnection (OSI) concept for computer networking. As its name implies, the OSI concept is based on the use of open systems, such as the UNIX operating system, rather than on proprietary systems under the control of any manufacturer. If technical standards for corporate network management were to be based on the OSI concept, rather than on IBM's SAA concept, IBM's competitive position in the information systems industry as a whole would, almost certainly, be weakened. IBM would still be one of the very few firms able to supply complete information systems to its customers and, as such, would benefit from economies of scope; for each specific element of these systems, however, IBM would be forced to compete on more-or-less equal terms with niche market suppliers. In markets subject to continuing rapid technological change, technological leadership will be crucial to the outcome of any competitive battles between IBM and its rivals. We have already discussed the reasons why IBM, despite the vast resources that it can devote to R&D, has found it impossible to maintain its technological lead over its smaller, more innovative rivals in any of the market segments considered in this chapter.

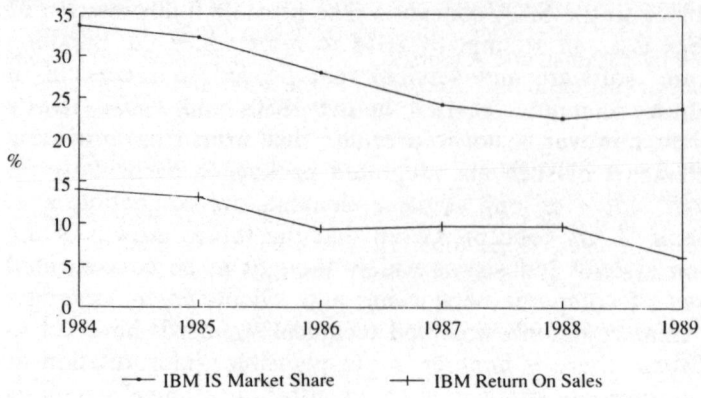

Figure 3.7 IBM's performance. (From *Datamation*, 1985–90.)

CONCLUSIONS

In this chapter we have demonstrated that, in a revised form, the Gilbert and Strebel framework can be used to analyse IBM's current competitive strategy in the market for microcomputers. In particular, based on our analysis of IBM's competitive strategy in the mainframe computer market in the 1960s, we have formulated a number of specific hypotheses relating to the competitive strategy of the dominant firm in an industry subject to rapid technological change; and we have shown that our analysis of IBM's competitive strategy in the microcomputer market does not lead us to reject these hypotheses. A number of caveats are in order: our analysis has been mainly qualitative, rather than quantitative; and it is concerned with two different segments of the same industry. Further research is needed to restate the hypotheses in a form enabling more powerful statistical tests to be performed, and to apply the analysis to a wider range of industries.

NOTES

1 In its June 1990 issue, *Datamation* introduced the following changes to its classification: microcomputers were renamed personal computers ('PCs'); minicomputers were decomposed into 'midranges' and 'workstations'. In this chapter we have maintained the old classification and terminology.
2 In the late 1960s IBM had to 'unbundle' the prices of much of its software and service offerings because of legal actions from some of its competitors.

3 Although the System/360 family of computers represented a major improvement in price/performance ratio over older models, it was essentially based on existing skills and know-how; and it was therefore classified by Tushman and Anderson (1986) as a 'competence-enhancing technological discontinuity'. According to the latter authors this kind of discontinuity tends to be associated with a decreased entry-to-exit ratio in the industry; we shall argue, however, that their hypothesis is somewhat misleading as is demonstrated by the large-scale entry of the PCMs into the information systems industry.

4 The royalty payments on the MCA bus typically ranged between 1 and 5 per cent of sales. In addition, IBM was known to demand a 'one time entrance fee' of 1 per cent on all prior sales of IBM-compatible products.

5 A small number of other manufacturers, for example Apricot, sell MCA machines.

6 For instance, users are still constrained by the 640K limit on RAM when running MS/PC DOS applications under OS/2.

7 Unfortunately, many computer manufacturers promote their own 'proprietary' versions of UNIX which tend to be mutually incompatible; for example, IBM's 'AIX'. However, AT&T's UNIX System V Rel.4 may well become the basis for an industry-standard version of UNIX (*Guardian*, 3 January 1991, p. 27).

8 In 1990 NCR announced a seven-level range of systems from laptop PCs to mainframe computers, all based on Intel 80386/486 microprocessors running DOS and/or UNIX (*Guardian*, 27 December 1990, p. 31.)

9 'Clients are any intelligent desktop systems capable of running a robust application in concert with a server, whether it be a dedicated print- or fileserver or a minicomputer or mainframe acting in such a capacity' (*Datamation*, 15 June 1990, p. 43).

REFERENCES

Brock, G. W. (1986) 'The computer industry', in W. Adams (ed.) *The Structure of American Industry*, 7th edn, New York, Macmillan, pp. 239–60.

Chow, G. (1967) 'Technological change and the demand for computers', *American Economic Review* vol. 57, no. 5, pp. 1117–30.

Chposky, J. and Leonsis, T. (1989) *Blue Magic: People, Power and Politics behind the IBM Personal Computer*, London, Grafton.

Datamation (1989) 1 January, vol. 34, no. 26.

Datamation (1990) 15 June, vol. 36, no. 12.

DeLamarter, R. T. (1986) *Big Blue: IBM's Use and Abuse of Power, London*, Macmillan.

Gilbert, X. and Strebel, P. (1988) '*Developing competitive advantage*', in J. B. Quinn, H. Mintzberg and R. M. James (eds) *The Strategy Process: Concepts, Contexts and Cases*, Englewood Cliffs, NJ, Prentice-Hall, pp. 70–9.

Johnson, G. and Scholes, K. (1988) *Exploring Corporate Strategy*, 2nd edn, London, Prentice-Hall.

Kotler, P. (1986) *Principles of Marketing*, 3rd edn, Englewood Cliffs, NJ, Prentice-Hall.

Langlois, R. N. *et al.* (1988) *Microelectronics – an Industry in Transition*, Boston, Unwin Hyman.

McAdams, A. K. (1982) 'The computer industry', in W. Adams (ed.) *The Structure of American Industry*, 6th edn, New York, Macmillan, pp. 249–97.

McKenna, R. (1989) *Who's Afraid of Big Blue? How Companies are Challenging IBM – and Winning*, Reading, Mass., Addison-Wesley.

Mercer, D. (1987) *IBM: How the World's Most Successful Corporation is Managed*, London, Kogan Page.

Mueller, D. C. (1988) 'The corporate life cycle', in S. Thompson and M. Wright (eds) *Internal Organisation, Efficiency and Profit*, Oxford, Philip Allan, pp. 38–64.

Porter, M. E. (1980) *Competitive Strategy*, New York, Free Press.

Porter, M. E. (1985) *Competitive Advantage*, New York, Free Press.

Quinn, J. B. Mintzberg, H. and James, R. M. (1988) *The Strategy Process*: **Concepts, Contexts and Cases**, Englewood Cliffs, NJ, Prentice-Hall.

Schofield, J. (1988) 'The nightmare logic of failure', *Guardian*, 10 October.

Shaw, R. W. and Sutton, C. J. (1976) *Industry & Competition*, London, Macmillan.

Tushman, M. L. and Anderson, P. (1986) 'Technological discontinuities and organizational environments', *Administrative Science Quarterly* vol. 31, pp. 439–65.

4 'Spain – the EC and 1992:

Marketing implications for Scottish Industry'.

Marilyn A. Stone

INTRODUCTION

The chapter examines trading patterns between Spain and the UK over the period 1970–89. It reviews trade developments that have taken place over the period including the effects of Spain's entry into the EC and assesses the likely marketing implications of the 1992 Single European Market.

The development from the Protectionist approach of the Spanish economic fiscal controls towards a greater level of European harmonisation since 1986 has demanded considerable changes in marketing management and approach. Threats and opportunities for UK and Spanish management in industry, commerce and the service sector are highlighted. Recommendations are made as to methods that would be appropriate to further enhance the benefits of closer economic and cultural links between the two countries that have been traditional 'outsiders' in 'Europe'.

The two have had a long history of misunderstandings (reflect on the Spanish Armada disaster and beyond) which over the last decade has been lessened considerably. Not only has tourist traffic increased substantially; so, too, has trade, inter-country investment, multinational activity, financial services support and cross-cultural exchanges. Yet British (and Scottish) industry has not fully taken up the marketing opportunities which are apparent.

ANALYSIS OF UK TRADING PATTERNS (1970–89 INCLUSIVE)

Over the period 1970–89 UK visible exports worldwide have increased from £8,063 million to £93,249 million, while UK imports have increased from £9,052 million to £120,788 million. This 'growth' has been influenced by UK membership of a number of trade blocs, namely the Commonwealth, the Organisation of Economic Cooperation and Development (OECD) Europe, OECD., European Free Trade Association (EFTA) and, since 1973, the EC.

The OECD was originally an association of European developed economies in 1970 (EC, EFTA., Irish Republic, Spain, Canary Islands, Spanish Ports in North Africa, Greece and Turkey). In 1973 it expanded to encompass most of the developed economies of the Western world to include North America, Japan and Australasia. This sector of the developed world is taking a steadily increasing share of UK trade, which is offset by declining trade with the Third World, including the Central Planned Economies as well as the Middle East and North African countries (since the heydays of the late 1970s). Imports from oil-exporting countries have fallen as North Sea UK oil production has come 'on-stream'. However, it is worth noting that UK exports have still had a significant benefit from the oil-related expansion of Middle East and North African countries despite their taking a declining share of overall UK export trade since the peak of 1976–9.

Over the period in question the EC has been enlarged (EC, 1987; Nicholson and East, 1987). From the initial six nations, it increased on 1 January, 1973 to include Ireland, Denmark and the UK. On 1 January 1981 it expanded to include Greece, and on 1 January 1986 Portugal and Spain joined. Whilst the EC has been increasing the number of European countries it encompasses, EFTA has had to contract as members cannot be aligned to both trade blocs. When Britain joined the EC in 1973 some special arrangements were made for Commonwealth agreements. Nevertheless, traditional trading patterns between Commonwealth countries and Britain were constrained in favour of EC markets.

In this way, while the membership of the EC over the period since 1970 has widened, the trading importance of the Commonwealth and EFTA has contracted. These factors have led increasingly to the UK turning to the EC for trading, which is reflected by the trend towards steady growth in the share of UK exports and imports.

Interpretation of trade statistics

The trade statistics presented in this chapter use current values and make no allowances for inflation, changes in exchange rates or any other variations that have occurred over the period in question. However, examination of the relative shares of the trading areas

Table 4.1 Trade by area/trade bloc: Exports from UK (as a percentage of total UK exports).

Trade bloc	1970 (%)	1975 (%)	1980 (%)	1987 (%)	1988 (%)	1989 (%)
EC	21.75	32.21	43.37	42.27	43.90	50.55
Rest Western Europe	19.34	16.91	14.25	9.54	90.76	8.71
North America	15.27	11.70	11.25	16.27	15.67	15.38
Other developed	n.a.	9.43	5.62	5.07	5.50	5.80
Latin America	3.51	3.45	2.24	1.49	1.35	1.24
Middle East & North Africa	n.a.	11.19	9.30	7.11	6.77	6.73
Other developing	n.a.	11.46	10.90	8.60	8.58	8.71
Centrally Planned Economies	3.21	3.34	2.76	1.93	19.75	1.92
EFTA	15.92	13.21	11.84	8.42	7.99	7.77
OECD	45.36	66.53	72.22	78.91	78.89	79.12
Oil exporters	n.a.	11.43	10.10	6.54	6.15	6.26
Commonwealth	21.02	16.29	13.01	10.91	10.94	11.19
Total trade (£million.)	8,063	19,922	47,363	79,849	81,654	93,249

of nations highlights trends in UK trading patterns. The period from 1970 to 1989 is a long one and a number of factors require to be taken into consideration when interpreting apparent changes in trading patterns. In some instances the countries comprising the trading bloc under examination have changed; similarly, factors such as the political and economic climate of a country, currency controls and key industries are likely to have altered. Critical changes have taken place in the membership of the associations of trading nations that have had their effect on UK trading patterns over the period 197C onwards.

Table 4.1 shows the relative increase in share of the EC of total UK exports from 22 per cent in 1970, to 32 per cent in 1974 and 51 per cent in 1989. In 1989 these UK exports to the EC amounted to £47.1 million.

Table 4.2 shows a similar, even more pronounced, trend for UK imports from the EC. These rose from 20 per cent in 1970 to 36 per cent in 1975, 52 per cent in 1988 but fell to 44 per cent in 1989. The 1989 imports to the UK amounted to £53.5 million (giving an adverse balance of trade for UK of £6.4 million).

Tables 4.1 and 4.2 indicate that the UK has changed her pattern of trading to favour the EC and OECD at the expense of traditional

Table 4.2 Trade by area/trade bloc: imports to UK (as a percentage of total UK imports)

Trade bloc	1970 (%)	1975 (%)	1980 (%)	1987 (%)	1988 (%)	1989 (%)
EC	20.13	36.42	41.34	52.70	52.37	44.29
Rest Western Europe	30.08	14.80	14.60	13.70	13.16	12.71
North America	20.51	13.29	15.00	11.47	12.11	12.57
Other developed	n.a.	7.67	6.77	7.75	7.99	7.70
Latin America	3.60	2.60	2.05	1.53	1.42	1.47
Middle East & North Africa	n.a.	12.53	9.51	2.27	2.32	2.25
Other developing	n.a.	9.50	8.40	7.89	8.09	8.24
Centrally Planned Economies	4.02	3.05	2.15	2.23	1.91	1.89
EFTA	15.60	12.62	12.69	12.82	12.44	12.03
OECD	41.32	69.10	76.15	84.86	84.82	84.73
Oil exporters	n.a.	13.59	8.54	1.81	1.96	1.92
Commonwealth	23.84	13.57	11.19	7.75	7.95	7.99
Total trade (£million)	9,052	24,128	49,773	94,026	106,571	120,788

partners in the Commonwealth. Share of trade from the Commonwealth has fallen for exports from 21 per cent in 1970 to 11 per cent of all UK exports in 1989. Similarly, for share of UK imports the Commonwealth has fallen from 24 per cent in 1970 to 8 per cent in 1989.

The traditional North American market has remained important for UK exports (15 per cent in 1970 as well as 1989) but has contributed to a fluctuating and declining share of UK imports (21 per cent in 1970 falling to 13 per cent in 1989).

The OECD, representing the major, developed economies is contributing to an increasing share of total UK trade. The share of UK exports going to the OECD increased from 45 per cent in 1970 to 67 per cent in 1975, remaining steady until 1982, since when it has grown to 79 per cent in 1989. The substantial increase from 1970 to 1973 is due to changes in the countries included in the OECD. The 1970 statistics covered only OECD Europe, but from 1973 onwards OECD worldwide was encompassed in the statistics. From 1973 onwards a more stable proportion of 71 per cent or so share of UK exports went to OECD countries. The pattern is similar for UK imports from the OECD which increased from 41 per cent in 1970 to 69 per cent in 1975 and 85 per cent in 1989.

By comparison EFTA has shown a declining share of trade over the same period with 16 per cent of UK exports in 1970 that fell to 8 per cent in 1989. Imports from EFTA to UK which were at 16 per cent in 1970 have declined, less severely than exports, to 12 per cent in 1989. EFTA has lost significance, as its one-time members have changed allegiance to join the EC (UK and Denmark on 1 January 1973). The likely application from Austria to join the EC will reinforce the trend.

Over the same period the Central Planned Economies (largely COMECON) have remained small contributors in UK trade, both in terms of exports and imports, and Latin America has reduced its share from a low initial base. The Middle East/North African countries have shown a fairly high share of UK trade. However, closer examination of the Middle East/North African trade statistics shows exports have fluctuated, generally falling slowly, from an 11 per cent to 12 per cent share over the period 1975–8 to 9 per cent in 1984 and 7 per cent in 1989. At the same time, the import trade to the UK from the Middle-East has fallen off, from 12 per cent in 1975 to 9 per cent in 1978 and more dramatically to 7 per cent in 1982, 4 per cent in 1984 and only 2 per cent in 1989. This trend is related to North Sea oil supplies replacing Middle Eastern sources, as well as a relative fall in the oil prices.

ANALYSIS OF TRENDS IN TRADING PATTERNS BETWEEN SPAIN AND THE UK

Share of UK exports

Among the three 'newest' EC members, Spain, Portugal and Greece, Spain has taken the larger share of UK exports (Figure 4.1). Spain received about 1.5 per cent of UK exports from 1970 to 1982, since when its share increased to reach 3.4 per cent in 1989 (£3,138 million). By comparison, Portugal's share of UK exports has fallen from the 1970/71 levels of 1.1 per cent to 1.0 per cent in 1989 (£916 million); Greece's share has been small and declining over the period 1970–89 (£571 million) from 0.7 per cent to 0.6 per cent.

From this cursory examination, it would seem that Portugal's entry into the EC on 1 January 1986 has had little effect on its share of UK exports, and certainly Greece's entry on 1 January 1981 does not seem to have had any positive effect on Greece's share. However, Spain's share of total UK exports has steadily increased since 1982, especially between 1986 and 1989, the period covering Spain's entry to the EC.

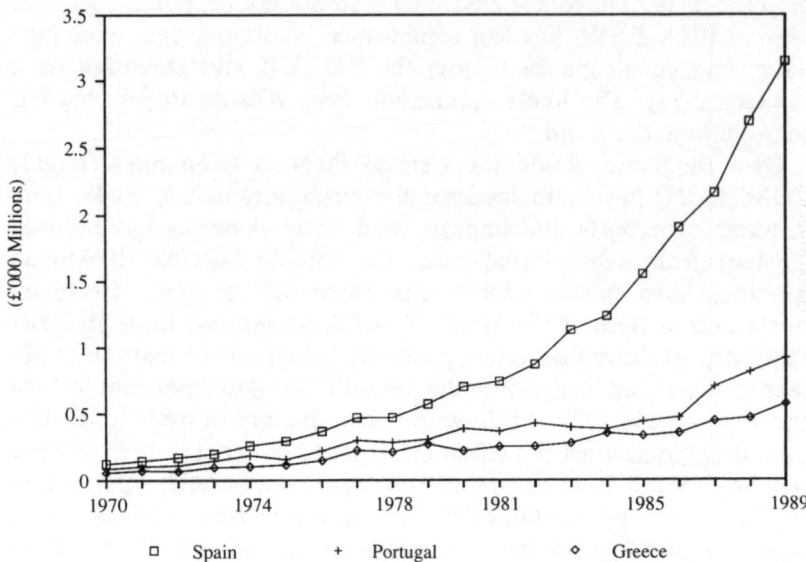

Figure 4.1 Exports from the UK to Spain, Portugal and Greece, 1970–89

Share of UK imports

Figure 4.2 shows similar trends for the share of UK imports from Spain, Portugal and Greece over the period 1970–89 as was shown for exports. Spain has provided a low but increasing share of total UK imports, rising from 1.2 per cent in 1970 to 2.0 per cent in 1984; 2.1 per cent in 1986 and 2.3 per cent in 1989 (£2,772 million) which is more than double the share of imports from Portugal (£1,041 million) and seven times the share of imports from Greece in 1989. Interestingly, in the early 1970s Spain and Portugal contributed to similar levels of UK imports. However, after 1973 when the UK joined the EC, the share of UK imports from Portugal fell, although subsequently there has been a small increase in the 1982–9 period. Imports from Greece have been at a steady, extremely low level (0.2 per cent in 1970 rising only to 0.3 per cent from 1984 to 1989 at £395 million).

Thus, in terms of contribution to total UK exports and imports Spain has had a low share since 1970 but this has increased, especially since Spain entered the EC. By comparison Portugal's share of

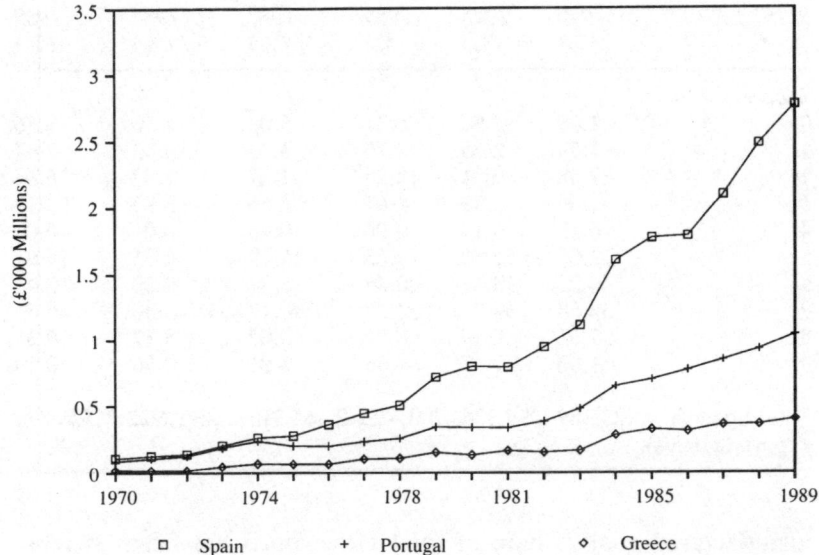

Figure 4.2 Imports to the UK from Spain, Portugal and Greece, 1970–89

exports and imports has been lower and falling, although a slight revival in the imports share is detectable since 1984. Greece, whose entry to the EC was initially associated with that of Spain and Portugal, has remained a country contributing only an extremely small share of UK trade in terms of visible exports and imports.

DETAILED ANALYSIS OF TRENDS IN EXPORTS FROM THE UK TO SPAIN (1970–89)

Product analysis of UK exports to Spain

Table 4.3 shows total exports from UK to Spain (in percentage terms) subdivided into the nine Standard International Trade Classifications (SITC), and depicts the changes that have occurred in the relative importance of the SITC groups over the period 1970–89.

Table 4.4 emphasises the concentration of UK exports on manufactured goods. In 1970 manufactured goods (SITC 6, 7 and 8 – detailed below) accounted for almost three-quarters (74 per cent) by value of all UK exports to Spain. However, since then, the

Table 4.3 Exports from UK to Spain by SITC (as percentage of total exports)

SITC	1970 (%)	1975 (%)	1980 (%)	1987 (%)	1988 (%)	1989 (%)
Section						
0	1.68	2.50	6.31	5.08	4.50	3.86
1	1.79	2.65	2.76	3.76	3.53	2.97
2	7.48	9.31	18.85	7.87	7.43	6.64
3	1.40	2.79	4.67	8.66	3.93	2.19
4	0.13	0.15	0.06	0.03	0.04	0.06
5	12.05	12.89	11.25	16.19	14.35	14.07
6	30.22	19.42	10.46	8.84	9.20	10.47
7	36.58	39.23	32.67	40.17	48.30	49.89
8	7.62	9.59	8.91	8.62	8.17	9.35
9	1.06	1.47	4.06	0.81	0.56	0.50
Total Spanish exports (£1000s)	123,169	294,734	700,429	2,164,316	2,691,662	1,526,821

manufactured goods' share of total UK exports has fallen steadily as shown below: their share fell to less than half (by value) in the 1984–6 period, although since then it rose to reach 70 per cent in 1989 (£1,060 million).

Of the categories SITC 6, 7 and 8, it is SITC 7, machinery and transport equipment, that predominates. This SITC 7 had 37 per cent by value of UK exports in 1970 and reached 39 per cent in 1977 but, thereafter, fell back to 33 per cent in 1980, 28 per cent in 1983, and 30 per cent for 1985 and 1986 (when Spain joined the EC on 1 January 1986). However, the share suddenly jumped in 1987 to 40 per cent of UK exports to Spain and to 50 per cent in 1989. This reflects the effect of changes in Spanish import regulations to the advantage of UK manufactures. The value of machinery and transport equipment exports from the UK to Spain in 1988 was £1,300 million, but this fell in 1989 to £762 million.

Further detailed analysis of SITC 7 shows that exports fall predominantly into the divisions 78 (road vehicles), 75 (office machines and data-processing machines), 72 (machinery specialised for particular industries), 76 (telecommunications and sound-recording equipment), and 77 (electrical machinery). Division 78 (road vehicles) has the largest contribution of any division, with a steady growth of share of total exports to 14 per cent in 1987, falling to 10 per cent in 1988,

Table 4.4 Contribution of specific SITC categories to total UK exports to Spain (as percentage of total exports)

SITC	1970 (%)	1975 (%)	1980 (%)	1987 (%)	1988 (%)	1989 (%)
2 *Crude materials*	8	9	19	8	7	7
3 *Mineral fuels*	1	3	5	9	4	2
5 *Chemicals*	12	13	11	16	14	14
6, 7 & 8 *Manufactured goods*	74	68	52	58	66	70
Total share of UK exports to Spain (in % terms)	95	93	87	91	91	93

Source: Calculations using Overseas Trade Statistics of United Kingdom, 1970–89, Dept of Trade and Industry, HMSO, Table 1a.

but increasing to 11 per cent in 1989 (£349 million). Division 75 (office machines etc.) accounted for 8 per cent (£241 million) in 1989.

On the other hand, SITC 6, manufactured goods classified chiefly by material, had a 30 per cent share of UK exports in 1970, since when its share has steadily fallen to 11 per cent in 1980, 8 per cent in 1984 and 9 per cent in 1986, 1987 and 1988, with a small rise to 11 per cent in 1989. This could be a reflection of changes in the classification of UK exports from the more general SITC 6 to those in SITC 7, machinery and transport equipment.

SITC 8, miscellaneous manufactured articles, is a catch-all and has been steady between 6 per cent to less than 10 per cent by value of UK exports to Spain over the period 1970–89.

Contrary to the trend for the dominant manufactured goods' divisions, SITC O, food and live animals chiefly for food, contributed less than 2 per cent by value of UK exports to Spain in 1970, which increased to 3 per cent in 1973 and 6 per cent by 1980. Since then it has fluctuated considerably. SITC O had a much higher contribution of 9 per cent in 1983, fell back to 3 per cent in 1984 and 1985, but suddenly increased to almost 11 per cent in 1986, falling again in 1988 to the 5 per cent level and in 1989 to 4 per cent (£59 million). Much of the variation can be related to the changes in import regulations for grain which has benefited UK trade to the disadvantage of North America.

SITC 1, beverages and tobacco, (primarily beverages) has been steady around 2–3 per cent share of total UK exports, increasing slightly to 4 per cent in 1986, 1987 but in 1989 dropping to 3 per cent (£45 million).

SITC 2, crude materials, inedible, excluding fuels, has made a relatively high, although fluctuating contribution towards UK exports to Spain. This category contributed 8 per cent of total exports by value in 1970 which increased to 10 per cent in 1973 and 19 per cent in 1980, since when its contribution has fallen back, especially from 1986 onwards, having only a 7 per cent share in 1989 (£101 million).

SITC 3, mineral fuels, lubricants and related materials, exports from UK to Spain were extremely low during the 1970–4 period at 1 per cent level, but since then have increased steadily to reach 4 per cent in 1978, 12 per cent in 1982, and a peak of 20 per cent in 1983 which fell off to 15 per cent in 1986 and 9 per cent in 1987 and the much lower 2 per cent in 1989 (£33 million). Presumably, Spain sources its mineral fuel needs (petroleum-based products) from the Middle East/North African countries rather than from the UK. Virtually all the exports in this sector fall into division 33 (petroleum, petroleum products and related materials) which has had a declining share of total exports from 10 per cent in 1982 to 8 per cent in 1987 and 3 per cent in 1989 (£80 million).

SITC 4, animal and vegetable oils, fats and waxes, has amounted to an insignificant share of total UK exports to Spain in value terms over the period 1970–89 inclusive (£0.9 million in 1989).

SITC 5, chemicals and related products, has fluctuated between 10 per cent and 17 per cent of UK exports to Spain. It accounted for 12 per cent in 1970, 13 per cent in 1978 and 11 per cent in 1980 and 14 per cent in 1989 (£215 million). Trends in the exports of SITC 5 are likely to be related to prices in the world chemicals market as well as in the petrochemicals market. The exports in this sector fell predominantly in division 52, inorganic chemicals, growing remarkably for 1986 and 1987 to 7 per cent of total exports, but falling off to 3 per cent in 1989 (£90 million). Division 51, organic chemicals, has made a steady contribution of just under 4 per cent of exports (£104 million in 1989 at 3 per cent).

Product analysis of imports to UK from Spain

Table 4.5 showing total imports to UK from Spain (in percentage terms) by SITC, highlights the dramatic change in the components of trade from predominantly agricultural products in 1970 to industrial manufactures in 1988/9. The contribution of SITC 0, food and live animals, has fallen from 45 per cent in 1970 to 14 per cent in 1989 (£377 million); while by contrast SITC 7, machinery and transport

Table 4.5 Imports to UK from Spain by SITC (as percentage of total imports)

SITC Section	1970 (%)	1975 (%)	1980 (%)	1987 (%)	1988 (%)	1989 (%)
0	45.07	33.08	16.69	16.82	13.21	13.60
1	10.18	11.52	5.94	3.39	2.91	2.30
2	6.34	4.53	4.29	5.37	4.79	4.97
3	6.59	3.75	5.55	4.64	2.29	1.75
4	2.37	0.16	0.09	5.37	0.14	0.16
5	4.67	4.56	3.75	4.42	4.49	4.95
6	13.03	17.75	22.55	16.76	17.97	18.05
7	6.36	12.24	31.28	33.19	44.13	43.28
8	5.15	11.41	8.06	9.76	9.80	10.77
9	0.23	0.99	1.80	0.27	0.27	0.18
Total Spanish imports(£1000s)	108,490	274,519	795,228	2,099,033	2,482,308	2,772,011

equipment, changed from 6 per cent in 1970 to 33 per cent in 1987 and 43 per cent in 1989 (£1,200 million). SITC 6, manufactured goods classified chiefly by material, rose from 13 per cent in 1970 to 18 per cent in 1989 (£500 million). SITC 8, miscellaneous manufactured articles, increased from 5 per cent in 1970 to 11 per cent in 1989 (£299 million), continuing the trend towards a greater share of total imports from Spain to UK from the manufactured sector.

Within SITC 7, machinery and transport equipment, division 78 predominates, accounting for 24 per cent of total imports in 1989 (£657 million). This reflects the growing importance of Spain as a base for multinationals' car production. Otherwise the spread of imports among the remainder of SITC 6, the rest of 7, and 8 is wide at about the 3 per cent level or less. The other divisions of particular note are within SITC O, food and live animals, division 05, fruit and vegetables, with 13 per cent in 1978 and 12 per cent in 1989 (£322 million). Within SITC 4, animal and vegetable oils and fats, division 42, fixed vegetable oils and fats (including olive oil), made hardly any contribution to imports between 1972 and 1985, in 1986 had 2 per cent, and in 1987 5 per cent, but this fell again in 1989 to 0.1 per cent. Worthy of comment is the fluctuation in imports of division 33, petroleum and petroleum products, being 0.5 per cent in 1978 but increasing steadily to a high of 17 per cent in 1984 and falling again to 2 per cent in 1988 and 1989 (£48 million).

GENERAL TRENDS IN THE SPANISH ECONOMY

Summary of key Spanish economic indicators

Spain, with a population of 38.8 million, is among Europe's fastest growing economies, with GDP growth 5.0 per cent in 1988 compared to 1987 (and 2.9 per cent average annual volume growth over the previous five years). However, it does have problems to overcome. Consumer prices/spending increased to 6.8 per cent in August 1989 compared with the previous year. Industrial price increase was lower at 4.6 per cent in August 1989 compared to the previous year (OECD 1990). There is a serious problem of high unemployment which reached 19.5 per cent in 1988, but fell to 17.3 per cent in 1989 and is projected to drop to 16.8 per cent by 1992 (OECD 1990).

Principal destinations for exports from Spain

From Table 4.6, France, West Germany and UK are key markets for Spanish exports, with France as the dominant importer increasing its share from 17 per cent in 1978 to 18 per cent in 1986, while West Germany increased its share from 11 per cent to 12 per cent over the same period. The USA has fluctuated around the 9 per cent level, while the UK in fourth position has increased its share of Spanish imports from nearly 7 per cent in 1978 to almost 9 per cent in 1986. It is to be anticipated that these imports to EC countries may well have increased since 1986 when Spain entered the Community and this will be reflected in later statistics.

Principal sources of imports to Spain

Similarly, looking at Table 4.7, it can be seen that by 1986 West Germany with 15 per cent in value terms of Spanish imports had replaced the USA as the prime supplier. France, too, increased its share steadily to 12 per cent and the UK in fourth position increased its share from 5 per cent in 1978 to nearly 8 per cent in 1986, a trend that can be expected to continue as the effects of Spain's entry to the EC become more evident.

Table 4.6 Exports from Spain by principal countries of destination (as percentage of total exports).

	1978 (%)	1980 (%)	1982 (%)	1984 (%)	1985 (%)	1986 (%)
France	16.61	16.52	16.47	14.85	15.50	18.00
West Germany	10.66	10.24	8.14	9.39	9.53	11.69
USA	9.26	5.31	6.38	9.65	9.93	9.14
UK	6.45	7.05	7.03	8.98	8.48	8.81
Italy	4.98	7.81	5.70	5.94	7.01	7.93
Netherlands	3.68	3.83	4.78	5.21	5.48	5.68
Portugal	2.04	2.73	2.78	2.37	2.18	3.38
Belgo/Lux	2.84	2.68	2.38	2.50	2.52	2.79
Saudi Arabia	1.52	2.26	2.71	2.46	1.89	1.31
Japan	1.52	1.28	1.26	1.56	1.30	1.11
Algeria	2.54	2.22	3.34	1.38	0.65	0.90
Mexico	0.85	2.03	2.46	0.88	1.01	0.75
Egypt	0.64	1.21	2.44	2.68	1.80	0.68
Iran	1.98	1.60	1.64	1.23	1.14	0.62
Libya	0.96	1.73	1.31	1.14	0.73	0.46
Total %	66.53	68.51	68.81	70.22	69.16	73.24
Total top 5 %	47.96	46.94	43.72	48.80	50.46	55.57
Total exports (in millions of pesetas)	1,001,383	1,493,187	2,233,935	3,743,453	4,108,751	3,815,893

UK PREPARATIONS FOR 1992 AND SINGLE EUROPE MARKET (SEM)

National versus regional studies

The Single European Act which came into force on 1 July 1987 has set out the necessary political impetus and legal framework to achieve a unified Community market by 1992 (EC 1989). It may be that full implementation of the Act will not take place in its entirety by the end of 1992, yet most certainly much of the detail will be in force, benefiting mostly the leaders in the market.

The increasing importance of Spain as a UK trading partner presents opportunities for UK exporters. A further enhancement might be expected from the SEM and a number of studies (for example, Mori 1989; Albemarle Yankelovich 1989) have reviewed the state of preparations of UK industry to match the potential opportunites and challenges. These studies generally have a UK-wide database and

Table 4.7 Imports to Spain by principal countries of origin
(as percentage of total imports)

	1978 (%)	1980 (%)	1982 (%)	1984 (%)	1985 (%)	1986 (%)
West Germany	9.95	8.20	9.47	9.90	10.52	15.12
France	9.09	8.26	7.99	8.60	9.21	11.84
USA	13.28	13.01	13.87	11.21	10.87	9.85
UK	5.38	4.70	4.93	6.07	6.45	7.72
Italy	4.72	4.93	4.48	4.22	4.56	7.26
Japan	2.80	2.47	3.20	3.07	3.40	4.92
Netherlands	2.81	2.15	1.87	2.01	2.13	3.04
Libya	3.63	3.71	3.47	3.68	3.75	2.68
Belgo/Lux	1.78	1.59	1.41	1.46	1.67	2.67
Mexico	0.65	3.80	5.95	6.02	5.73	2.62
Saudi Arabia	8.62	9.45	9.10	3.41	1.17	1.44
Algeria	0.89	1.61	2.13	1.69	2.98	1.33
Portugal	0.30	0.48	0.48	0.78	0.79	1.29
Iran	4.87	3.10	3.44	4.18	2.95	1.16
Egypt	0.08	0.53	0.21	0.97	0.58	0.25
Total %	68.86	67.97	71.99	67.25	66.74	73.19
Total top 5 %	41.25	40.35	41.83	36.11	36.82	51.80
Total (in millions of pesetas)						
	1,431,033	2,450,653	3,474,813	4,630,106	5,114,687	4,954,607

Source: Estadistica del Comercio Exterior, Tomo II, (Comercio por Paise 1978–86).

relatively low sample sizes, giving conclusions that have been drawn accordingly.

A number of localised/regional surveys (Barker 1989; Scott 1989) have shown more specific problems to be overcome which, in particular, highlight factors arising from the north–south division of British industry, with much of the north now dominated by branch economies. Scotland provides an example of an area faced with such structural difficulties where the manufacturing industry is very much operated as a branch economy subject to the screwdriver effect, with large numbers of manufacturers concentrating on assembly work for major operators, even multinationals, whose headquarters are elsewhere – frequently in south-east England or in North America.

Concentration on nationwide studies gives results typical of the average but these conclusions are not really descriptive of situation in the extreme 'regions'. The Scottish situation would be more adequately covered in a localised study such as the Peat Marwick McLintock survey of manufacturing industry in Scotland.

Peat Marwick McLintock survey

This postal questionnaire survey of Scottish manufacturing industry (Clarkson *et al.* 1989) investigated a wide variety of issues concerning Scottish industry. The high response rate to this survey (over 290 companies, about 45 per cent of the total number of business units in Scotland employing over 100 people) gave the researchers confidence that the findings were representative.

Almost a third (31 per cent) of the business units covered were Scottish, most of which are privately owned. A further two-thirds (63 per cent) were subsidiaries, mostly of UK-based companies (41 per cent), with a significant proportion (16 per cent) being subsidiaries of US companies. Among the responses there were only a handful of business units which are owned by EC or Japanese companies, reflecting the pattern of ownership in Scotland rather than a cultural bias.

The major challenges highlighted by this study are felt to be coming from the structural problems of industry and centre on maintaining profit margins against increased foreign competition, rising costs (reflecting government worries concerning increased inflation) and increased domestic competition. Of much less concern to the respondents was the increased involvement with export trade, more especially penetrating export markets and factors related to the changes in EC trade policy aiming towards the SEM by 1992. This is particularly worrying when taken into the context of this particular chapter relating to 1992 and the SEM.

Of the total number of respondents, 74 per cent were exporters to some extent. Involvement with European trade is still relatively low for Scottish manufacturers. Over half of the replies were from business units that did not export to Europe at all at present. Only 44 per cent had links with European firms, and, ostensibly, there is not a major readiness for 1992, the more especially as half of these links are only through sales agency agreements.

Views seem evenly divided by Scottish industrialists between the SEM in 1992 being seen to have little impact on businesses (38 per cent) or being a major opportunity (40 per cent). Surprisingly, few consider the SEM to be a major threat. It would appear that the plethora of information about 1992 is getting through to businessmen, although a quarter (24 per cent) of replies felt insufficient information was available. A fifth of replies (22 per cent) were cautious and felt that it would take until the year 2000 to fully implement the SEM – but then on the optimistic side almost a half (43 per cent) expected it to take much less time.

Possible barriers to operating in Europe at present are largely regulatory, rather than cultural. The greatest concern is fluctuating exchange rates which are felt to be especially problematic by almost three-quarters of the respondents (74 per cent). Generally, language and cultural differences are considered to be, at most, minor hindrances in developing European links. However, differences in standards and regulations between European countries (and in particular, compared with British standards) do pose major problems for 22 per cent of respondents, and, related to this, protectionist policies are considered to be a major problem for 27 per cent of respondents. Varying VAT rates present only minor problems for a quarter of respondents in the survey, but varying inflation introduces more problems for 41 per cent of the respondents. Related to these 'restrictions' differences in legal and customs practices give rise to problems for about half of those surveyed.

In the Peat Marwick McLintock study public procurement policies were considered to present a problem for half the respondents, which suggests a feeling at least that government bodies within the EC do attempt to protect home industry in practice, if not by formalised means. Capital movement was considered to be a problem by more than a quarter, which is surprising bearing in mind the free movement of capital that is purported to be possible within the EC.

Indicators of strategic direction of Scottish industry

From the Peat Marwick McLintock study, most Scottish business units appear to be basing their growth plans for the next five years on increasing market share in existing markets (86 per cent). Clearly, this is worrying as there is unlikely to be room for all manufacturers to grow in this manner in markets of relative stability and maturity in many sectors. Furthermore, there seems little obvious strategic planning to expand towards Europe. New markets and new products are major factors in anticipated growth: most respondents expect such developments to be within home markets (77 per cent) or with familiar products (71 per cent) in which the manufacturer has expertise. A lower but still high proportion (58 per cent) propose the much more risky strategy of introducing new products to new markets, but not, it seems to European markets.

Over a third of the responses (36 per cent) were from those who expect to grow by acquisition over the next five years. Such growth is easier and more rapid than growth by organic market development.

Nearly a fifth (19 per cent) were expecting some form of retrenchment to take place over the next five years and, by the same token, 35 per cent of responses indicated that rationalising of the present product range was likely. Again this 'negative' growth was directed towards the home market.

In the main, the major marketing barriers to expanding within Europe are associated with transport costs and getting into the market. Market research, finding a suitable sales agent or partner as well as overcoming difficulties related to the distance of the market from the manufacturing base, and gaining access to the most appropriate channels of distribution are all factors which at least half the respondents felt posed difficulty.

From the Peat Marwick McLintock survey critical factors considered by the respondents necessary for a manufacturer to achieve a competitive edge over the next three years concentrated very heavily on quality and related issues; marketing, in the form of sales representation; identifying a market niche for a range of products, and new product introduction; as well as cost containment aimed at the home market.

Interest in developing links with European firms is much less apparent. Only 23 per cent of the replies expressed interest in progressing joint venture arrangements with European businesses, although a small, but significant 13 per cent of replies were interested in takeover activity in Europe.

Three-quarters of the respondents conduct foreign business transactions, with over 70 per cent of them working in foreign currencies. The US dollar and West German mark are the most frequently used currencies, being used by about half the respondents.

The Spanish dimension: implications for trade development between Spain and Scotland

Although the Peat Marwick McLintock survey did not directly consider Spain as an export market for Scottish industries, many of its findings can be extrapolated into a Spanish scenario. Indeed, most of the perceived barriers will be accentuated since Spain is still in the process of reducing its tariffs in the run up to full membership of the EC by 1992. For example, the Spanish government procurement policy has operated within an economy which has a long-standing tradition of protectionism. This is unlikely to change quickly whatever the theoretical easing of government sourcing philosophy. State nationalised industry monopoly continues in many spheres but is beginning to be broken, for example, the recent liberalising of the petrol distribution/retail sector.

The Spanish peseta is not a commonly used trading currency. However, Spain has joined the European Monetary System (EMS) aimed at stabilising exchange rates through the Exchange Rate Mechanism (ERM) countries (EC, 1989). Furthermore, the peseta has been the strongest currency in the EC from 1989 onwards and pressure is being put on Spain to devalue/realign the peseta against the German mark.

Nevertheless, the Spanish banking industry is still traditional in outlook and performance. The Madrid stock exchange is going through the 'Big Bang' process but still is not a major European source of industrial capital. All of these factors could combine to make the raising of capital as well as capital movement more of a problem in Spain than in some other European countries. Yet much interest in the Spanish financial scene has been apparent from both US and UK merchant and commercial banking groups. For example, a financial link up has been established between Banco de Santander and the Royal Bank of Scotland. Chase-Manhattan has been involved in setting up retail charge card operations in Spain and, in a different sector of the financial market, Abbey National has introduced mortgage credit operations in Spain, notably in Madrid. Perhaps predictably, Abbey National is finding difficulty in overcoming traditional Spanish support for local Spanish savings banks in this field.

Trends in trading between Spain and Scotland

The Scottish Council for Development and Industry (SCDI) is aware of the potential opportunities presented by Spain for UK manufacturers. The SCDI survey (1988) in 1987/1988 showed that in real terms the value of Scottish manufactured exports increased by 13 per cent in 1987/88, compared with a fall of 11 per cent in 1986/1987. Nearly all of the major export industries in Scotland shared in this recovery in fortunes, but exports from the mechanical engineering industry continued to decline. Whisky and computers remain, by far, Scotland's most important exports. These trends continued in 1989 and are detailed by Scott in his assessment of the implications of SEM for the Scottish economy (Scott 1989).

Exports from Scotland to Greece, Spain and Portugal have grown rapidly during the last four years (see Table 4.8) and this rapid growth is expected to continue.

Table 4.8 Exports to Spain from Scotland in £ million (rank order of destination)

	1985	1986	1987	1988
Spain	121 (12)	170 (7)	230 (8)	307 (7)

Source: Scottish Council for Development and Industry, Scottish manufactured exports in 1987/1988/1989 surveys.

There has been some fluctuation concerning the relative ranking of Spain as a destination for Scottish exports, into seventh position in 1988. However, Scottish industry has increased its exports to Spain substantially since 1985.

Government bodies (such as the Scottish Development Agency) are attempting to prepare Scottish industry for the challenges of 1992 (DTI 1988; Scottish Office, 1988), but local initiatives are needed to counter some of the perceived difficulties. Hence, one concerted taskforce in the east of Scotland attempting to promote acceptance of this challenge is the recently formed EAST (the Euro Action Specialist Team), set up with backing from the Scottish Development Agency, Lothian Region and Edinburgh District Council as well as the private sector (EAST, 1989). It aims to act as a single point of contact for a wide range of consultancy services for businesses in the Edinburgh area to exploit the opportunities of 1992. Clearly one prime area could be Spain, and with this in mind, the SCDI organised a European trade mission to Spain in June 1989 with the Royal Bank of Scotland as principal sponsor.

One encouraging sign of efforts being made to improve trade relationships has been visits such as that by a delegation from the Chamber of Commerce in Vitoria, northern Spain to Edinburgh District Council to develop links between the two (April 1989). Such a visit would have been extremely unlikely a decade or so ago.

CONCLUSION

General trading trends

The UK is turning more and more towards the EC for trading, which is reflected by the trend towards steady growth in the share of UK exports and imports with the EC. These are standing presently at about 50 per cent by value of trade.

The UK has changed her pattern of trading to favour the EC and OECD at the expense of traditional partners in the Commonwealth.

The North American market has remained important for UK exports but has contributed to a fluctuating and declining share of UK imports.

Trade with Spain has been at a low level but has increased steadily since 1979: especially since 1 January 1986, when Spain joined the EC.

UK exports to Spain are predominantly manufactured goods (SITC 6, 7 and 8). However, this concentration has been reduced from the 74 per cent level in 1970 to 50 per cent or so between 1982 and 1986. Most of these exports fall into division 78, road vehicles, and at a lower level, division 75, office machines.

Chemicals (SITC 5) have remained important, actually increasing their share of total Spanish exports from the UK with some fluctuation from 12 to 14 per cent. Inorganic chemicals (division 52) have the larger share.

Mineral fuels (SITC 3) from a low 1–4 per cent level over the 1970–8 period suddenly jumped to account for 12 per cent in 1982, 20 per cent of UK exports in 1983, but then fell to 15 per cent in 1986 and only had 2 per cent share in 1989.

Crude materials (SITC 2) started at 8 per cent in 1970, increased suddenly between 1978 and 1982 to 15 per cent, but then fell in 1989 to 7 per cent of UK exports to Spain.

General trends in the Spanish economy

Spain is among Europe's fastest growing economies but faces problems associated with increasing inflation and serious unemployment.

Principal destinations for exports from Spain are France, Germany and the UK. The latter is taking an increasing share of Spanish imports.

Principal sources of imports to Spain are Germany, France and the USA. The UK was ranked fourth in 1986, and has increased its share of Spanish imports from 5 per cent in 1978 to 8 per cent in 1986.

UK preparations for 1992 and the Single European Market

Localised/regional surveys have shown specific problems to be overcome which highlight factors arising from the north–south division of the British economy.

A survey of Scottish manufacturing industry (Clarkson, *et al.* 1989) indicates that challenges are coming from structural problems of Scottish industry facing increased foreign competition and rising costs. Increased domestic competition is of more concern to industry than preparations for 1992 and the SEM.

Barriers to operating in Europe seem to be largely regulatory and, to a lesser degree, cultural. Exchange rate fluctuations pose particular problems.

Scottish industry appears to be basing five-year growth plans on increasing market share within existing markets. There is little evidence of strategic planning to expand towards Europe. Rather, anticipated growth is expected to be within home markets.

Major marketing barriers to expanding within Europe are associated with transport costs and getting into the market. Market research, finding a suitable sales' agent or partner, and gaining access to appropriate channels of distribution pose problems.

Interest in developing links with European firms is less apparent than overcoming home market problems.

Spanish dimension

It is likely that the general reticence of Scottish manufacturers to developing European markets and the problems highlighted by the PMM/Clarkson, Stone and Shaw survey will be even more apparent when considering the Spanish market.

Spain is still in the process of reducing its tariffs in the run-up to full membership of the EC by 1992. With the tradition of protectionism entrenched in the Spanish economy, it is likely that the Spanish market will pose as many, if not more, barriers to UK exporters than other EC members.

However, when looking more specifically at trade, Scottish exports to Spain have increased substantially since Spain joined the EC. Detailed trade statistics are not available but the general SCDI export survey suggests that the exports taking place are predominantly in the product sectors covering whisky and computers within SITC 1 and SITC 7. From the general trends, opportunities exist for exporting products falling into the machinery and transport equipment (SITC 7) section, in particular within division 78 (road vehicles). In this context, there should be potential to increase exports of the heavy commercial vehicles produced in Scotland. Opportunities also exist to export goods falling into division 75 – office machines and data-processing equipment; and division 72 – machinery specialised for particular industries; for example, heavy engineering equipment as well as division 77 – electrical machinery.

EC export initiatives

Government policy, backed by regional and local administration, encourages export activity to Europe and has led to a number of catalytic initiatives being set up in Scotland.

These include BOTB advice services as well as SDA, SCDI in the encouragement of trade missions and the locally formed EAST management consultancy services. It is hoped that these will help to prepare Scottish manufacturing industry to take up the opportunities and challenges associated with 1992 and the SEM and the potential of the enlarged EC – in particular the attainment of full membership by Spain. However, it is apparent from the Peat Marwick McLintock study that generally Scottish industry knows the mechanics of how to export but presently is not putting its full concentration towards concerted effort to win the 1992 and SEM race. Nevertheless, changes are taking place. Recent initiatives suggest that the climate may be right to develop and encourage trading links with Spain.

REFERENCES

Albemarle Yankelovich Clancy Shulman (1989) 'Doing business with the British: a study of European executives' attitudes', Confederation of British Industry Initiative, June, pp. 1–42.
Barker, Lynton (1989) 'Survey of industries' preparation for 1992 in Greater Manchester area conducted by Coopers & Lybrand for Greater Manchester Economic Development agency', reported in *The Financial Times*, 5 April 1989, p. 6.
CL-Alexanders Laing & Cruickshank (1988) 'Economic and monthly review', reported in *The Financial Times*, 22 August 1989, p. 7.
Clarkson, A. H., Stone, M. A. and Shaw, W. N. (1989) 'Peat Marwick McLintock survey of Scottish manufacturing', April, pp. 1–42.
Department of Trade & Industry (1988) 'Survey of awareness that 1992 is the date when the Single European market is set for completion', April 18–29, reported in *The Financial Times*, 11 May 1989, p. 8.
Department of Trade & Industry (1970/1989) *Overseas Trade Statistics of United Kingdom*, London, HMSO, Tables 1b and 5.
Dudley, J. W. (1989) *1992: Strategies for the Single Market*, London, Kogan Page.
EAST (1989) 'Survey undertaken by Price Waterhouse on behalf of Euro Action Specialist Team – Edinburgh District and Lothian Regional councils', Scottish Development Agency and Edinburgh Chamber of Commerce, March.
EC (1987) *Steps to European Unity: Community Progress to Date: a*

Chronology, 6th edn., Luxembourg, Office for Official Publications of the European Communities, 6th edn, pp. 1–99.

EC (1989a) *The EMS: Ten years of Progress in European Monetary Cooperation*, Brussels, Commission of the European Communities, March, pp. 1–20.

EC (1989b) *Europe without Frontiers – Completing the Internal Market*, 3rd edn, Luxembourg, Office for Official Publications of the European Communities, April, pp. 1–68.

Euromonitor (1987) Spain: European market for the 1990s, Euromonitor, London, pp. 1–175.

Metra Martech (1988) *Spain: Business opportunities*, 3rd edn, Metra Consulting Group Ltd, 1 Queen Anne's Gate, London, SW1H 9BT, pp. 1–453.

Moman, Praveen (1988) *Europe Without Frontiers: Completing the Internal Market*, 2nd edn, Luxembourg, Office for Official Publications of the European Communities, pp. 1–67.

Mori (1989) 'What's stopping British firms from winning in Europe: a survey of preparations for 1992', Confederation of British Industry Initiative, May, pp. 1–15.

Nicholson, Francess and East, Roger (1987) *From Six to Twelve: the Enlargement of the European Communities*, London, Longman.

OECD (1989) OECD Economic Surveys – Spain 1988/1989, Paris, pp. 1–113

OECD (1990) *OECD Main Economic Indicators*, Paris, August.

Paliwoda, Stanley (1986) *International Marketing*, London, Heinemann, pp. 247–60.

Scott, Andrew (1989) 'Completing the internal market: some implications for the Scottish economy', *Royal Bank of Scotland Review* No. 162, June, pp. 25–46.

SCDI (1988) 'Scottish manufactured exports in 1987/88 survey summary', Scottish Council Development and Industry in association with the Scottish Development Agency, December, pp. 1–14.

Scottish Office (1988) 'Economic impact of the Single Market', pp. 1–7.

Tsoukalis, Loukas (1981) *The European Community and its Mediterranean Enlargement*, London, George Allen & Unwin, pp. 1–256.

APPENDIX 4.1 DIVISION AND SECTION TITLES OF THE STANDARD INTERNATIONAL TRADE CLASSIFICATION (REVISION 3)

Division 00 Live animals other than animals of division 3
          01 Meat and meat preparations
          02 Dairy products and birds' eggs
          03 Fish, (not marine mammals), crustaceans, molluscs and aquatic invertebrates and preparations thereof
          04 Cereals and cereal preparations
          05 Vegetables and fruit
          06 Sugar, sugar preparations and honey
          07 Coffee, tea, cocoa, spices, and manufactures thereof
          08 Feeding stuff for animals (not including unmilled cereals)

	09	Miscellaneous edible products and preparations
Section	0	Food and live animals

Division	11	Beverages
	12	Tobacco and tobacco manufactures
Section	1	Beverages and tobacco

Division	21	Hides, skins and furskins, raw
	22	Oil seeds and oleaginous fruit
	23	Crude rubber (including synthetic and reclaimed)
	24	Cork and wood
	25	Pulp and waste paper
	26	Textile fibres (other than wool tops) and their wastes (not manufactured into yarn or fabric)
	27	Crude fertilisers other than those of division 56 and crude minerals (excluding coal, petroleum and precious stones)
	28	Metalliferous ores and metal scrap
	29	Crude animal and vegetable materials, NES
Section	2	Crude materials, inedible, except fuels

Division	32	Coal, coke and briquettes
	33	Petroleum, petroleum products and related materials
	34	Gas, natural and manufactured
	35	Electric current
Section	3	Mineral fuels, lubricants and related materials

Division	41	Animal oils and fats
	42	Fixed vegetable fats and oils: crude, refined or fractionated
	43	Animal and vegetable oils and fats, processed, and waxes of animal or vegetable origin; inedible mixtures or preparations of animal or vegetable fats and oils NES
Section	4	Animal and vegetable oils, fats and waxes

Division	51	Organic chemicals
	52	Inorganic chemicals
	53	Dyeing, tanning and colouring materials
	54	Medicinal and pharmaceutical products
	55	Essential oils and resinoids and perfume materials: toilet, polishing and cleansing preparations
	56	Fertilizers, (other than those of group 272)
	57	Plastics in primary forms
	58	Plastics in non-primary forms
	59	Chemical materials and products, NES
Section	5	Chemicals and related products, NES

Division	61	Leather, leather manufactures, NES and dressed furskins
	62	Rubber manufactures, NES
	63	Cork and wood manufactures (excluding furniture)
	64	Paper, paperboard, and articles of paper pulp, of paper or of paperboard

65 Textile yarn, fabrics, made-up articles, NES and related products
66 Non-metallic mineral manufactures, NES
67 Iron and steel
68 Non-ferrous metals
69 Manufactures of metal, NES

Section 6 Manufactured goods classified chiefly by material

Division 71 Power generating machinery and equipment
72 Machinery specialized for particular industries
73 Metal working machinery
74 General industrial machinery and equipment, NES and machine parts, NES
75 Office machines and automatic data-processing machines
76 Telecommunications and sound recording and reproducing apparatus and equipment
77 Electrical machinery, apparatus and appliances, NES and electrical parts thereof (including non-electrical counterparts, NES, of electrical household type equipment)
78 Road vehicles (including air cushion vehicles)
79 Other transport equipment

Section 7 Machinery and transport equipment

Division 81 Prefabricated buildings; sanitary, plumbing, heating and lighting fixtures and fittings, NES
82 Furniture and parts thereof: bedding, mattresses, supports, cushions and similar stuffed furnishings
83 Travel goods, handbags and similar containers
84 Articles of apparel and clothing accessories
85 Footwear
87 Professional, scientific and controlling instruments and apparatus, NES
88 Photographic apparatus, equipment and supplies and optical goods, NES: watches and clocks
89 Miscellaneous manufactured articles, NES

Section 8 Miscellaneous manufactured articles

Section 9 Commodities and transactions not classified elsewhere in the SITC

Source: Overseas Trade Statistics of United Kingdom, Department of Trade and Industry, HMSO.

5 The implications of 1992 for companies in technological collaboration

Claire Shearman

The likely impact of 1992 on corporate strategies for technological collaboration has been the subject of some debate. The Commission's White Paper on 1992 and its subsequent economic research programme on the 'Cost of non-Europe' both saw industrial collaboration as being facilitated and encouraged by 1992. The Cecchini Report (Cecchini *et al.* 1988) argued that the relatively low level of Community joint ventures by comparison with those set up with non-EC partners would be raised with the removal of non-tariff barriers to trade. Proponents of the alternative view – that is, that the direct effects of 1992 will be to reduce such collaboration – have argued that collaboration agreements are typically devices of the last resort for firms. The elimination of non-tariff barriers to trade, therefore, would reduce both the need to collaborate with EC partners to gain market access and the willingness to collaborate with firms which are increasingly likely to be potential rivals.

This chapter seeks to explore the issues surrounding the implications of 1992 for companies in technological collaboration in more detail. What, for example, are the nature and underlying incentives of current trends in European technological collaboration? How appropriate to these are conventional notions of the competition/collaboration relationship? What are the political as well as economic implications of 1992 and how might these shape and alter responses at the governmental (national or European) and corporate levels? To what extent would the achievement of a uniform single market framework truly effect intra-European market access?

The arguments presented here follow four main lines. First, the growth of national and international interfirm agreements relating in one way or another to technology represents a significant and novel development of the 1980s. Moreover, they involve a much wider and more flexible range of activities than is suggested by the industrial economists' definition of 'joint venture' and, within the context of Europe at least, they are increasingly seen by managers not as a device of the last resort but as one of an increasingly widening range of available instruments through which strategic corporate policy decisions can be effected.

Secondly, conventional analysis of the competition/collaboration relationship is seen to be increasingly inappropriate. Competitive modes of behaviour can and do exist on a variety of levels, but so too do cooperative interactions. Competition may reach a peak at a particular stage of an industry's development but it tends to co-exist at the same time with close, cooperative modes of interaction. Firms may, therefore, compete and cooperate simultaneously with other firms in the same industry. The precise nature and balance of such relationships change as an industry matures (Shearman and Burrell 1987), and thus the particular stage of industrial development of a given industry may well be a crucial determinant of the extent to which technological collaboration of one form or another might figure in managerial perceptions of strategies for dealing with the turbulence, restructuring and change engendered by the developments towards a European internal market.

Thirdly, 1992 is as much a political and symbolic initiative as it is an economic one. Consequently corporate activity in high technology sectors will be shaped and constrained by political as well as economic forces. State intervention of one form or another is commonplace in such strategic and defence-related areas of high technology as space and satellite communications, aeronautics and electronics. The boundaries between civil and defence-related R&D in the so-called 'dual-use' technologies and industries are increasingly blurred and the effects of 1992 cannot be totally divorced from the shifting geo-political patterns between and within the East and West.

Finally, it is important to differentiate between the uniformity of a single European market framework and the diversity of intra-European markets. Europe is culturally and linguistically heterogeneous and harmonisation of language and culture are not on the agenda. Indeed moves to create a greater general level of homogeneity across Europe on the one hand may well be tempered by nationalistic and/or regional attempts to protect and reinforce cultural identities. Consumer demands are not and will not be uniform across Europe, and intra-European collaboration may well be required to facilitate local market access.

We begin then with a consideration of the nature of technological collaboration before going on to examine the underlying incentives behind current trends in European collaboration and the conflicting views with regard to the impact of 1992. These give rise to a number of issues which are then explored – namely, the role of collaboration as a corporate strategy instrument, the changing nature of the relationship between competition and cooperation, the wider context and geo-political implications of 1992 and the likely nature of the resulting markets.

THE NATURE OF TECHNOLOGICAL COLLABORATION

The concept of technological collaboration is broad, covering a spectrum ranging from university-based pre-competitive research on the one hand to joint production agreements between firms (sometimes involving governments) on the other. Indeed, one of the characteristics of the literature on technological collaboration or interfirm agreements is the high degree of flexibility in the definitions proposed by authors and in the range of agreements included in different studies. This reflects in part the fact that the responses firms can give through cooperation with other firms and organisations to the need for a broadened base of scientific and/or technological resources and ensured access to important markets are very varied and will often differ from one industry supply structure and/or major type of technology to another.

The most commonly used term for interfirm agreements – joint venture – is often applied with some ambiguity. The OECD Committee on Restrictive Business Practices (1987), for example, defined joint ventures as all forms of agreements through which 'the operations of two or more firms are partially, but not fully, functionally integrated in order to carry out activities in one or more areas' – a wide-ranging approach which covers *inter alia* buying or selling operations, natural resource exploitation, development and/or production operations, manufacturing, engineering and R&D in a variety of forms, ranging from non-equity cooperation research agreements to technology sharing and customer-supplier agreements. For industrial economists meanwhile, joint ventures are operations whereby a legally independent and autonomously managed business enterprise is established by two or more parent companies to run a clearly defined set of activities in the common interest of the founding firms. While this kind of agreement is undoubtedly the oldest and principal form of interfirm agreement in particular industries such as petrochemicals, for example, it is no longer the sole, or indeed necessarily even the most characteristic, form of technological collaboration agreement.

Licensing agreements are a further form of conventional categorisation of interfirm agreements. These encompass a variety of situations, ranging from isolated or *ad hoc* one-off operations to ongoing and steady relationships between, say, larger and smaller firms or cross-licensing between firms of comparable size and strength within the same industry. By definition though, licence agreements concern existing 'proven' technology, in contrast with those forms of agreements aimed at the development of *new* knowledge or combinations of technology.

Perhaps more useful is the approach developed by Ricotta and Mariotti (1986) which defines technological collaboration as those 'intercompany cooperation agreements, which are formal and informal, agreements between two or more companies providing for a certain degree of collaboration between them (and) involving equity participation or the creation of new companies (as well as) non-equity agreements'. Thus a broad spectrum of industrial cooperation agreements are encompassed which excludes only those arrangements which become *de facto* acquisition or merger.

Table 5.1, building on Hacklish (1986) and Ricotta and Mariotti (1986), illustrates the range of agreements which firms may establish with a view to producing, acquiring and/or commercially exploiting new technology in common. The spectrum covers:

Pre-competitive stage

(A) University-based cooperative research projects

These are collective R&D undertakings established and financed by firms in universities with or without public support. R&D is located in academic structures and extensively supported and directed by firms.

(B) Government–industry cooperative research projects

These national or international research projects are collective R&D undertakings on the basis of joint initiatives by governments and firms, and are located in universities, public research institutes and in firms. Distinctive characteristics of this type of cooperative agreement are the fairly strong government initiatives and financial support, and the heterogeneous nature of the R&D location and execution.

(C) Research corporations

These are private sector joint ventures financed by a number of firms on a shareholder basis. Research is conducted in separate laboratories or in research facilities established specifically for the purpose, and generally focusses on generic technology directly related to the competitive interests of the joint venture partners.

Competitive stage

(D) Corporate venture capital agreements

Agreements involving the use of corporate venture capital are used by large firms to identify innovative processes within smaller organisations and to monitor the development of new technologies on the market. They represent the direct and continuous involvement of industrial firms in the financial activity of small innovative firms so as to acquire strategic benefits without depriving SMEs of autonomy in their R&D and management decisions.

(E) Non-equity cooperative research agreements

These are highly flexible forms of cooperation without shareholder participation, used by a small number of firms to deal with specific research projects. Of limited duration, they are intended to attain strictly defined results which may be exploited commercially by each of the participating firms or through the establishment of a separate joint venture manufacturing and/or marketing firm.

(F) Technical agreements on completed technology

Technical agreements between firms concerning completed 'proven technologies' manifest themselves in a variety of forms ranging from technology-sharing and second sourcing agreements to two-way exchanges of licences and cross-licensing in separate product markets.

(G) Joint venture firms and R&D/manufacturing/marketing consortia

Comprehensive R&D, manufacturing and marketing consortia comprise joint ventures with a fairly large number of parties. They are

Table 5.1 Patterns of collaboration

Pre-competitive stage			Competitive stage					
Research and development cooperation			Technological cooperation			Manufacturing/marketing cooperation		
A	B	C	D	E	F	G	H	I
University based cooperation research financed by associated firms (with or without public support)	Government/industry cooperative R&D projects with universities and public research institute involvement	Research and development corporation on a private joint-venture basis	corporate venture capital in small high tech firms (by one or by several firms otherwise competitors)	Non-equity cooperative research and developments between two firms in selected areas	Technical agreements between firms on completed technology *inter alia* technology sharings and cross licensing agreements in product markets	Industrial joint-venture firms and comprehensive R&D manufacturing and marketing consortia	Customer/supplier agreements, notably partnerships	One-way way licensing and/or marketing agreements inc. OEM sales agreements
Many partners		Several partners	Few or very few partners			Few or very few partners		

established in response to predetermined technical and economic objectives, or as a result of initial technical and marketing studies. Industrial joint ventures between a very small number of firms are frequently aimed at the same kind of objectives – that is, the joint development, production and marketing of a specific product.

(H) Partnerships

Customer-supplier agreements or partnerships can involve a strong technological component. They represent a significant interdependence or reliance of the partners on one another and provide a mechanism for leveraging critical technical and financial resources for the partners.

(I) Licensing and/or marketing agreements

'Classic' one-way licence agreements and technology transfers are a traditional, but nevertheless frequent form of interfirm technical cooperation agreement.

Cooperation and/or technology exchange between firms (or between firms and other categories of research organisations) then can take place at any single given point of the R&D to commercialisation process or indeed cover the whole development, innovation and commercialisation cycle. It can concern either the creation of new technology or the acquisition and use of an existing one or, again, both. An example within Europe of university-based cooperative research is the European Molecular Biology Laboratory in Heidelberg. European Community programmes such as Esprit and Brite/Euram are major examples of government/industry cooperative R&D programmes with university and public research institute involvement. The Siemens/ICL/Bull Research Laboratory at Munich is an example of an R&D corporation run on a private joint venture basis and European Silicon Structures (ES2) represents the investment of corporate venture capital by several firms into one small high-tech firm. The Phillips/Siemens semiconductor Megaproject represents a non-equity cooperative R&D agreement between two firms in a selected area and Airbus an R&D manufacturing and marketing cooperation.

The dividing line between the pre-competitive and the competitive is blurred. Firms, for example, may jointly fund so-called 'generic' research, which precedes commercial applications, but try via patent and other means to appropriate that knowledge for themselves for competitive reasons. Similarly, when firms get together to form a private R&D corporation producing proprietary generic technology for the partners in the joint venture, they may not be doing 'competitive R&D' from the perspective of their own joint venture relations. They are nevertheless quite definitely doing 'competitive R&D' from the standpoint of their relations with other firms in the industry. Inevitably too, strong pressures for continued subsidy and collaboration come from those firms which, having worked effectively together at the so-called 'pre-competitive' stage, find it desirable to continue to do so as the technology becomes more market-oriented.

A recent OECD review (1988) of interfirm cooperation found agreements on the joint production, sharing and two-way exchange of technology to be characteristic of the 1980s. One-way transfers of technology, two-way exchanges and/or sharing and pooling of technology, along with agreements involving R&D and the production of new technology, now represent a central feature of a large proportion of agreements – either as their main objective or as a component of a more complex arrangement involving production and marketing. Having examined the nature of technological collaboration, let us turn now to the incentives underlying the major European collaboration initiatives.

EUROPEAN COLLABORATION: THE UNDERLYING INCENTIVES

Incentives for collaboration have traditionally been explained in terms of the costs, scale or inherent nature of the technological development involved. These, together with the increasing frequency of technological convergence, the need for capabilities spanning both technological disciplines and business experience and the search for access to potential new markets have certainly played a role in increasing global interest in collaboration generally. They provide insufficient insight, however, into the reasons why intra-European collaboration has become an increasingly attractive option in the 1980s. Here it is also useful to examine the promotion and development of technology in its wider political context. The development and exploitation of technology tends to alter the nature of power relationships, whether social, economic, political or military. Shifts in international economic and political power derive, to a large extent, from differential access to, and facility with, technological developments (Williams 1984).

Consequently, the maintenance of relative economic, and therefore political, influence of West European states in the international sphere is inextricably tied up with the acquisition of significant shares of major global markets.

Many of the collaborative ventures in the 1980s fall into strategically important sectors and the context within which they have developed is inevitably somewhat politicised. In the IT-related field, for example, where considerations of national and international perceptions of status and prestige have combined with the pressures of global recession, falling market shares and budgetary constraints, the concept of European collaboration began in the early 1980s to constitute an increasingly attractive element of political rhetoric. Individual European states' attempts to acquire a substantial foothold in global communications markets had been somewhat impeded by their relative disadvantage in terms of size and resources. At the same time West European governments were experiencing a collective sense of threat in response to the steadily increasing penetration of European markets by American multinationals. Though economic actors in principle, such corporations tend in practice to accrue a more political role. Consolidation of their presence within Europe ultimately deprives the host nations of some of their political influence. The close links between the IT and telecommunications sectors and national defence policies moreover exacerbated the feelings of European vulnerability.

Expression of these political and economic fears focussed on the concept of the 'technology gap' that was perceived to exist between Europe on the one hand and the US and Japan on the other. The belief that individually, European states lacked the capability to close this so-called 'gap' was fuelled by the Japanese fifth-generation computer program and the American Strategic Defence or 'Star Wars' Initiative. Some form of concerted action at the European level was deemed necessary if Europe's position of technological imbalance was to be altered. Degrees of commitment to the idea varied – British ambivalence contrasted with French enthusiasm and German caution – but the mid-1980s onwards nevertheless witnessed an unprecedented spate of European initiatives within and outside of the European Community.

The interests of commercial logic do not always coincide with those of political ends as is evidenced by the higher number of extra rather than intra-European agreements negotiated at the corporate level. The proportion of the latter, however, is currently increasing. From the company's point of view, complementarity of technical know-how, resources and markets provide the key to successful collaborative ventures. As far as many industrialists were concerned, such complementarities were located outside Europe. By the mid-1980s, however, these perceptions were in the process of changing – first because levels of awareness of existing available competencies within Europe were steadily rising and secondly because European industrialists were in fact beginning to think collectively in terms of a European dimension to their activities in much the same way as their scientific counterparts had done in the 1960s. This change of attitude was facilitated by the European Commission, whose efforts over the previous decade to involve industrialists in Community policies had had the side effect of providing a European forum for discussions and contacts. The result, in the economic climate of the 1980s, was the emergence of a greater sense of a 'European' industrial consciousness, which served to reinforce the trend towards intra-European collaboration not only within the context of European Community programmes but in industry-led initiatives too (Sharp and Shearman 1987).

Indeed, the effects of what might be termed a collaboration 'community' were evident. European Community programmes in particular facilitated the establishment of formal and informal channels of communication between the various participants from industry and academia. A momentum has now been achieved through the actual process of collaboration, the spin-off and definitive effects of which may prove more important in the long term than the programmes themselves in terms of the contacts generated, the experience gained and the increasing acceptance of common standards. The extent of such a 'community', however, should not be exaggerated. Although it is certainly quite marked by comparison with former levels, many European companies still have little knowledge of each other and consequently fail to exploit much of the potential that Europe might offer them.

CONFLICTING VIEWS ON THE IMPACT OF 1992 ON TECHNOLOGICAL COLLABORATION

The European Commission's White Paper on 1992 sees the achievement of intra-European industrial collaboration as a major objective. It argues that while the removal of internal boundaries and the establishment of free movement of goods and capital and the freedom to provide services are clearly fundamental to the creation of the internal market, Community action must go further and create an environment or conditions likely to favour the development of cooperation between undertakings. It suggests that as barriers to industrial cooperation are reduced by the single market, industrial cooperation will consequently increase. The absence of a Community legal framework for cross-border activities by enterprises and for cooperation between enterprises of different member states is seen to have led – if only for psychological reasons – to numerous potential joint projects failing to get off the ground. As the internal market develops, enterprises are likely to become increasingly involved in intra-Community operations. Current Community policies moreover – particularly in the competition, regional and technology areas – were already encouraging this development of cross-border collaborative activities.

Subsequent to the publication of the 1992 White Paper, the European Commission initiated a research programme in 1986 on the 'Costs of non-Europe'. Detailed microeconomic and macroeconomic analysis of the likely effects of 1992 were carried out, with particular attention being directed to key industrial sectors. Broadly speaking, the conclusions generated by this research suggested that 1992 would provide benefits in terms of (i) cost reductions due to scale economics; (ii) improved efficiency and reduced prices due to competitive pressure; (iii) facilitation of real cooperative advantages in market competition, and (iv) increased innovativeness (Cecchini *et al.* 1988; Commission of the European Communities 1988).

The findings of this research into the 'Costs of non-Europe' reiterate the emphasis on technological collaboration in the Commission's 1992 White Paper. Cecchini *et al.* (1988), for example, noted that Europe-wide standards are an essential lever both for prising open national markets and then welding them together through technological alliances (Cecchini *et al.* 1988: 89). EC-sponsored R&D programmes like Esprit were considered a crucial focus for the fusing of cross-frontier innovation and business (Cecchini *et al.* 1988: 89). Nevertheless, the research results pointed to a certain 'paradox' in the existing patterns of cooperative behaviour – cooperation with Community partners has been less frequent than cooperation with partners in non-member countries (Cecchini *et al.* 1988, Commission of the European Communities 1988). However, with the implementation of the internal market such a paradox was likely to disappear since European cooperation could grow substantially as a result of the removal of some of these barriers (Commission of the European Communities 1988: 137) and market integration would bring with it a number of factors giving European firms the chance to regain technological leadership including the rapid development of cross-frontier business cooperation for R&D (Cecchini *et al*. 1988: 75). Indeed, the 'Cost of non-Europe' research programme concluded that firms of all sizes displayed a similar desire for cooperation. Two main corporate strategies for dealing with 1992 were in the process of emerging – namely, measures to improve productivity and to increase the number of international cooperation agreements (Commission of the European Economy Communities 1988: 133).

This link between the attainment of the internal market and an increase in European industrial collaboration is disputed by Kay *et al* (1989), who suggests instead that the direct effects of 1992 will be to reduce such agreements. Their argument is based on two basic premises. First, that the more open a market is, the more likely firms will be able to operate within it without partners and to view in-house expansion and/or mergers and acquisitions as strategies for extending unilateral control. Secondly, the more open a market is, the greater the possibility that potential collaborators are also potential competitors. Firms would thus be increasingly reluctant to enter into cooperative agreements which might act to diffuse their technological knowledge. By eliminating non-tariff barriers to trade, the impact of the single market will be to reduce both the need to collaborate with EC partners to gain market access and the willingness to collaborate with potentially rival firms.

This discrepancy of views relating to the impact of 1992 on technological collaboration raises a number of issues with regard to the role of collaboration as a corporate strategy instrument, the relationship between competition and collaboration, the wider context and geopolitical implications of 1992 and the likely nature of the resulting markets. We go on now to examine each of these in turn.

COLLABORATION AS A CORPORATE STRATEGY INSTRUMENT

How then do companies perceive collaboration as a strategic policy instrument? Kay's analysis takes as its starting point the traditional stance of the industrial economist with regard to the raison d'être for collaboration. In Kay *et al*. (1987), he has argued that in analysing industrial cooperative behaviour it is essential to understand that for firms joint ventures are typically a device of the last resort. Firms generally prefer to perform ventures on their own. Open markets facilitate trade and exporting strategies, while barriers to trade encourage access through multinational location. Cooperative arrangements by contrast are often expensive and cumbersome to establish and administer and crucially may erode firms' competitive advantage by giving potential rivals access to valuable know-how.

Yet, as the preceding sections have shown, the range of activities under the umbrella of industrial collaboration in the 1980s are not only much wider than the industrial economist's notion of 'joint venture' might suggest, but are also not necessarily devices of the last resort. Nor are they always motivated by the search for market access. European programmes like Esprit and the Eureka initiative are about putting money into the process of collaboration. Financial support for such ventures can encourage firms to pursue cooperation which they might not otherwise have considered. The case for European governments actively promoting collaboration between European firms is from a narrow *economic* point of view relatively weak. Benefits are gained from a wider exchange of information and higher R&D expenditure level but costs are also imposed. *Political* and *strategic* factors, though, swing the balance the other way. The world does not operate according to benign free-trade rules. Given the current performance of US and Japanese multinationals and the trading policies pursued by their governments, it is impossible to be confident that what might seem benign trading partnerships today will not result in technological dependency tomorrow. European collaboration then offers a constructive alternative to protection. Completion of the internal market will help to improve the competitiveness of European firms but in turn will expose firms to considerable competitive strain. The cementing of intra-European partnerships will help to prevent European firms being victims of a 'weakness take-out' – that is, selling out to the USA or Japan (Sharp and Shearman 1987).

THE RELATIONSHIP BETWEEN COMPETITION AND COLLABORATION

The second issue in technological collaboration considered here is that of the relationship between competition and collaboration. While much emphasis has been placed on the difference between 'pre-competitive' R&D collaboration on the one hand and 'competitive' R&D on the other, the maintenance of these distinctions in practice has not always proved easy. From a competition policy regulatory point of view, this can cause problems. Generally the European Commission has made a distinction between 'pre-competitive' or basic industrial research (for which a level of subsidy of 50 per cent or more can be granted) and R&D nearer to the market for which progressively lower levels of assistance are approved. Joint exploitation of R&D results, however, requires specific exemption. To accommodate changing interfirm collaborative patterns though, the European Commission has since 1985 awarded automatic exemption from EEC competition rules under a limited 'block exemption' regulation for agreements relating to collaborative R&D (including that combined with joint exploitation of results) and to joint exploitation of results prior R&D between the same partners. To qualify, collaborators must not jointly hold more than 20 per cent of the market for the products resulting from the collaboration.

While completion of the internal market will continue to require the development of a coherent competition policy, the premises upon which this is built may need some reassessment. Experience gained under Esprit, Brite/Euram and other European Community R&D initiatives would seem to indicate that an increasing level of cooperation between companies has not hampered their competitive activities. Competition and cooperation are not necessarily mutually incompatible. Indeed it may be that the predominant view of 'competition' depicting individual firms, clearly demarcated one from the other, engaged in cut-throat competition is not entirely accurate. Competitive modes of behaviour can and do exist on a variety of levels as do cooperative interactions. While 'competition' may reach a peak at a particular stage in an industry's development, it generally tends to co-exist with a variety of closer cooperative relationships. Indeed, the very nature of the cooperation/competition relationship alters as an industry develops (Shearman and Burrell 1987).

In a model outlined elsewhere (Shearman and Burrell 1987), Gibson Burrell and I have characterised the changing nature of the cooperation/competition interrelationships (among other things) into four ideal typical terms which are taken to mark the process of industrial evolution – namely, the community, the informal network, the formal network, and the club. In the cycle of industrial development, the features inherent in each of these 'stageposts' are ever present and crucially impact upon interorganisational and competitive relationships.

The 'community' represents the early stage of an industry's development.[1] It resembles a *Gemeinshaft* in which individuals, firms and groups are all engaged in a relatively unstructured set of complex and multi-faceted relationships, which in certain important ways reflects a social 'community'. Little 'competition' in its conventional sense exists between groups of individuals for the nature of the 'industry', 'product' and 'market' are as yet ill-defined. Companies on the whole are newly established and trust levels are high between firms and between individual entrepreneurs. The industry approximates what Burns (1981) has termed 'a collaborative system' in which bonding processes may be enhanced by cultural and regional factors. Geographical proximity, along with shared perceptions and values, generates a set of social interactions in which little sense of the economic 'cost' of any transaction is apparent.

With time, the 'community' evolves into an 'informal network' where elite groups of key individuals and organisations serve to focus the still relatively fluid relationships. The basis for *'Gemeinschaft'* breaks down and is replaced by a movement towards *'Gesellschaft'*, in which the common ideologies and value orientations characteristic of the community phase begin to disintegrate. Trust begins to decline between members of the networks as the 'collaborative system' declines in importance. Interfirm relationships assume the form of a 'negotiated order' in an ongoing day-to-day manner (Strauss, 1978). A calculative approach begins to develop as linkages with other firms are increasingly perceived in terms of economic costs. Information is now bartered rather than relatively freely disseminated and knowledge within the industry becomes, for the first time, subject to control and limitation. As specialisation between firms develops, 'competition' between firms begins to assume more significance. Inevitably, the increasing numbers of interfirm transactions assume a more strictly economic and/or legalistic character until the relationships within the industry begin to take on the form of the 'formal network'.

The 'formal network' is the so-called 'mature' stage of industrial development in which competition takes the form frequently discussed in economic theories of the firm. The 'collaborative system' has been replaced by a managerial structure (Burns 1981) based on mistrust and coercive sanctions. Relationships within the network are formalistic and monofaceted, occurring between rigid and well-defined entities in predictable stylised ways. Loyalty to the firm is consciously fostered by corporate management and interactions carrying no perceived gains for the firm are actively discouraged. Information is exchanged, managed and 'traded' and the barriers governing its dissemination are well established. The formal network stage may last for decades or even generations.

The 'club', meanwhile, develops out of the periods of crisis which eventually assault every industry. It represents the structural form many declining industries have taken. The 'club' is defensive with a well-defined sense of external threat and self-interest. It is wholly purposive and essentially pragmatic in nature. Less rigid in some ways than the formal network, it may enrich the range and type of cross-organisational relationships. Where the sense of crisis is not perceived to be imminent, 'community-clubs' may develop. Less defensive groupings than clubs, such entities may, through their joint activities encourage the development of new industries.

Many of the European-level initiatives may be characterised as 'club-type' developments. What distinguishes the club style in particular is not the output as such – for, as in the case of pre-competitive collaborative R&D, this is merely the perceived strategy of the moment – but the fact that the activity is a defensive response to a serious crisis. This is certainly the case for sections within the European IT industry. The notion of so-called 'new' technology and/or sunrise industry is sometimes mistakenly equated with that of an embryonic or emerging industry. But in Europe, as elsewhere, the IT industry displays the characteristics of a mature industrial sector and indeed as outlined above, many of the incentives underlying government and industry promotion of European technological collaboration reflect exactly that sense of crisis characteristic of the club. Programmes such as Esprit are in effect a defensive response to the threat to Europe posed by Japanese and US technological leadership and their increasing European market penetration.

AN INDUSTRY-LEVEL APPROACH TO TECHNOLOGICAL COLLABORATION AND 1992

Such an industry-level approach to the analysis of technological collaboration affords some useful insights into the potential impact of 1992. First, both the underlying incentives for collaboration and the nature of the cooperation sought may be shaped not so much by the opportunities and/or threats generated by 1992 itself as by the state of maturity reached by the industry to which a particular firm or group of firms belong. This has important implications not only for the promotion or otherwise of European technological collaboration but also for the development of economic and industrial policy objectives at the national and European levels.

Secondly, the survival of Europe's collective manufacturing base depends on the creation and maintenance of a variety of industries which ultimately generate wealth, high levels of employment and taxable revenues. Clearly, all four types of industrial structure need to be encouraged within a framework of European, national and regional industrial strategy, though the balance between them may shift with the changes in political objectives (Shearman and Burrell 1987). All four, moreover, involve quite different cooperation/competition relationships and policy approaches. 'Communities' are inevitably difficult to replicate and occur only in very special circumstances. Their long-term economic potential is great but their ability to generate high levels of wealth and employment in the medium to short term is low. 'Communities' involve an *ad hoc* informal type of cooperation best facilitated by infrastructural supports rather than direct policy intervention. It is here then that implementation of the single market could help to encourage the development of community-style industries through, for example, the availability of transnational venture capital funding and a barrier-free corporate environment.

'Informal networks' represent those industries which are moving towards a sustainable point of development. They constitute the target of much of Japan's industrial strategy. Collaborative arrangements with non-European partners might be employed to try and effect the acquisition and transfer to Europe of the know-how and expertise fostered in community-type industries located elsewhere. Intra-European collaboration may serve to facilitate the transition from community to informal network of industries within Europe. The impact of 1992 on such arrangements is difficult to determine. Much would depend on the global location of community-type industries, the ease with which industry structures could be transferred across cultures and the global market content. The single market could serve to reinforce European competencies or alternatively to underline European technological and economic dependency.

The formal network stage of industrial development perhaps most closely approximates the usage of collaboration portrayed by Kay and others. Firms here are clearly demarcated one from the other and engaged in cut-throat competition, and collaborative ventures are more likely to be devices of the last resort. In such circumstances it is reasonable to assume that where intra-European collaborative agreements currently exist, the direct effects of 1992 would be to reduce the incentives for increasing them.

This is not to suggest, however, that the post-1992 pattern of collaborative behaviour within Europe will be one of diminishing rather than increasing activity. First, as has been noted above, commercial logic is not the sole factor at work. Secondly, many of the industrial sectors in Europe are, in the context of global markets, fast reaching the club rather than formal network stage. Europe's strengths relative to the USA and Japan lie in aerospace, chemicals, mechanical engineering and nuclear reactors. Its weaknesses are to be found in computing, electrical machinery and components, radio, television and telecommunications (Patel and Pavitt 1987; Sharp and Shearman 1987). While the extent of these weaknesses may vary within Europe according to country and sector, collectively they represent a defensive position *vis-à-vis* the United States and Japan.

The creation of clubs, meanwhile, is a defensive posture suggesting that the initiative already lies elsewhere in the field of international capital. Yet it is this very defensiveness that in some ways created the momentum for achieving the internal market. Part of the incentive underlying European-based collaboration initiatives was a desire to counter US and Japanese protectionism and circumvent the imperfections of the European home market (Sharp and Shearman 1987). While in economic terms, the obvious solution for achieving the latter is to remove such internal barriers, governments are not, when it comes down to it, willing to sacrifice national champions in their high-tech industries or to really indulge in the market free-for-all that this would imply. Collaboration therefore offered a useful compromise: it secured some of the benefits without comprising national sovereignty and spread some of the costs of adjustment.

Collaboration, although a compromise between maintaining national capabilities and achieving the full internal market, does nevertheless help to promote the achievement of the internal market itself. Governments are inevitably sensitive about national sovereignty issues and overestimate their importance and consequently create artificial barriers to the achievement of the internal market without fully realising the cost which has to be paid in terms of long-term competitiveness. National champions traditionally connive with governments to keep it this way and as their competitiveness in global markets increasingly diminishes, protection at home assumes increasing importance. The advantage of intra-European collaboration is that it makes national champions aware of what might be achieved if a unified European market were fully exploited – that is, it creates a constituency which puts pressure on individual governments to back those moves which help create a more unified internal market.

Sectors within Europe, therefore, that approximate to the club rather than formal network stage of industrial development are by virtue of their defensive posture *vis-à-vis* the US and Japan and their strategic salience to European economies likely to generate intra-European collaborative activities. The process of Europeanisation effected by inter-governmental and Community initiatives to date and by the 1992 programme itself, moreover, is likely to reinforce the

European nature of collaboration for industries in both of these stages of the development cycle. Firms contemplating collaboration need to be able to identify appropriate partners. Inevitably, there is often a natural bias towards firms that are known to each other. The tendency to treat the European, US and Far Eastern markets as separate entities, and for European firms to run European operations from their home base, means that until recently cross-licensing and markets arrangements have been *more likely* to be biased towards non-European rather than European firms. Considerable competencies however do exist *within* Europe and mechanisms such as Esprit and Eureka have encouraged a wider search for European opportunities and successfully forged links in sectors where participants freely admit that lack of knowledge had inhibited earlier contacts. Similarly, links between companies and academic and/or technological research institutes have to date been largely nationally based but the momentum towards 1992 is slowly encouraging more cross-European links. These in turn will serve to develop and reinforce an awareness within Europe of Europe's *own* range of competencies and assets so that on economic or commercial grounds alone, the search for collaborative partners may not necessarily be directed to sources outside Europe.

1992: THE WIDER CONTEXT AND GEO-POLITICAL IMPLICATIONS

The primary motivation for the launch of the 1992 programme in 1985 was economic. A belated acknowledgement that Europe needed to adapt to mounting pressure generated by structural changes occurring in the world economy and international markets, the plan was perceived to offer the best chance – or indeed the last hope – of revitalising European economies afflicted with sluggish growth rates, high unemployment and declining international competitiveness which were obstinately refusing to respond to national policy prescriptions. Since then, 1992 has acquired a powerful political and symbolic importance. Though frequently only loosely articulated, the force of 1992 as an *idea* has to a large extent already overshadowed the expected impact of the specific legislature proposals contained in the EC programme and the somewhat notional deadline set for their implementation. Part of this is accounted for by the political rhetoric whipped up by the EEC, governments and industry, but the force of 1992 as an idea is also being driven by the underlying changes in European business perceptions and market behaviour manifested in the surge of cross-frontier acquisitions, mergers and alliances of recent months. Indeed, the current willingness of European firms to venture across borders is contributing to a somewhat irreversible re-shaping of market structures and suggesting that to a certain extent the vision of an economically more integrated, barrier-free Europe may be starting to become something of a self-fulfilling prophecy.

Underlying the symbolic and economic potency of the 1992 initiative is the political debate on the future of Europe which it inevitably generates. The founders of the European Community were inspired by the political desire to eliminate forever the threat of another war in Europe. They envisaged a unified federal structure within which the powers of national governments would steadily wither away. The creation of a single market was viewed as a necessary stage on the road to that ultimate goal rather than as an end in itself.

The process of achieving the single market is inevitably raising new issues for debate which will colour discussions on Europe's future for some time to come. To what extent, for example, have EC governments fully acknowledged the wider political consequences of increased economic integration and what kind of longer-term direction will the Community – and the rest of Europe – take after 1992? The way in which Europe deals with these political challenges will to a large extent ultimately determine whether 1992 will amount to a limited exercise in removing a number of market barriers or develops into the first stage of a much more ambitious and far-reaching drive towards comprehensive integration. Already it is clear that the apparently straightforward task of removing trade barriers is difficult to complete and unlikely to yield its full potential economic benefits until and *unless* EC member governments commit themselves more wholeheartedly to common policies in the economic and political sphere. Similarly, the Community has yet to forge a consensus on the extent to which its pursuit of further integration implies a more forceful assertion of its own economic and political identity at the possible expense of its traditional relationships with the rest of the world.

Discussions of the impact of 1992 on technological collaboration, therefore, cannot be separated from the wider political and economic issues associated with the process of implementing the internal market. The nature and quality of the changes effected by the 1992 programme are crucially dependent on the level of progress that is achieved on the political front. To date, the political debate has touched on such issues as 'fortress Europe', 'reciprocity' and 'European preference' but has shed little light on the substantive underlying issues. Increasingly, implicit uncertainties are being articulated and echoed outside the economic sphere. In the arenas of defence and foreign policy, for example, the task of finding a coherent response to the difficulties facing Europe over the next few years is complicated not just by differences of views with Europe, but also by the fact that it must take account of rapid and continuing changes in the international political and economic landscape.

Many of the forces underlying Europe's current position originated outside its borders and lie beyond its direct control. The growing detente between the US and the Soviet Union and the '*glasnost*' momentum within Eastern Europe, for example, have major long-term implications for Europe's role in international relations. The extent to which West European interests and priorities are still shared by the US is open to question as is the rationale for US military presence in Europe. Secondly, the erosion of the overwhelming margin of international economic, industrial and technological advantage enjoyed by the US for the majority of the post-war period has led to concerns within Europe that the battle for economic and industrial supremacy which is developing between the US and Japan may be partly fought out in European markets. The fact that the US economy and trade are becoming more closely integrated with those of Asian countries in the Pacific Rim reinforces the feeling that the US disposition to view Europe as its most natural economic ally is now diminishing. Thirdly, developments in world financial and capital markets have stimulated increased interdependence between industrialised economies, reshaped the way in which international resources are allocated and deprived national governments to a large degree of their former policy autonomy. Fourthly, the changing economics of many product markets meanwhile makes it increasingly hard for most industries to survive merely on the basis of domestic demand and forces them to compete for world market share in a context where the rapid diffusion of knowledge and technology requires innovations to make ever-bigger investments to protect their position. In semiconductors, for instance, the costs are so high that it is doubtful whether even the whole of the Western European market is sufficiently large enough to enable them to be recouped profitably. Finally, there is the question of the influence of state intervention within the economy. The assumption that governments are able to control the economic output, competitiveness and growth of their national economies through direct intervention has been undermined by external pressures and structural shifts within the economies themselves. Consequently, post-war corporatism and intervention-ism has in the 1980s largely given way to an increased emphasis on market-oriented policies. Liberalisation and de-regulation have become part of the economic orthodoxy espoused by governments on both the Right and the Left of the political spectrum.

Thus parallel changes and pressures are underway in most European countries but the future direction of EC development remains to be seen. Successful implementation of the internal market calls for a political as well as economic consensus. Many in the UK favour a Community open to international influences with a distinctly Atlanticist emphasis. France views a unified community as a bulwark against the rest of the world and a means of covering trade concessions from the rest of the world. As Europe's largest economic and trading bloc, the Community is a powerful centripetal force exercising substantial influence over the broad direction of developments in the whole of the region. Some EFTA countries may well opt to apply for EC membership to avoid political and economic marginalisation. The shape of future relations between Eastern and Western Europe too is of growing importance.

It is clear at the moment that the future definition of Europe even as a geographical unit is somewhat blurred and some distance from the goal of being a coherent political, strategic and economic entity. Defence groupings further complicate the issue. The Community currently excludes a number of West European countries, several of which belong to the NATO alliance. Of the EC partners, Ireland is neutral and France and Spain lie outside NATO's integrated command structure. Yet the boundary between civil and defence interest is becoming increasingly difficult to draw. The subject of so-called 'dual-use' technologies and industries and their role in promoting not only better defence capabilities but economic competitiveness has captured the attention of policymakers associated with *both* NATO and the European Community. Whatever the outcome of debates on the complexion of the post-1992 European Community, political factors will continue to militate in favour of intra-European collaboration of one sort or another.

THE POST-1992 EUROPEAN MARKET

Finally, it is important to differentiate between the uniformity of a single European market framework and the diversity of intra-European markets. As noted above, harmonisation of Europe's heterogeneous culture and language are not on the agenda. The consumer of 1993 will not look very different from the consumer of 1989. Basic national differences of language, climate, custom and culture will still be there and habits of shopping, eating, working and leisure will change only slowly – if at all. The kind of changes that the European public is currently undergoing are social and demographic – smaller households, more working women, fewer teenagers and more pensioners. Many manufacturers will be tempted to standardise their procedures to achieve the cost-economies of high-volume runs but few will be able to design products with equal acceptability from Athens to Amsterdam. So called 'European' brands of products currently differ from country to country in formula, price, positioning and competitive climate – and post-1992 will no doubt continue to do so. Moves to create a general level of homogeneity across Europe may well be tempered by nationalistic and/or regional protection of cultural identities. The broadcasting and media industries, for example, are finding entry into the 'European' market difficult despite the obvious boost to internationalisation from satellite technology. The real barriers are language and culture, and the smaller the country and its population, the greater is the determination to oppose 'cultural imperialism'.

Markets themselves, moreover, are becoming more complex. In the field of computing there is no longer a single, more or less homogeneous computer market of the kind which existed in the 1970s and early 1980s and which was IBM-dominated. Instead, a series of specialisations is emerging, each with its market leader. In these changing and unsettling conditions, the rationale for a series of new and innovative links between Europe's major players is clear. Such links could take a variety of forms from joint ventures and marketing agreements to mergers or acquisitions. The need to gain access to each others' geographic markets could be supported through bilateral marketing agreements. The impact of 1992 is unlikely to reduce the need for European high technology firms to seek out intra-European marketing as well as technical collaboration agreements. Where the nature of markets is radically changing, it will be the internationally competitive, financially sound, innovative and flexible companies that will be best placed to meet the challenge. A more open European market is likely to increase the vulnerability of firms such as those in the European computer industry which are traditionally tied to national markets, relatively lacking in commercial innovation and slow to react to fundamental changes in the industry. Too small to compete effectively with the global US and Japanese players and too large and inflexible to emulate new companies creating new niche markets, intra-European collaboration may well represent their only real strategic option.

CONCLUSIONS

What then are the implications of 1992 for companies in technological collaboration? This paper has sought to show that the role of collaboration in corporate strategy is no longer necessarily a device of the last resort. The past decade has witnessed a spectacular growth in collaboration agreements. As the OECD (1986: 6) has noted, the growth in international, interfirm technical cooperation agreements represents one of the most important novel developments of the first half of the 1980s. The range of activities involved, moreover, is much wider than that generally associated with the notion of 'joint venture'. It has also been argued here that the experience of European collaboration to date suggests that not only are conventional analyses of the competition/collaboration relationship somewhat inappropriate but that the precise nature and balance of such relationships between firms alter as an industry matures. The particular stage of industrial development of a given industry, therefore, may well be a crucial determinant of the nature of corporate responses to the challenges of 1992. Equally important though will be the salience of the political factors associated with technological collaboration at any given point in time, features which in turn will be shaped by the shifting intra-Community relationships and extra-European geo-political structures and patterns. Finally, achievement of the internal market framework does not necessarily imply a homogeneity of intra-European markets. Cultural, linguistic and psychological barriers combined with changing industrial and market developments may well serve to reinforce rather than diminish the need to extend technological R&D agreements into the arena of intra-European collaborative marketing and distribution.

NOTE

1 For further details on the 'community' and other stages in this model, see Shearman and Burrell (1987).

REFERENCES

Burns, T. (1981) 'A comparative study of administrative structure and organisational processes in selected areas of the National Health Service', SSRC Report HRP 6725.
Cecchini, P. *et al.* (1988) *The European Challenge 1992*, Aldershot, Wildwood House.
Chesnais, F. (1986) *Technical Cooperation Agreements Between Firms: Some Initial Data and Analyses*, DSTI, OECD.

Commission of the European Communities (1988) 'The economics of 1992', *European Economy*, 35.

Hacklish, C. (1986) Technical alliances in the semiconductor industry, Centre for Science and Technology Policy, New York University, unpublished report.

Kay, N. Robe, J. and Zagnoli, P. (1987) 'An approach to the analysis of joint venture', European University Working Paper.

Kay, N. (1989) 'Competition in technological change and 1992', unpublished draft discussion paper.

OECD (1987) 'Committee report on restrictive business practices', Paris.

OECD (1988) 'Science, technology, industry review', No. 4, Paris.

Patel, P. and Pavitt, K. (1987) 'Is Europe losing the technology race?', *Research Policy*, 1.

Ricotta, E. and Mariotti, S. (1986) 'Diversification agreements among firms and innovative behaviour', paper presented at the Venice Conference on Innovative Diffusion.

Sharp, M. and Shearman, C. (1987) *European Technological Collaboration*, Chatham House Papers 36, London, Routledge & Kegan Paul.

Shearman, C. and Burrell, G. (1987) 'The structures of industrial development', *Journal of Management Studies* 24, 4.

Strauss, A. (1978) *Negotiations: Varieties, Contexts, Processes and Social Order*, San Francisco, Jossey-Bass.

Williams, R. (1984) 'The international political economy of technology', in S. Strange (ed.) *International Political Economy*, London, Allen & Unwin.

6 A new kind of marketing for Europe

Barry Witcher

INTRODUCTION

This chapter argues that the incomplete acceptance of marketing ideas results from an organisational segmentalist view of the marketing function. A new type of marketing is required which can be implemented throughout the whole organisation. This is probably more suited to European conditions than conventional 4-P-based marketing. It is suggested that total quality management (TQM) provides a way forward, particularly if it results in improved organisational market responsiveness. This is very important for industrial products and services where non-marketing personnel are involved in direct contact with employees in customer companies. The implications for strategic marketing are outlined, as well as the role for a wider form of internal marketing. The chapter ends with observations that marketing should be closely involved in the design and implementation of TQM.

THE MARKETING FUNCTION

'Marketing is the management process responsible for identifying, anticipating and satisfying customers' requirements profitably' (Chartered Institute of Marketing). Marketing is broader than just those activities which are encompassed by a marketing department, those things which are traditionally understood as marketing – such as selling, advertising and branding. This is because commercial organisations have to match the aspirations of customer requirements with the internal capacity of what can actually be produced. This is not a simple question of physical capacity but it is also about the factors which determine overall organisational market responsiveness and corporate image.

MODERN MARKETING AND ITS FAILURE

Thirty years ago marketing came of age and the profession began to talk about a marketing concept which put the interests of the consumer and customer at the centre of all of an organisation's activities. 'Companies revolve around the customer, not the other way around. . . . As the concept gains every greater acceptance, marketing is emerging as the most important single function in business.' (Keith 1960:35)

However, marketing's hope for a central place in any organisation's priorities has only seen partial fulfilment. The discipline's ideas were adopted not as an organisational philosophy which had relevance to the whole organisation, but in the form of a specialised, and often marginalised, organisational function – the marketing department. This was an improvement on what had gone before, in the sense that marketing activities were now integrated as part of marketing plans or programmes, which were targeted at groups of customers or consumers according to the principles of market segmentation (a sort of Smithsonian specialisation based upon a division of markets). These ideas were propagated in textbooks which emphasised the importance of the 4-P model of marketing management (see McCarthy 1960), under four categories labelled product, price, place (or distribution) and promotion. The idea was to design different combinations of these so that a total package might be offered to suit the needs of separate parts of a market. Thus the marketing organisation would be meeting the needs of its market more closely than a competitor which might be supplying only one kind of offer to the whole market. In this sense the role of the marketing function was clear: it was to identify, analyse and break down markets into segments on the basis of market requirements, and to design appropriate marketing mixes for each target segment. However, even these ideas seem to have met with only partial adoption in the United Kingdom.

'It was . . . alarming to discover that 47 per cent of British and 40 per cent of the US companies (vs 13 per cent of Japanese) acknowledged that they were unclear about the main type of customers in the market and what their needs were' (Doyle *et al.* 1987: 11–12). The report from which this quotation is taken presented evidence which suggested that British (and American) organisations have been slow to adopt marketing principles. This seems to have been particularly true for some industrial markets, where segmentation has meant a simple division of markets based upon the convenience of the supplier, rather than upon the needs of customers – such as a categorisation of customer by geographical area or product category, and leaving it simply at that. There is also some evidence which suggests that marketing programmes have relied too heavily on a short-term and superficial manipulation of the marketing mix, which has been detrimental to radical inno- vation and product change (see Witcher 1988). Other observers have pointed to a kind of 'can't-see-the-wood-for-the-trees' syn- drome, for example, a survey of managers in the USA suggested that marketing was too difficult to separate out in the abstract because it was something which seemed to them to be so basic to everyday business. Some European marketers have suggested that marketing is, anyway, too broad to be confined solely to a marketing department.

EUROPEAN MARKETING

During the 1980s a new view of European marketing has been developed for industrial and services markets. This has included the work of the International Marketing and Purchasing Group, (see, for example Hakansson's (1981) report of research into European user–supplier relationships) and follow-up reports of similar research presented at IMP's conferences (for example, Turnbull and Paliwoda 1988). Similar work has been conducted by Scandinavian researchers into services marketing, (see particularly, research from Gronroos 1983). This work in general takes an interaction or network approach to understanding trading behaviour, and emphasises two things: that marketing activity is company-wide and is not confined to a specialist department, and that the main marketing job does not focus upon a single market transaction, but is instead about the establishment of a customer–supplier relationship over a long period of market transactions. Gronroos (1989) has been particularly vehement in arguing that Western marketing practice has been based too much on ideas which had come originally from North American experience, where the socio-economic and market infrastructures differ markedly from the European. He has argued for a new understanding based on the existence of a broad organisation-wide marketing function, and a new definition of marketing which is based on relationships, where the establishment of mutual trust between customer and supplier is the main aim of marketing. He reports that European companies are closing down their marketing departments. This sounds rather drastic.

There are signs that American marketing is responding to relationship marketing ideas. Some marketing academics there have begun to write about relationship marketing for services markets. Berry and his colleagues have probably gone the furthest in examining how relationship marketing can actually be translated into organisational activity (see, for example, Zeithaml *et al.* 1990). This has always been the basic weakness of the marketing concept and marketing planning: the question of how marketing ideas can be integrated with the activities of non-marketing employees (or as Gronroos terms them, part-time marketers). Berry and his colleagues have suggested appraisal frameworks for services based in essence on quality management ideas (see for example, Berry *et al* 1985, 1988), and other American academics are now developing similar quality-based ideas, as instanced in Orsini's recent work (1990, 1991). While Europeans were quick to research and describe relationship marketing, they have been much slower to see any link between marketing and quality.

QUALITY MANAGEMENT

The last decade saw a widespread and growing interest in Japanese quality management ideas from both European and American companies. An important reason for this was the success of the Japanese in seeming to solve inter-functional conflicts between production and marketing. Conventionally, a Western marketing department working to the principles of market segmentation will tend to seek variety in products, so as to add value. Production usually resists this as product complexity makes for shorter production runs, increased buffer stocks, and generally increased operational costs. Yet the Japanese had generally managed to increase product variety and reduce production costs at the same time. This had been achieved through the principles of company-wide quality, which had permitted practices like just-in-time (JIT) management and the extension of these ideas to suppliers (see the work of Abeglen and Stalk 1985, and the very good prescriptive accounts by Schonberger 1986, 1990).

Japanese quality management had its roots in the years after World War 2 with the pioneering quality-control ideas of two Americans: W. Edwards Deming (1986) and Joseph Juran (1989). This later evolved into what became known across the Western world as total quality control (TQC), the idea that quality management can be extended to every organisational activity. In the UK TQC came to be called by its now popular name, total quality management (TQM). A journal, '*The TQM Magazine*', was first published in 1988, and several books had been published by the end of 1990 (for example, Oakland 1989), which is probably the best one and firmly based on the ideas of Deming and Juran; Cullen and Hollingum 1987; Collard 1989; Atkinson 1990; and two collections of papers edited by Chase 1988, and Dale and Plunkett 1989. An American text has also been published (see Berry 1990).

A major weakness of this work is that TQM is presented in ways which suggest a variety of sometimes conflicting approaches to implementation. This might not be too serious if Oakland is right when he writes that while the so-called quality gurus seem to present different solutions, this really only reflects differences in dialect rather than language (Oakland 1989: xi). A more serious problem is that most of these writers are from an operations or manufacturing background, which means that they have tended to exaggerate the quality control aspects while under-playing what TQM is really all about, which is its involvement of everybody, mainly through progressive human resource management policies. Putting TQM simply: 'total' means that every person in the company works together, 'quality' means meeting market requirements exactly, and 'management' is management by a set of principles.

Central to the idea of TQM is the quality chain, where jobs are conceptualised as linking processes in a chain which stretches from primary input sources to the final consumer. This includes people who are working with no obvious contact with the external market. They do have immediate internal customers, however, and these are those people who work on the follow-up process which forms the next link in the chain. The quality of everybody's work has consequences for the work of others later on, and eventually it will determine the quality of the end-products in the final market place. Thus the concept of an internal customer is all-important: it is the needs of this customer which must be satisfied exactly.

The most interesting aspect for marketers is that TQM is about creating a customer-responsive philosophy for the whole company, in a way which ensures that the achievement of quality is achieved first time in the form in which the customers want it. This is virtually the same thing as the marketing concept. TQM uses the language of marketing for everyone's job, no matter how far the operator or performer of that job is from the external customer. The value of TQM for marketing is that it produces market-responsive organisation, and so it is a new way to implement the marketing concept. It is particularly useful for industrial and service marketing, where non-specialist marketing staff meet with employees from customer organisations on a continuing relationship basis. This integrated view of marketing has been a feature of Japanese industrial practice for a long time. Shoichi Saba, an ex-CEO of Toshiba, has written about the importance of market analysis and sales promotion as sub-fields of marketing but that

> real marketing is just commonsense. . . . What I mean by that is that every employee should share in having a common sense for the market. To have sensitivity to what is happening in the market, and what is needed there, is the origin of all marketing and every employee should share a common sensitivity to the market.
>
> (Saba 1989: 87)

Sensitivity required the 'intimate cooperation' of everybody, so that operations and employee attitudes are harmonised throughout all areas of corporate activity. At Toshiba this was done by a process he described as 'management engineering', which were his words for TQM. In this sense TQM is a far wider idea than the assurance or control of product and service quality. Oakland has written that it is 'the new way of managing for the future . . . it is a way of managing the whole business or organization to ensure complete customer satisfaction at every stage, internally and externally' (Oakland 1989: x).

Of course, putting it this way is strong stuff, and claims like this have been heard before, thirty years ago, for the marketing concept, (see Keith 1960, for example). The marketing concept never quite came off as a company-wide approach to management. Perhaps the 'customer-is-always-right' evangelicalism of fundamentalist marketing seemed to run counter to other people's work. A market-led philosophy can place an exaggerated emphasis on the welfare of the external customer which is likely to result in adversarial relations with other functions (see Price 1984: 211–12); waste from over-stocking (see Dear 1988: 16); or in a tendency to cut corners (as suggested in Groocock 1986: 82).

ORGANISATIONAL SEGMENTALISM

Inter-functional and other disputes between units and individuals are organisational facts of life. Managers in different parts of a large organisation can be expected to agree over very little, particularly when it comes to the appropriateness of competing strategies, (see Johnson and Scholes 1984). Organisational behaviour texts give many instances of the importance of political factors in management (see, for example, Pettigrew 1985) and marketing (see Piercy 1985). Many causes of inter-functional conflict were documented in early studies of organisational decision-making processes (see, for example, Crozier 1964; Burns and Stalker 1961), which drew attention to professional barriers between departments, particularly research and development's separation from marketing and production, which had insulated managers from customer needs. More recently, Kanter (1983) has attacked what she has called organizational segmentalism, for its resulting over-specialisation and insularity as barriers to innovation and change. Studies of Japanisation have also singled out related problems, for instance:

> Quality is about power sharing: about giving power to the customer and to subordinates. If you allow people to influence you, you give up expert power. But people build up their reputations with expert power. To give it up goes against the organisation's power culture.
>
> (Giles and Starkey 1988: 43)

The marketing department, itself often physically located far away from manufacturing operations at a head office, is perhaps too prone to suspicions and dark imaginings of company engineers sitting around in cosy quality circles, who are inventing new versions of Concorde or Sinclair's C5. Marketing's reaction to present-day aspirations of quality people has had some reserve about it:

> The recent interest in quality concept is a good example of a traditional approach that . . . falls short of moving the company to being more market-responsive . . . the quality concept may even serve to drive the company further away from being market responsive.
>
> (Masiello 1988: 87)

This is most likely to be true if the quality function itself is compartmentalised into a specialist department. It is least likely to happen if quality management is true TQM and involve everybody equally and top management in particular. It must involve marketing specialists, who are in contact with the external customer, and their participation must be felt in the TQM support infrastructure. At the present time very few (and it has to be noted here that many of them look very doubtful versions) TQM programmes involve marketers very closely.

QUALITY'S CONTRIBUTION TO MARKETING

Things might be changing, however. Articles have begun to appear in the specialist marketing literature which discuss the application of quality ideas to processes in marketing. Kohoutek has reviewed the application of quality assurance (1988). The work of Berry and others in services marketing was noted above: they have emphasised the importance of appropriate performance specifications (Bery *et al.* 1985, 1988). Bertrand (1987) and Cravens *et al.* (1988) have gone furthest by sketching out the stages for implementing a TQM programme in marketing itself. This involved the identification of marketing processes so that the techniques of statistical process control (SPC) might then be used to ensure consistency in conformance to external customer quality specifications. These authors do not examine the nature of the marketing function in terms of its relevance to the whole organisation, instead their primary concern was to describe the stages in a total quality implementation programme in the marketing department. In this work there is a strong implication that TQM transfers from a production context to specialist marketing activities without modification. This is questionable given the open-endedness of many marketing activities, particularly with regard to the soft or intangible attributes of many products and most services. In some markets, quality may be difficult to specify, because competitive success depends upon brand personality, people-based services and a corporate image. It is true that organisations may be able to specify some of the main indicators of quality, and design these into their products and services, but the essence is sometimes difficult to catch, and its secret remains very much in the fickle creativity of the marketer.

TOTAL MARKETING

A total management approach to better marketing can be summarised in the following way.

1 TQM can improve the narrow marketing function as performed by marketing specialists if the principles of quality control and assurance are applied directly to specialist processes inside the marketing department or marketing's areas of responsibility.
2 In a similar way, the application of TQM principles to inter-departmental or functional relationships will also improve the quality of service from other support operations in the organisation, including sales, delivery, warehousing and so on.

3 Quality principles can also be applied to those processes which link into market information systems, and need marketing to provide marketing research information which the organisation will actually use, perhaps for planning and new production development.

4 There is the direct consequence of higher quality working in other parts of the organisation, and what this means for final product and service reliability – perhaps lower costs, increased reliability and a better market offer with respect to the competition.

5 There is the effect on corporate culture and identity, which are prime determinants of employee motivation, corporate image, and how people outside the organisation feel about an organisation, its products and its services.

STRATEGIC MARKETING

The relevance of TQM to strategic marketing is that total approaches represent a business rather than a functional type of management. In Japan managers have been thought of more often as general managers rather than as functional specialists. Recently, Peter Drucker (1990) has argued this is likely to be the case in the future for Western managers, with the rise of the 'business manager'. This thinking is consistent with Kanter's ideas that organisations must become less deterministic in their approaches to planning.

> [M]ost organizations have attempted to deal with forthcoming change and with environmental contingencies by evermore elaborate mechanisms for strategic planning – essentially designed to help organizations feel in control of their futures. There will always be a need for this, of course, but the balance between planning – which reduces the needs for effective reaction – and structural flexibility – which increases the capacity for effective reaction – needs to shift toward the latter. The era of strategic planning (control) may be over; we are entering an era of tactical planning (response).
>
> (Kanter 1983: 41)

TQM shifts the focus of responsibility for quality to the people who actually do the work and makes wide use of teams and other forms of participative action. As such it represents a transformation from traditional authoritarian, top-down decision-taking to task-oriented ideals. This would call for marked changes in the strategic thinking of most European companies, since TQM brings together a management concern with managing change strategy, with the routine efficiency improvement activities of the shopfloor, in one total approach to organizational management. It can be extended to the wider marketing system if, as Porter has suggested (1985), suppliers, customers and facilitators are brought together in a value chain, perhaps in the form of strategic partnerships.

STRATEGIC INTERNAL MARKETING

In all of this there is a special contribution for the marketing department to make in terms of the development of the long-term organisational marketing culture. This requires that TQM includes the participation of specialists so that they take special responsibility on a long-term basis for those things which determine an organisation's competitive advantage in the market place, particularly where it links up with corporate image, product and service positioning. It requires a broader view of traditional internal marketing, which in the past has been understood as a short-term promotion of a particular policy, or message to a company's employees. In this narrow sense, it uses promotions such as employee competitions, suggestion schemes, videos, posters and in-house communication media (see Arnott 1987). These activities have been the preserve of a public relations function, but when training is involved, as for customer care programmes, then a personnel function has often taken over the primary responsibility. An instance of this is provided by Houghton (1988) in the case of Prudential Insurance, which changed its corporate identity and image. One of the few books to consider a strategic role for internal marketing is Thomson (1990), which has taken general marketing ideas and proposed their use for internal marketing, but from a human resource management perspective.

Masiello (1988) is a rare example of a marketing academic who reviewed ideas for market-sensitising organisational employees. He has used TQM-related ideas, although the link with TQM was not explicitly recognised in the article, which emphasise the need for employees to talk to each other about customers, and he outlined a programme which would involve management commitment and communication. The programme would include management strategy sessions and forms of rough planning which would use research or focus groups; the identification of business issues; the use of cross-functional training or work sessions; a mission definition for each department; system or process formalisation, and how the whole programme might be implemented.

Many of these ideas touch on issues of leadership and organisational climate, all of which have received popular acclaim in recent business literature (for example, in McBurnie and Clutterbuck, 1987), and most notably in the ideas of Peters (1988) and what he calls 'total customer response'. These books give anecdotal rather than systematic accounts of strategic internal marketing implementation. A rare exception is a work by Robson (1986), which has taken much from the ideas of Ouchi (1981) and the strategic internal use of mission statements. Robson emphasised how these can be used through stages to implement teamwork, motivate and to make all employees more market-responsive. The role for internal marketing, in the narrow sense, is discussed as a means to create a favourable corporate climate for programmes which aim to change corporate culture in the long term. A useful general text about mission statements is Campbell and Tawadey (1990).

COMPETITIVE ADVANTAGE

An excellent quality culture is not by itself enough to win and hold markets. The advantages of consistent quality at a standard required by the market is, of course, central to commercial success, and marketing's promotional activities must ensure that the market knows and understands the advantages of TQM. Nevertheless, there has to be something which is additional and unique in terms of market-place perceptions, both about the organisation itself, and the products and services it offers, which clearly distinguishes them in the market from competitors over the long period.

Quality should not be restricted to functional attributes but must have additional perceptional attributes built into it, which give colour and meaning to external customer benefits. Corporate image should have designed into it a differential advantage in terms of what the individual customer or consumer should feel about corporate personality, and this should be coordinated throughout the range of its products and services in a way which positively sets them apart from the competition. Built-in differentials begin life in an organisational mission statement, and are reinforced at every stage of production, and beyond the boundaries of the organisation through strategic partnerships, customer closeness and training. Matters of perceptual quality are central to positioning and success in external markets, and if for this reason only, then TQM and marketing must come together.

SUMMARY OF THE ADVANTAGES OF BRINGING MARKETING INTO TQM

Marketing people should be involved with the design of TQM programmes. This is necessary for the following reasons:

1 Marketers should understand TQM to be able to bring it into their teaching and training – it is a way of implementing the marketing concept throughout the whole company.
2 TQM is a user-friendly way of getting non-marketers to see the importance of marketing leadership.
3 Marketing is more aware of intangible quality factors.
4 Involvement of general personnel in contacts with outsiders and external customers makes TQM seem less like brainwashing.
5 Marketing information must be relevant to people who have to use it and involves its own marketing; TQM facilitates this.
6 Marketing skills and materials are relevant to internal customers and markets.
7 General employees should understand what is unique about their organisation and its products to the market – the competitive dimension.
8 TQM should be applied to specialist marketing processes and its integration with other functions.

REFERENCES

Abeglen, J. C. and Stalk, G. (1985) *Kaisa, The Japanese Corporation*, New York, Basic Books.
Arnott, M. (1987) 'Effective employee communication', in N. Hart (ed.) *Effective Corporate Relations*, New York, McGraw-Hill, pp. 59–89.
Atkinson, P. E. (1990) *Creating Cultural Change: The Key To Successful Total Quality Management*, Kempson, IFS Publications.
Berry, L. L. Zeithaml, V. A. and Parasuraman, A. (1985) 'Quality counts in the services, too', *Business Horizons* 28, 44–58.
Berry, L. L., Parasuraman, A. and Zeithaml, V. A. (1988) 'The service-quality puzzle', *Business Horizons* 31, 35–43.
Berry, T. H. (1990) *Managing the Total Quality Transformation*, London, McGraw-Hill.
Bertrand, K. (1987) 'Marketers discover what quality really means', *Business Marketing*, April, 58–64, 66, 70, 72.
Burns, T. and Stalker, G. (1961) *The Management of Innovation*, London, Tavistock.
Campbell, A. and Tawadey, K. (1990) *Mission and Business Philosophy*, London, Heinemann Professional Publishing.
Chartered Institute of Marketing (n.d.) *Marketing as a Career*, Cookham, Berks, CIM.

Chase, R. L. (ed.) (1988) *Total Quality Management*, IFS Executive Briefings, Kempson, IFS Publications.

Collard, R. (1989) *Total Quality: Success Through People*, London, Institute of Personnel Management.

Cravens, D. W., Lamb, C. W. and Moncrief, W. C. (1988) 'Marketing's role in product & service quality', *Industrial Marketing Management* 17, 285–304.

Crozier, M. (1964) *The Bureaucratic Phenomenon*, Chicago, University of Chicago Press.

Cullen, J. and Hollingum, J. (1987) *Implementing Total Quality*, London, IFS Publications.

Dale, B. G. and Plunkett, J. J. (eds) (1989) *Managing Quality*, London, Philip Allan.

Dear, A. (1988) *Working Towards Just-In-Time*, London, Kogan Page.

Deming, W. E. (1986) *Out of the Crisis*, Cambridge, Mass., Center for Advanced Engineering Study.

Doyle, P., Saunders, J. and Wright, L. (1987) *A Comparative Study of US & Japanese Marketing Strategies in the British Market*, Report, Warwick University.

Drucker, P. (1990) 'The emerging theory of manufacturing', *Harvard Business Review*, May–June, 94–102.

Giles, E. and Starkey, K. (1988) 'The Japanization of Xerox', *New Technology, Work & Employment* 3 (2) 125–33.

Gronroos, C. (1983) *Strategic Management and Marketing in the Service Sector*, Bromley, Chartwell Bratt.

Gronroos, C. (1989) 'Defining marketing: A market oriented approach', *European Journal of Marketing* 23 (1) 52–60.

Groocock, J. M. (1986) *The Chain of Quality: Market Dominance Through Product Superiority*, New York, John Wiley.

Hakansson, H. (ed.) (1981) *International Marketing & Purchasing of Industrial Goods: An Interaction Approach*, London, John Wiley.

Houghton, P. (1988) 'Insurance: Larger than life', *Marketing*, April, 14, 20–2.

Johnson, G. and Scholes, K. (1984) *Exploring Corporate Strategy*, Englewood Cliffs, NJ, Prentice-Hall.

Juran, J. M. (1989) *Juran on Leadership for Quality*, New York, Free Press.

Kanter, R. M. (1983) *The Change Masters – Corporate Entrepreneurs at work*, London, Allen & Unwin.

Keith, R. (1960) 'The marketing revolution', *Journal of Marketing*, January.

Kohoutek, H. J. (1988) 'Coupling quality assurance programs to marketing', *Industrial Marketing Management* 17, 177–88.

McBurnie, T. and Clutterbuck, D. (1987) *The Marketing Edge*, London, Penguin.

McCarthy, E. J. (1960) *Basic Marketing: A Managerial Approach*, Homewood, I11. Richard Irwin.

Masiello, T. (1988) 'Developing market responsiveness throughout your company', *Industrial Marketing Management* 17, 85–93.

Oakland, J. S. (1989) *Total Quality Management*, London, Heinemann Professional Publishing.

Orsini, J. L. (1990) 'The application of quality function deployment to services: a financial example, *Proceedings of the 1990 AMA Services Marketing Conference*.

Orsini, J. L. (1991) 'Quality function deployment: marketing participation in product/service design, *Proceedings of the 1991 AMA Winter Educators' Conference*.

Ouchi, W. G. (1981) *Theory Z: How American Business Can Meet the Japanese Challenge*, Reading, Mass. Addison-Wesley.

Peters, T. (1988) *Thriving on Chaos*, London, Macmillan.

Pettigrew, A. M. (1985) *The Awakening Giant*, Oxford, Basil Blackwell.

Piercy, N. (1985) *Marketing Organization – An Analysis of Information Processing, Power and Politics*, London, Allen & Unwin.

Porter, M. E. (1985) *Competitive Advantage: Creating & Sustaining Superior Performance*, New York, Free Press.

Price, F. (1984) *Right First Time*, London, Gower.

Robson, M. (1986) *The Journey to Excellence*, Chichester, John Wiley.

Saba, S. (1989) 'The difference between Japanese and Western companies', *The Roundel*, April, 84–8.

Schonberger, R. J. (1986) *World Class Manufacturing: The Lessons of Simplicity Applied*, London, Collier Macmillan.

Schonberger, R. J. (1990) *Building a Chain of Customers*, London, Hutchinson Business Books.

Thomson, K. M. (1990) *The Employee Revolution: The Rise of Corporate Internal Marketing*, London, Pitman.

Turnbull, P. W. and Paliwoda, S. T. (eds) (1988) *Research Developments in International Marketing*, Proceedings of the 4th IMP Conference, September, Manchester School of Management, UMIST.

Webster, F. E. (1981) 'Top management concerns about marketing issues for the 1980s', *Journal of Marketing*, Summer.

Witcher, B. (1988) Innovation & Marketing, in M. J. Thomas and N. E. Waite (eds) *The Marketing Digest*, Heinemann, London, pp. 171–86.

Zeithaml, V. A., Parasuraman, A. and Berry, L. L. (1990) *Delivering Quality Service: Balancing Customer Perceptions and Expectations*, New York, Free Press.

Part II

Corporate performance and management control

7   Typologies of corporate recovery

Peter Grinyer and Peter McKiernan

INTRODUCTION

This chapter extends the earlier work of Grinyer *et al.* (1988) in the area of corporate recovery. The aim is to specify typologies of recovery based upon common characteristics and conditions faced by the companies. The theoretical debate that follows suggests that the timing of the recovery is an important dimension for defining the related typologies. Hence the chapter examines the characteristics and conditions facing early, intermediate and late recovery situations. These stages are illustrated by case evidence and supported by statistical analysis. The results suggest that there is not one strategic gestalt for corporate recovery. On the contrary, at each stage a different design is required.

The remainder of this chapter is divided into four sections. An introduction to classification schemes is provided for the general reader in the next section. The recovery-specific theoretical debate is highlighted in the second section. The third section explains the methodology involved and this is followed in the fourth section by a discussion of the results.

CLASSIFICATION SCHEMES

Contingency theory has triggered a significant number of classification schemes in the strategic management (and related) literatures. These schemes, or more accurately systems[1], have been developed for the corporate (Miles and Snow 1978), business (Buzzell *et al.* 1975; Hofer and Schendel 1978; Abell 1980; Porter 1980, 1985; Galbraith and Schendel 1983; Chrisman *et al.* 1988) and the functional (Kotler 1965) levels of strategy. Significant attention and publicity have been given to their general applicability (Porter 1980, 1985) but serious attempts have also been made to focus upon classifications for specific circumstances. These latter studies have focussed on variables that best explain business strategy. The product life cycle has a perennial significance (Hofer 1975; Anderson and Zeithaml 1984; Thietart and Vivas, 1984) and logically the specific classifications have concentrated on its stages. Particular emphasis has been placed on the stage of maturity (Harrigan 1982; Schofield and Arnold 1988) with a focus on low share businesses (Hamermesh *et al.* 1978; Woo and Cooper 1981), and stagnating industries (Hamermesh and Silk 1979). Schemes for the decline stage have concentrated on end-games (Harrigan 1980; Harrigan and Porter 1983), exit decisions (Harrigan 1982) and types of market (Robinson 1986). A closely related specific scheme involves turnarounds. The academic and practitioner literature is extensive (Schendel and Patton 1976; Schendel *et al.* 1976; Hofer 1980; O'Neil, 1981, 1986; Bibeault 1982; Hambrick and Schecter 1983; Slatter 1984; Melin 1985; Zimmerman 1986, 1989; Hardy 1987). Turnarounds involve a severe financial predicament with a credible threat of extinction for the organisations. However, organisations can, and do, significantly improve their performance from positions of relative stagnation or decline without this immediate extinction threat (see Grinyer *et al.* 1988; Grinyer and McKiernan 1990: Stopford and Baden-Fuller 1990). Differences between the literature relating to such organisations relates primarily to whether they are able to manage substantial change either sharply (Grinyer *et al.* 1988) or gradually[2] (Stopford and Baden-Fuller 1990). Significantly, the general results of this research and the evolved model are consistent whether the label is recovery (as here) or rejuvenation (Stopford and Baden-Fuller 1990).

General classification schemes (or systems) have their merits in enabling differentiation, generalisation, identification and information retrieval. They are influential in the evolution of our knowledge by facilitating the theory development-theory testing cycle. But as Chrisman *et al.* (1988) emphasise, all the taxonomies that have emerged for business strategies to date, including the most popular ones (Porter 1980, 1985), are so fraught with problems, such as the omission of variables and measurement error, that their general applicability is placed in question. Admirably, these authors construct a theoretically optimal classification system containing fourteen strategies. The complexity of several dynamic contingency variables coupled with fourteen (as yet untested) business strategies is severe. This raises a fundamental question. Is it possible to build useful, testable classification systems for business strategies?

This issue has been addressed in some of the literature on turnarounds. Classificatory schemes (e.g. Schendel *et al.* 1976; Hofer

1980) distinguish between strategic and operating taxa relating to turnarounds. The difference is between 'doing different things' and 'doing things differently'. Hambrick and Schecter (1983) have challenged this distinction, which becomes blurred as the unit of analysis shifts from the corporate to the business level. Moreover, Hofer's two market share turnaround strategies (100 per cent and 200 per cent growth) are considered too optimistic for mature and declining industries. Hambrick and Schecter established the existence of three primary turnaround gestalts – two small clusters representing asset/cost surgery and selective product–market pruning and a third, much larger, cluster representing piecemeal strategies. The significance of the size of their latter taxon suggests that the dominant turnaround strategy may not be a gestalt at all but varies from business to business and hence is very difficult to generalise properly.

Similar problems of adequate distinctions occur in work on sharp recovery of stagnating companies such as Grinyer *et al.* (1988). It has been argued (see Taylor 1989; Stopford and Baden-Fuller 1990) that at one extreme the sample of 'sharp-benders' includes organisations that are into turnaround situations, and the other extreme, it contains many organisations that are far removed from the threat of extinction and yet are still in decline relative to their industry. However, across this spectrum, all organisations achieved a sharp (less than two years) and sustained (greater than five years) recovery. Yet the very breadth of the sample companies in terms of sizes of organisations, their industries and their distances from possible extinction makes it useful as a basis for a detailed examination of the types of recovery employed by its twenty six organisations, and how these are related to contextual variables. Hence it provides the basis for an empirically based classification system.

THEORETICAL BACKGROUND

Literature on decline and crises is well established (Whetten 1987; Cameron *et al.* 1988). However, underpinning the identification of recovery taxa is an understanding of the process of corporate decline – whether relative or absolute (see, for instance, Nystrom and Starbuck 1984 and Starbuck *et al.* 1978, 1988). Briefly, organisations' perceptions of internal and external events is never accurate. Signals on threats can become distorted through the organisation's reception system. This system incorporates a decoding mechanism referred to as a 'repertoire' (Shrivastava and Mitroff 1983), 'template' (Pondy 1984) or 'programme' (Starbuck *et al.* 1978, 1988) – an integral part of organisational learning. Past success helps to form and reinforce these programmes that are used to interpret and react to internal and external signals. These programmes are formalised in organisational procedures; the greater the success, the more integrated, trusted and reinforced the programme becomes. This success allows organisations to build buffers (e.g. in inventories) which effectively reduce its sensitivity to environmental events. These may not be interpreted accurately nor responded to timeously. Moreover, power centres in organisations tend to resist strategic change to avoid dissolution or dismissal (Grinyer and Spender 1979) and cling to programmes that have worked in the past. Failure to act appropriately may then precipitate crises. Information signalling crisis is often delayed by a reliance on historic accounting systems; poor performance is blamed on external economic factors; temporary tightening is seen as sufficient; real crisis is denied, the truth is adjusted and concealed; morale deteriorates and good managers leave; crisis deepens and the related cost of recovery is increased as the delay is prolonged; disintegration occurs as failure is expected; beyond a certain point, organisations cannot save themselves and external intervention, including top management removal, is necessary. Hambrick and D'Aveni (1988) have appropriately referred to large corporate failures (not recoveries) as 'downward spirals'.

The above process has been witnessed in many organisations. Its complexity can be increased by the type of decision-making system and the nature of the individual (and collective organisational) aspiration levels (Cyert and March 1963; Grinyer and McKiernan 1990). If environmental decoding programmes incorporate sequential decision-making sub-routines, the associated increased search responses to signals can prolong the delay in the effective identification and treatment of true causes of problems (see Cyert and March 1963; Grinyer and Spender 1979; Grinyer and McKiernan 1990). Three further issues add gravity to this situation. First, sub-routines contain a local urgency to take action on operational issues (Ansoff 1969). This can lead to the treatment of symptoms of problems rather than true causes (Starbuck *et al.* Hedburg 1978, 1988; Muller 1985). Secondly, the number and variety of threatening signals (or causes of decline) can overload sequential systems, increasing the probability of symptom rather than problem treatment. Finally, the wider search procedures of such systems mean that strategic solutions are considered only finally and therefore very rarely. Hence threatening events need to be amplified to crisis proportions before change occurs (Nystrom and Starbuck 1984).

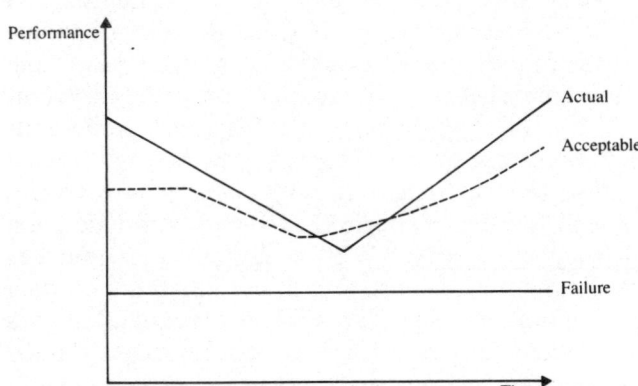

Figure 7.1 Actual performance affects acceptability

The literature on crises has failed to incorporate organisational response to environmental events via higher level learning rules (e.g. strategic planning), decision-making systems (e.g. parallel decision making, Ansoff 1969) or imitation of new programmes found to be successful in the industry. All of these could, theoretically, increase the speed and effectiveness of response to both strong and weak environmental signals, providing they are unhindered by the inflexibility of other internal programmes or mind sets.

Increased individual (or collective) aspirations (Cyert and March, 1963; Grinyer *et al* 1988; Grinyer and McKiernan 1990) can sometimes outweigh the inertia associated with existing, now inadequate, structured, formalised programmes. Grinyer *et al.* (1988) argue that there is an acceptable level of performance that faces all organisations. This level is determined by a coalition of external and internal perceptions of what the organisation, as a Penrosian bundle of resources, is capable of achieving. This level can vary with actual performance (see Figure 7.1). On the other hand, a period of relatively inferior performance (compared with other organisations) can sometimes lead to a revision downward of general perceptions of the organisation's capabilities. Similarly a period of relatively superior performance can lead to an upward revision. However, the delicate interrelationship between acceptable levels or aspiration levels of organisational performance and actual performance could mean that there is a simultaneous dependence of one on the other. It is unclear at present, without extensive empirical examination,

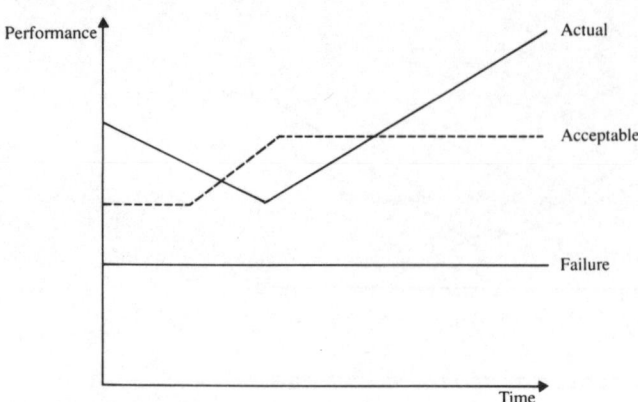

Figure 7.2 A change in acceptability leads to a change in actual performance

which is the stronger influence on the other. Added to this systematic interrelationship are other explanatory variables that can influence the level of aspirations, e.g. managerial perceptions of new opportunities, changes in top management or the chief executive, or competitive benchmarking. These influences can shift acceptable levels quickly (see Figure 7.2).

The model of downward spiral explains observed corporate histories of early signals, delay, inadequate response and the eventual severity that incorporates acute financial exigency and threatened extinction. This process, together with its suggested recovery taxa, is depicted in Figure 7.3. It is now appropriate to superimpose the level of acceptability onto this depiction and, for reasons of pedagogic parsimony, to show it in a constant format (horizonal line). Such an extension enables the model to explain the phenomenon of sharp recovery or 'sharp-bending' as well as that of turnarounds.

Four organisational cases are shown in Figure 7.3. Case A represents those organisations in relative decline whose performance is above that which is perceived to be acceptable. These organisations are anticipatory rather than reactive and make incremental operational or strategic changes to reverse decline (see Nadler and Tushman 1989). Anticipation of performance falling to unacceptable levels, i.e. below the aspiration level, is here a sufficient trigger to induce action. Action to achieve recovery comes in advance of the decline in performance to unacceptable levels and well before

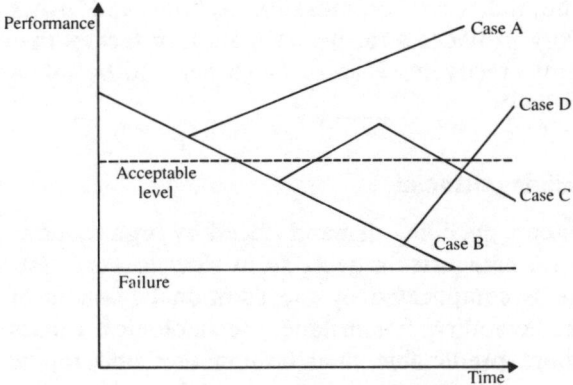

Figure 7.3 Reactions to declining performance

any threat of extinction. Case B organisations have experienced the long slide of relative decline. Their system has failed to react to all the environmental signals. Their plight becomes so critical that extinction is inevitable. Case C represents organisations in an intermediate position. Performance has breached the acceptable level and passed beneath it, triggering alarm signals. Actions are taken, in a reactive sense, that boost performance. Case C companies may recover fully. However, inappropriate actions in response to symptoms rather than problems may cause organisational performance to decline again. These organisations may later use wider search criteria for problem identification and solution. They may still have time to take appropriate action and recover strongly. Case D represents organisations that have declined to the state of near extinction. The threat is so great and the problem now of such crisis proportions that intervention (probably external) is required to force them into a recovery position. The recovery taxa suggested by this process is made up of anticipatory (Case A) and reactive (Cases C and D) organisations. The purpose of this study is to examine the conditions and characteristics of each of these classes of recovery. Is there a typology of corporate recovery?

EXTENSION OF THE PRELIMINARY MODEL

The process described above suggests a number of taxa of corporate recovery incorporating an anticipatory/reactive dimension related to acceptable levels of performance and actual performance over the decline phase.[3]

Research from the industrial organisation school and other contingency-based work provides a further indication of factors that may influence corporate recovery. Factors which need to be taken into account are as follows:

(a) The nature of declining demnad

Harrigan (1980) segments declining demand (faced by organisations in their industries) into categories ranging from slow to very fast. The speed of decline is complicated by the additional features of its variability and predictability. For instance, technological causes of decline are far more predictable than fashion or demographic changes. Unpredictable rates of decline can induce delay as organisations find it difficult to interpret their situations through the iterative routines in their existing programmes and are inclined to adopt more optimistic interpretations of events which allow the status quo to continue. Slower, more predictable rates of decline could induce lethargy and delay but alternatively, may provide a buffer for buying time for a planned strategic recovery. Organisations, with their specific programmes, respond in different ways to these features of decline. Pro-active organisations (anticipatory) are better placed to make either quick operational adjustments or even embark on strategic reorientations.

(b) Exit barriers

Industrial economists have long been interested in the level of exit barriers (Bain 1956; Harrigan 1982; Harrigan and Porter 1983) that influence the ability of organisations to leave their strategic group, markets or industries. The higher the exit barrier (e.g. sunk cost, asset specificity) the greater the difficulty for all types of organisations (anticipatory or reactive) to make strategic reorientations. There may be a long delay in divestment as organisations fail to achieve desired resale values of the investments in fixed assets and become reluctant to sell. As time passes, this resale value diminishes as marginal competitors also seek and achieve exit (Rafferty 1987). If the exit barriers are of the strategic (image destruction) or managerial (emotion) kind, lengthier delays can be expected as organisations' reluctance becomes entrenched in individual managerial attitudes. Exit barriers can be largely responsible for continued decline and the speed of decline at later stages. If barriers are low, organisations can more easily pursue cost-based rationalisation tactics followed by eventual diversification strategies. If barriers are high organisations may choose to remain, buying up the excess capacity of competitors who exit the market/industry.

(c) Industry concentration

Declining environments can prove volatile in concentrated industries as oligopolists compete vigorously for diminishing customer bases (Caves and Porter 1977). If the industry is in rapid decline, panic behaviour, including destructive price cutting, can ensue as organisations try to fill their excess capacity to breakeven levels. An interaction of high industrial concentration plus high exit barriers could intensify competition and hinder recovery. The situation is more complex in fragmented industries. Although individual players may enjoy some monopoly power in specific market niches, their smaller size may imply insufficient resources or reserves for major restructuring operations if local or national demand diminishes quickly. On the other hand, without the intense competition of oligopolistic structures in homogeneous markets, organisations in fragmented industries may have more opportunity for innovation without immediate competitor reaction. These first-mover advantages may well be the key to forming a sustainable competitive advantage and hence superior consequent performance.

(d) Concentration of buyers: consumer-industrial markets

Related to industry concentration is the structure of buyers. Organisational products can be delivered into consumer or industrial markets – each presenting a different challenge to organisations when they are in decline. Consumers in the former markets may make small, repeated purchases where advertising may then be important to maintain sales. Industrial markets are characterised by fewer, arguably more specialist buyers, and personal selling and after-sales service are important. Woo and Cooper (1981) found that in industrial markets and in high valued-added industries organisations could sustain profitability even with low market shares. It may be that organisations providing standardised industrial components or supplies can, through a closer personal relationship with their buyers, gain time during the decline phase in order to plan and augment recovery.

(e) Market share

The choice of turnaround strategy is dependent in part on the competitive position of the organisation, especially with regard to capacity utilisation (Hofer 1980). Hence Hambrick and Schecter (1983) argue that market share is a key factor in recovery. Organisations with high market shares tend to make only minor, 'piecemeal' changes to strategy to remain profitable. Low market share organisations in declining industries are likely to operate close to breakeven – where cost-cutting tactics are appropriate – or below breakeven where asset-reduction tactics are normally the only viable options. However, organisations with low market shares may operate on a specialised rather than on a volume basis. They may rely on high quality, localised, with (Hamermesh *et al*, 1978) or without (Woo and Cooper 1981) innovative products.

(f) Organisational structures/organisational size

Organisational structure and size are important theoretical contingency variables. Arguably, more decentralised organisational structures imply a closer proximity of the decision-takers to the same market signals, and a more immediate and flexible response to external causes of decline. Thus organisational structure should influence speed of response and indeed anticipation of environmental changes early on in the decline phase. Yet, leadership by a strong centre of power is a widely acknowledged form of crisis management (Mintzberg 1988). This no doubt reflects the need to impose strong controls over cash and all forms of expenditure; 'rationalising' reduction of overheads; and introduction of changes that may challenge vested interests during the effort to turnaround. However, even if centralised organisational structures may still be the best means of achieving recovery at the crisis stage, it is still probable that they will delay further responses to threatening environmental signals.

Size is a closely related issue. Clifford (1977) and others have argued that small and medium sized enterprises share a flexible, reactive strength over larger organisations, which inevitably centralise major strategic decisions even if decentralising operational ones (Grinyer and Yasai-Ardekani 1981). Their more formal systems add to the degree of inflexibility. The latter organisations may well decline at a slower rate because of organisational slack but may well take longer to respond to threats because of inherent inflexibilities and slower responsiveness than their smaller counterparts. By contrast, smaller organisations can combine centralisation of major decision taking, and faster response times from strong leadership (Khandwalla 1978), with closer proximity of the chief executive officer to the market and internal operations.

(g) Speed of recovery

Neither the theoretical process model of decline nor the burgeoning empirical literature on turnarounds gives much attention to the speed or rate of recovery. Grinyer *et al* (1988) have referred to sharp or fast recovery as being within one to two years. For the twenty-six sharp-benders in their sample this was an average figure. It is possible that there are different rates of recovery associated with early or late recovery stages. Early recoveries (Case A), without the stimulus provided by the threat of extinction, may well enjoy slower rates than organisations (Case D) who leave it late. In the latter case, massive asset-reduction tactics (e.g. rationalisation) together with stringent cost control may well lead to a faster recovery.

(h) Other variables

A number of other plausible variables that impinge upon organisational recovery have been suggested that, unfortunately, we have been unable to incorporate into our study. For instance, Hambrick and D'Aveni (1988), building on the earlier work of Argenti (1976), Miller and Friesen (1977) and Harrigan (1980), argue that the extent of product market initiatives (and their inherent risks) introduced by the organisation can be a significant deterrent to recovery. They found no strong support, however, from their empirical analysis for their hypothesis, although organisations that failed were either too inactive or too hyperactive in this respect. Again, further industrial organisation variables might ideally have been added, such as the degree of product differentiation, import competition, volatility of price levels, government regulations and factors that impinge on competitiveness in the industry (e.g. buyer/supplier power, substitutes). The focus of the data collection by Grinyer *et al.* (1988) was, however, the company, which meant that a number of wider industry structure factors were omitted.

The original Grinyer *et al.* (1988) model incorporates a framework of sharp recovery that consists of causes of decline, triggers for action, actions taken and sustained characteristics of corporate recovery. The first three characteristics are important for this attempted classification. We incorporate types of causes, triggers and action to reflect the work of previous researchers discussed earlier. We also incorporate the absolute numbers of causes, triggers and action taken as surrogates for the intensity of activity at each stage.

The general propositions emanating from the previous discussion are as follows:

1 Companies in relative decline can be grouped, based upon common characteristics, into early, intermediate and late recovery types.
2 Early recoveries are likely to be characterised by few causes, low rates of decline, internal triggers, strategic and operating actions, flexibility given by size and organisational structure, low exit barriers, low levels of industry concentration, consumer final markets and have slower recovery rates.
3 Intermediate recoveries are likely to be characterised by an increase in the number and complexity of the causes of decline, medium rates of decline, internally dominated triggers, operating actions, average market shares, entry barriers and rates of recovery.
4 Late recoveries are likely to be characterised by a high number and complexity of causes of decline, external triggers, operating actions with an emphasis on rationalisation, high exit barriers, high levels of industrial concentration, industrial buyers in final markets, mature/declining industries and have faster rates of recovery.

METHODOLOGY

This study draws upon and extends the original 'sharp-benders' study (see Grinyer *et al* 1988). New variables were measured and added to the original data on the twenty-six companies. These variables, together with their mode of calculation, are shown in Table 7.1.

The analysis was in three phases. First, initial descriptive statistics and data-plots were produced for the individual stages of recovery and the independent variables. Secondly, Spearman's rank correlation (appropriate for categorical variables) was calculated pairwise for all the variables included in the study, to identify the strength and direction of potential relationships. Finally, discriminant analysis was conducted on the whole data set and then on a parsimonious selection of variables. The results of each of these phases of analysis are shown in the Appendix.

Table 7.1 Contextual variables associated with the early, intermediate and late stages of recovery

Variable[a]	Categories/scale
Stage of recovery	Early–Intermediate–Late
Causes of decline	External–Internal
Number of causes	Actual number
Decline rate	1. Very Low
	5. Very High
Number of triggers	Actual number
Actions	See Table 3
Number of actions	Actual number
Organisational	1. Decentralised
structure	2. Centralised
Industrial life cycle	1. Growth
	2. Maturity
	3. Decline
Buyer type	1. Industrial
	2. Consumer
Size	1. Small
	2. Medium
	3. Large
Market share	1. Low
	2. Medium
	3. High
Industry concentration	1. Low
	2. Medium
	3. High
Exit barrier	1. Low
	2. High
Recovery rate	1. High
	2. Medium
	3. Low

[a] Measurement of the variables is given in the Appendix.

Discussion of the results

Summary results of the descriptive and bivariate analyses appear in Tables 7.A1 and 7.A2. It is useful to discuss these in relation to the stages of recovery.

Early stage

The four organisations that 'sharp-bent' early faced little threat of immediate extinction. Despite their relative decline, they could have continued trading in their existing market/industries for some time. Because they acted early, the agglomeration of causes of decline would tend to be less, according to the model. It is no surprise, therefore, that they had fewer causes (2.5) on average than organisations taking actions to recover at a later stage of decline. The descriptive statistics suggest strongly that their most frequent cause of decline was their poor marketing. Given that 75 per cent of them were in consumer products, this was a crucial weakness. Feedback from pricing and advertising decisions was frequently short term and such operational, functional maladies can usually be remedied by administrative changes as long as quality and consumer purchasing power remain strong. Internal triggers, especially the role of visionary or anticipatory existing management teams, were largely responsible for the appropriate remedies. These, as found by Grinyer and McKiernan (1990), bear a direct relationship to the cause of decline. Hence we witness improvements in marketing and, more important, the largest change in product-market focus of any of the groups. This is consistent with earlier suggestions that these organisations are better placed to make quick operational adjustments or strategic reorientations. This was particularly so because all four organisations faced low exit barriers, were in fragmented industries with low market shares (where innovation may not be quickly followed by competitors), and consequently had relatively low rates of decline. The interaction of this group of variables was significant in facilitating complete reorientations in product-market scope. Such dramatic changes are rare and organisations need the time and conditions necessary to carry them through successfully. Recoveries were sharp but not dramatic.

The motivating force for the actions of those early recoverers is important. Aspiration levels or performance targets were raised in half of these organisations by takeover threats, not those pertaining to extinction. This stimulus provoked existing management into a positive, anticipatory mode. It may be a myth that organisations can be immediately classified as anticipatory or reactive in the Tushman/Nadler sense without an examination of prevailing contingency factors that help to trigger events leading to positive action. In these companies wider search procedures were so driven by the threats of takeover that it shocked even their relatively safe managements into making major changes to the status quo. However, in the other 50 per cent of cases, the organisations were quite prosperous and had no threat of takeover. In these cases, it was a chance perception of major new opportunities that stimulated top management into raising their sights.

John Wood Group

The recovery of the John Wood Group in Aberdeen, Scotland is a typical example of this taxon. The organisation ran a traditional fishing fleet with associated support facilities out of a harbour which was destined to become the oil-capital of Europe. Members of the management team had been on a holiday/business trip to the USA and had visited Texas. They had witnessed at first hand the major impact that oil had had on the structure of industry. This event triggered ideas of product-market switching and diversification. They manoeuvred their assets from the declining North Sea fishing industry to oil-related offshore support services. They had a common knowledge of shipping and also an asset base in the existence of warehousing and dock facilities. Such a dramatic switch is rare in family-dominated companies. The trigger was wider experience and the facilitating mechanism was a fundamental bundle of non-specific assets that could be easily switched into alternative uses.

Intermediate Group

As to be expected, causes of decline were both more numerous and less operational for this group than the early 'sharp-benders'. Poor marketing was less of a problem than major market declines. Many of their industries had matured or were in decline with resultant problems of excess capacity and financial difficulties. Risky projects that went wrong, through poor control, accelerated the plight of these organisations. The triggers were all internal, with management perceiving problems in the predicted 'reactive' mode as actual performance fell below their perception of what was acceptable. These managers planned their own chief executive officer successions where this was deemed appropriate. The absence of threatened take-overs as an external stimulus to increased levels of aspirations, was consistent with with mature or declining markets, entry to which was less attractive to other firms seeking expansion by acquisition.

Against a background of relatively greater market decline, these organisations had larger market shares and faced higher exit barriers than the early group of 'sharp-benders'. However, industry concentration was low, which would suggest a lower likelihood of competitor reactions to major changes. As predicted, their reactive stance was largely to try to achieve an acceptable level of performance within their current markets by means of rationalisation and cost cutting. Consistently with this emphasis on rationalisation they tended to change their structures in the direction of greater centralisation, providing a trimmed-downed head office with greater decision-making power and a close monitoring of costs. Only in isolated cases was there evidence of strategic reorientation. Because the financial impact of rationalisation and cost cutting is fairly immediate, recovery rates were faster than for those organisations that 'sharp-bent' earlier; 82 per cent of these recoveries reflected the classic 'V' of sharp-bending. Unlike the pattern which follows many savage rationalisations in companies in a turnaround situation, these recoveries were sustained. It appears the majority of organisations in this taxon enjoyed excellent diagnostic power. A typical example of a recovery in this taxon is the one by William Collins.

William Collins PLC

William Collins was a long-standing, family-managed printing and publishing company based in Glasgow, Scotland. It had large market shares in some areas of the publishing market such as Bibles and dictionaries. It moved from old city-centre premises in the early 1970s to a new factory on a greenfield site on the outskirts of the city. This move created pressures and tensions among the largely female workforce who had developed strong social support groups in the old, but inefficient, multistorey premises. They could no longer shop at lunchtime and their travel time to work was longer.

Moreover, instead of taking the opportunity to re-equip the new factory with machines incorporating the latest technology, they merely transferred the old equipment to the new site. In addition, costs were a significant cause of décline. The historically low wages of the female labourforce were rising with the advent of equal pay legislation. Furthermore, the new factory had been financed with loans and, as interest rates climbed in the late 1970s, the company began to feel the squeeze.

These problems were compounded by a fundamental weakness in top and middle management. Collins had many of the succession problems associated with family-run businesses, where key managerial positions are reserved for family members who may not be as effective as their predecessors. The trigger for change was an internal recognition by management of its dangerous financial position. A non-family chief executive officer replaced the family incumbent after bitter and hostile boardroom politics. This major change was accompanied by a heavy rationalisation programme (50 per cent labour force reduction), tighter production and quality control and the closure and sale of expensive head offices. In fact, as a salient reminder to the employees of its financial plight, part of the remaining offices were bricked off to save rate payments.

Collins experienced a dramatic recovery, with the classic 'V' of 'sharp-bending'. This was based on increased productivity, larger investments in new technology and a more open management style. The success of its sustained recovery attracted predators and in 1988 Collins was taken over by News International.

Late stages

Organisations at this stage faced relatively sharp declines in their industries which were mainly in the mature or decline stages of their life cycle. Unfortunately the high exit barriers prevented immediate divestment and the improvement of performance was made manifestly more difficult by the high levels of industry concentration. As argued earlier, such levels tend to induce competitor infighting for market share as the decline spirals downward. On the other hand, most of the competitors faced industrial markets and their closer personal involvement with customers might have enabled them to buy some time.

The companies that took action to recover closer to the final turnaround crisis typically faced multiple, and more major, structural problems than those which did so earlier. They had to deal with the complexity of interacting causes. Major declines in their markets were compounded by failure of big projects with a resultant worsening of their financial problems. These were frequently exacerbated by cyclical declines in their markets. As predicted, in over half of these companies the external incentive was crucial. As in early 'sharp-benders' the threat of takeover, possibly initiated by dissatisfied bankers and/or institutional shareholders, triggered dramatic action in a large percentage (42 per cent) of the companies. A new chief executive officer was an important stimulus as in the previous two types. But in over half of the companies faced by the impending threat of extinction, management was prepared to move from its old programmes or the status quo. They perceived the now more glaring problems. Their actions involved both strategic and operating changes (see Hofer 1980): namely, heavy cost cutting, rationalisation and closure (50 per cent); improved marketing in the hope of capturing an increase in market share in the declining overall market (33 per cent); and strategic product-market switches in nearly

60 per cent of companies. As was the case for organisations at the intermediate stage, and common in turnaround strategies (Slatter 1984) those companies which were decentralised tended to move to centralised organisational structures to facilitate the recovery. After these changes, the great majority of those 'sharp-bending' late possessed a centralised structure.

Although the speed of recovery of late 'sharp-benders' was similar to that of the intermediate stage, the pattern was different. The classic 'V' shape of sharp-bending was present in only 66 per cent of cases (compared with 82 per cent at the intermediate stage) but the cyclical pattern is present in 33 per cent of cases (compared with 18 per cent for the intermediate stage). Whilst rationalisation and cost cutting boosted short-run performance in this 33 per cent, it was not, in itself, a solution to the complex causes of decline. More fundamental action was required to produce a second and sustained recovery. Closure of loss-makers was then combined with product-market reorientations. This combination of operating and strategic measures, although not fully synchronous, was clearly related to the circumstances facing each organisation. This could give rise to the perception of piecemeal measures rather than the existence of a coherent, internally consistent 'gestalt' (see Hambrick and Schecter 1983) in what is effectively a turnaround situation. The recovery at Fisons represents a classic example of this taxon.

Fisons story

By the late 1970s, Fisons faced increased competition in their traditional industry of fertilisers from much larger players such as ICI, which had greater economies of scale. Sales and profits suffered and Fisons, with poor financial controls, witnessed an escalation in debt to dangerous levels. Unfortunately, despite the fact that senior management had realised for some considerable time that the medium- and long-term future of its fertiliser and agrochemical businesses was poor, Fisons had not moved away from these strategically weak business areas. Managerial, strategic and other sunk costs had created immobility. The financial situation eventually became so grave that the company began to trade at a loss in the early part of the 1980s. At the same time, the existing chairman reached retirement age and was succeeded by a widely regarded, dynamic leader. Fisons merged their agrochemicals business with Boots plc in a 50–50 deal. They sold off loss-making businesses and those with poor prospects (fertilisers). They acquired new businesses in strategically healthy areas (scientific instruments). They overhauled their management accounting and cost control systems and rationalised their top management team. Head office was slimmed and strategic planning (higher level learning rules) was introduced. Although the company centralised initially to force through the recovery, it decentralised as soon as this turnaround was consolidated to give the divisions all but strategic autonomy.

Conclusion

These results are consistent with previous theoretical and empirical research. Relative decline can be a long process, but the rate of decline increases as the threat of extinction approaches. Market shares, a surrogate for managerial/strategic sunk cost, together with high exit barriers, prevent immediate escape. Organisations are locked into declining markets and industries. Their first moves are to try to stay in the industries they know best. However, as industry concentration increases there is less room to sustain shorter and tactical moves as competitor reactions accelerate the environmental intensity of the downward spiral. Internal/external causes usually act in combination (Schendel *et al.* 1976; Bibeault 1982). Clearly, the decline and especially the turnaround or late stage is a multi-faceted process (Zimmerman 1986) and the interaction of the many causes is a complicating feature. Recovery strategies bear a close resemblance to the asset/cost surgery, product-market pruning and piecemeal gestalts covered by Hambrick and Schecter (1983). They also reflect the multi-faceted decline process as, in later stages, coordinated actions need to be taken on a number of fronts yielding a number of custom-made recovery strategies (Ramanujan 1984). As decline progresses, adjustments to structure from decentralised to centralised appear to facilitate immediate recovery in this UK sample. This result contrasts with that of Melin's Scandinavian sample which, perhaps because of the number of international businesses in his sample, involved a more decentralised structure during recovery. Moreover, not all recovery strategies in our sample involved wholesale replacements of chief executive officers or top management teams in an attempt to break old programmes/practices. This result contrasts with that of Biteman (1979) and O'Neill (1986) where in all turnaround cases, top management was replaced. These were both US samples which perhaps yields a national cultural bias reflected in the different attitudes in the US and the UK to bankruptcy. Equally, it could reflect the fact that the majority of our 'sharp-benders' were short of the turnaround situation. Moreover, one of these studies dealt with

	Incremental	Strategic
Anticipatory	Tuning	Reorientation
Reactive	Adaptation	Re-Creation

Figure 7.4 Types of organisational change. (From Nadler and Tushman, 1989.)

specific assets (banking – O'Neill) and the other was too small a sample to allow generalisation.

The explanation may also lie in the nature of the change in triggers as the decline phase progresses. In early 'sharp-benders', the threat of extinction, or perception of major opportunities, was sufficient to induce change before multiple causes of decline became serious. In the intermediate stages existing management's reactive response (possibly due to an over-reliance on historic cost accounting data) was sufficient given the presence of good diagnostic qualities without wholesale change in the nature of the business, or its programmes. Later on, however, in what is more of a turnaround situation the threat of extinction together with threats of takeover, possibly induced by dissatisfied external share-holders, seems to trigger existing management into breaking their own programmes and practices as survival instincts take over. Changes in top management and the introduction of new chief executive officers are important but not necessarily sufficient in altering 'programmes'. Internal management teams given sufficient stresses from external threats can break their own 'programmes' or templates.

This research, including the discriminant analysis in the Appendix, demonstrates that stages of decline and their associated circumstances and strategies for recovery are interrelated. Immediate comparison with the turnaround literature is most appropriate at the later stages of decline. Hence Hofer's operating and strategic gestalts were identified but were used in parallel. Hence they were not mutually exclusive as some of the literature may suggest. More generally, when the recovery is early enough, operational tweaks need not precede strategic switches. Where organisations have the luxury of time, strategic switches sometimes take precedence over operational tweaks. Hence strategies for recovery need not depend on the operational/strategic health of the organisation in precisely the way suggested by Hofer.

Organisations do, however, appear to fall into an anticipatory or reactive category – a key ingredient of the Nadler/Tushman model of organisational frame-bending. However, our research on recovery suggests that their categories of tuning adaptation, reorientation and re-creation (see Figure 7.4) require a clear definition of incentives for change. The relationship between external/internal stressors (e.g. takeover, extinction, performance threats) and actual performance is significant in specifying the options facing organisations at each stage of decline. For instance, both strategies of reorientation and re-creation are available to our anticipatory companies (e.g. the John Wood Group) and tuning and adaptation are strategies used at the intermediate stage by our reactive organisations.

Our findings suggest that a wider definition of recovery is needed beyond that of the anticipatory or reactive organisations. For the purposes of classifying successful recovery strategies in organisations the suggestions by Miles and Snow of prospecters, analysers, defenders and reactors may well be an important one.

NOTES

1 A classification scheme only contains one category of entities or taxa, whereas a classification system contains two or more categories of taxa, where a category is a rank or level in a hierarchical classification. Most of the attempts at a classification of business strategies at the general and specific levels concentrate on competitive sub-strategies alone. Hofer and Schendel's (1978) definition of business strategies incorporates three sub-strategies – investment, competitive and political. It is arguable that any business strategy classification system must incorporate the often neglected investment and political levels. There is a strong argument for a hierarchical business strategy classification system in which the individual schemes form separate categories.
2 This gradual change should be distinguished clearly from the incrementalism associated with the propositions of Lyndblom (1959) or Quinn (1980).
3 Grinyer, *et al.* (1988, 1990) deal consistently with relative as opposed to absolute decline. Theoretically, there is little reason why this process should not apply to situations of absolute decline.

REFERENCES

Abell, D.F. (1980) *Defining the Business: The Starting Point of Strategic Planning*, Englewood Cliffs, New Jersey, Prentice-Hall.
Anderson, C.R. and Zeithaml, C.P. (1984) 'Stages of the product life cycle, business strategy, and business performance', *Academy of Management Journal* 27, 5–24.

Ansoff, H.I. (1969) 'Toward a strategic theory of the firm', in H.I. Ansoff, *Business Strategy*, Harmondsworth, Penguin.

Argenti, J. (1976) *Corporate Collapse: The Causes and Symptoms*, Maidenhead, McGraw-Hill.

Bain, J. (1956) *Barriers to New Competition*, Cambridge, Mass., Harvard University Press.

Bibeault, D.B. (1982) *Corporate Turnaround: How Managers Turn Losers into Winners*, New York, McGraw-Hill.

Biteman, J. (1979) 'Turnaround management: an exploratory study of rapid, total organisation change', doctoral dissertation, Harvard University, quoted in Hoffman (1989).

Buzzell, R.D., Gale, B.T. and Sultan, R.G.M. (1975) 'Market share: a key to profitability', *Harvard Business Review*, January/February, 97–106.

Cameron, K.S., Sutton, R.I. and Whetten, D.A. (eds) (1988) *Readings in Organisational Decline: Frameworks, Research and Prescriptions*. Cambridge, Mass., Ballinger.

Caves, R.E. and Porter, M.E. (1977) 'From entry barriers to mobility barriers: conjectural decisions and contrived deterence to new competition', *Quarterly Journal of Economics* 41, 241–61.

Chrisman, J.J. (1986) 'Strategy skills and success: an exploratory study', unpublished doctoral dissertation, University of Georgia, Athens.

Chrisman, J., Hofer, C. and Boulton, W.R. (1988) 'Toward a System for classifying business strategies', *Academy of Management Review*, 13 (3), 413–28.

Clifford, D.K. (Jnr) (1977) 'Thriving in a recession', *Harvard Business Review*, July/August, 57–65.

Cyert, R. and March, J. (1963) *A behavioural Theory of the Firm*, Englewood Cliffs, New Jersey, Prentice-Hall.

de Jong, H.W. (1988) *The Structure of European Industry*, 2nd edn., Dordrecht, Kluwer.

Doulton, D and Kesner I. (1985) 'Organisational performance as an anticedent of inside/outside chief executive succession: an empirical assessment', *Academy of Management Journal* 28 (4), 749–62.

Galbraith, C. and Schendel, D.E. (1983) 'An empirical analysis of strategy types', *Strategic Management Journal* 4, 153–73.

Grinyer, P.H. and McKiernan, P. (1990) 'Generating major change in stagnating companies', *Strategic Management Journal* 11, 131–46.

Grinyer, P.H. and Spender, J.C. (1979) *Turnaround: Managerial Recipes for Strategic Success*, London, *Associated Business Publications*.

Grinyer, P.H. and Yasai-Ardekani, M. (1981) 'Research note: Some problems with measurement of macro-organisational structure', *Organisation Studies* 2 (3), 287–96.

Grinyer, P.H., Mayes, D. and McKiernan, P. (1988) *Sharpbenders: The Secrets of Unleashing Corporate Potential*, Oxford, Blackwell.

Hambrick, D.C. and D'Aveni, R.A. (1988) 'Large corporate failures have downward spirals', *Administrative Science Quarterly* 33 (March), 1–23.

Hambrick, D.C. and Schecter, S.M. (1983) 'Turnaround strategies for mature industrial product business units', *Academy of Management Journal* 26 (2), 231–48.

Hamermesh, R.G., Silk, S.B. (1979). 'How to compete in stagnant industries',

Harvard Business Review, September/October, 161–8.

Hamermesh, R.G., Anderson, M.J. (Jnr) and Harris, J.E. (1978). 'Strategies for the low share businesses', *Harvard Business Review*, May/June, 95–102.

Hardy, C. (1987). 'Turnaround strategies in universities', *Planning for Higher Education* 16 (1), 9–23.

Harrigan, K.R. (1980) *Strategies for Declining Industries*, Lexington, Heath Books, Mass.

Harrigan, K.R. (1982) 'Exit decisions in mature industries', *Academy of Management Journal* 25 (4), 707–32.

Harrigan, K.R. and Porter, M.E. (1983) 'End game strategies for declining industries', *Harvard Business Review*, July/August, 111–20.

Hofer, C.W. (1975) 'Toward a contingency theory of business strategy', *Academy of Management Journal* 18, 784–810.

Hofer, C.W. (1980) 'Turnaround strategies', *Journal of Business Strategy* 1 (1), 19–31.

Hofer, C.W. and Schendel, D.E. (1978) *Strategy Formulation: Analytical Concepts*. St Paul, West Publishing.

Hoffman, R.C. (1989) 'Strategies for corporate turnarounds: what do we know about them?' *Journal of General Management* 14 (3), Spring, 46–66.

Khandwalla, P. (1978) 'Crisis responses of competing versus non-competing organisations', *Journal of Business Administration* 9, 151–78.

Kotler, P. (1965) 'Competitive strategies for new product marketing of the life cycle', *Management Science* 12 (December), B104–B119.

Lippitt, G.L. and Schmidt, W.H. (1966) 'Crisis in a developing organisation', *Harvard Business Review*, November/December, 102–12.

Lyndblom, C.E. (1959) 'The science of muddling through', *Public Administration Review*, Spring, pp. 79–88.

Melin, L. (1985) 'Strategies in managing turnaround', *Long Range Planning* 18 (1), February 80–6.

Miles, R. and Snow, C. (1978) *Organisational Strategy, Structure and Process*, New York, McGraw-Hill.

Miller, D. and Friesen, P.H. (1977) 'Strategy making in context: ten empirical archetypes', *Journal of Management Studies'* 14, 253–80.

Mintzberg, H. (1988) 'The simple structure', in J.B. Quinn, H. Mintzberg and R.M. James (eds) *Strategy Process: Concepts, Contexts and Cases*, Englewood Cliffs, New Jersey, Prentice-Hall.

Moulton, W.N. and Thomas H., (1990a) 'Turnarounds, financial restructurings and bankruptcy reorganisations: frameworks for analysis', paper presented at the Annual Academy of Management meeting, San Francisco, California, August 1990.

Moulton, W.N. and Thomas, H. (1990b) 'Firm growth, industry growth and business failure', Working paper, University of Illinois at Urbana-Champagne, Department of Business Administration.

Muller, R. (1985) 'Corporate crisis management', *Long Range Planning* 18 (5), 38–48.

Nadler, D.A. and Tushman, M.L. (1989) 'Organisational frame-bending: principles for managing reorientation', *Academy of Management Executive* 3 (3), 194–204.

Nystrom, P.C. and Starbuck W.H. (1984) 'To avoid organisational crises, unlearn', *Organisational Dynamics*, Spring.

O'Neil, H.M. (1981) *Turnaround Strategies in the Commercial Banking Industry*, Ann Arbor, Michigan, UMI Research Press.

O'Neil, H.M. (1986) 'Turnaround and recovery: what strategy you need?' *Long Range Planning* 19 (1), 80–8.

Pearson, B. (1977). 'A marketing orientated approach for turnaround situations', *Industrial Marketing Management* 6, 241–50.

Pondy, L. (1984). 'Union of rationality and intuition in management action', in Shrivastava and Associates, *The Executive Mind: New Insights on Managerial Thought and Action*, San Francisco, California, Josey-Bass.

Porter, M.E. (1980) *Competitive Strategy: Techniques for Analysing Industries and Competitors*. New York, Free Press.

Porter, M.E. (1985) *Competitive Advantage: Creating and Sustaining Superior Performance*. New York, Free Press.

Quinn, J.B. (1980) *Strategies for Change: Logical Incrementalism*, Homewood, Illinois, Urwin.

Rafferty, J. (1987) 'Exit barriers and strategic position in declining markets', *Long Range Planning* 20 (2), 86–91.

Ramanujam, V. (1984) 'Environmental context, organisational context, strategy and corporate turnaround', doctoral dissertation, University of Pittsburgh, cited in Hoffman (1989).

Robinson, S.J.Q. (1986) 'Strategies for declining industrial markets', *Long Range Planning* 19 (2), 72–8.

Sandberg, W.R. (1986). *New Venture Performance: the Role of Strategy and Industry Structure*, Lexington, Mass., Lexington Books.

Schendel, D.G. and Patton, R.G. (1976) 'Corporate stagnation and turnaround', *Journal of Economics and Business* 28 (3), 236–41.

Schendel, D.G., Patton, R.G. and Riggs J. (1976). 'Corporate turnaround strategies: a study of profit decline and recovery', *Journal of General Management* 3, 3–11.

Schofield, M. and Arnold, D. (1988) 'Strategies for mature businesses', *Long Range Planning* 21 (5), 69–76.

Schwartz, K.B. and Menon K., (1985) 'Executive succession in failing firms', *Academy of Management Journal* 28 (3), 680–6.

Shrivastava, P. and Mitroff I., (1983) 'Frames of reference managers use: a study in applied sociology of knowledge', *Advances in Strategic Management* 1, 161–82.

Slatter, S. (1984) *Corporate Recovery*, Harmondsworth, Penguin.

Starbuck, W.H., Greve, A. and Hedberg, B. (1978) 'Responding to crises', *Journal of Business Administration*, Spring.

Starbuck, W.H., Greve, A. and Hedberg, B. (1988) 'Responding to crises', in J.B. Quinn, H. Mintzberg, and R.M. James (eds) *Strategy Process: Concepts, Contexts & Cases*, Englewood Cliffs, New Jersey, Prentice-Hall.

Stopford, J.M. and Baden-Fuller, C. (1990) 'Corporate rejuvenation', University of Bath working paper.

Taylor, B. (1989) 'Sharpbenders book review', *Long Range Planning* 22 (3), 130–51.

Thietart, R.A. and Vivas, R. (1984) 'An empirical investigation of success strategies for businesses along the product life cycle', *Management Science*

30, 1405–23.

Whetten, D.A. (1987) 'Organisational growth and decline processes', *Annual Review of Sociology* 13, 335–58.

Woo, C.Y. and Cooper, A.C. (1981) 'Strategies of effective low share businesses', *Strategic Management Journal* (2), 301–18.

Zimmerman, F.M. (1986) 'Turnaround – a painful learning experience', *Long Range Planning* 19 (4), 104–14.

Zimmerman, F.M. (1989) 'Managing a successful turnaround', *Long Range Planning* 22 (3), 105–24.

APPENDIX 7.1

Table 7.A1 Summary descriptive results

	Stages of recovery					
Variable	*Early* (n = 4)		*Intermediate* (n = 11)		*Late* (n = 12)	
	No	*%*	*No*	*%*	*No*	*%*
Causes:						
Average number	2.5		3.5		3.9	
Market decline		25		55		75
Financial		25		55		67
Big project Failure		25		36		75
Strategic Problems		0		9		25
Poor Marketing		75		9		8
Triggers:						
Average number	2.0		1.2		1.8	
Internal		75		100		54
External		25		0		46
Ownership threat		50		0		42
New CEO		25		36		33
Management sees Problems		25		91		58
Management sees Opportunities		100		0		0
Actions:						
Average number	5.0		3.7		5.0	
Rationalisation/ Closure		25		46		67
Changes in Structure		25		46		50
Improved Marketing		75		9		33
New Product/ Market		75		18		58

Variable		Early (n = 4)		Intermediate (n = 11)		Late (n = 12)	
		No	%	No	%	No	%
Additional:							
Organisational	1 Cent.		50		36		58
structure	2 Decent.		50		64		42
Industry	1 Growth		25		0		17
Life	2 Mature		50		55		58
Cycle	3 Decline		25		45		25
Buyer type	1 Consumer		75		46		33
	2 Industrial		25		54		66
Decline rate		Very low		Medium		Medium	
Size		Small/medium		Small/medium		Small/medium	
Market share		Low		Medium		Medium	
Industry							
Concentration		Low		Low		Medium	
Exit barriers		Low		Medium		High	
Recovery rate		Low		Medium		Medium	

Table 7.A2 Summary bivariate results

Stages of recovery with:	rho	Sig-Level
Number of causes	0.32	0.030
Internal–external triggers	−0.51	0.004
Centralised/ decentralised	0.14	0.095
Low/high industry concentration	0.26	0.092
Consumer/industrial buyer	−0.26	0.099
Low/high exit barriers	0.31	0.049

Measurement of the variables

Many of the variables used in this study have already been defined in Grinyer *et al.* (1988). Further financial data were collected from the Datastream and Extel on-line electronic databases to create the following additional variables introduced in this study.

Variable	Measurement
Stage of recovery	Expert panel (company management, external analysts plus authors and researchers) Perception of distance from financial collapse.

	Supported by data on five year average below industry financial average over the same period.
Causes of decline	Segmented into external/internal based on the data in Grinyer *et al.* (1988).
Decline rate	Slope of OLS regression line on performance data during decline.
Organisational structure	Original Grinyer *et al.* scales split into decentralised and centralised.
Industry life cycle	Original Grinyer *et al.* data based upon internal managerial perceptions reinforced by external expert panel.
Buyer type	See industry life cycle above
Size	Total assets divided by industry sector average total assets for a period of five years before the 'sharp-bend'.
Market share	See industry life cycle above, based upon main product in main market.
Industry Concentration	See Industry life Cycle above, reinforced by de Jong (1988).
Exit barriers	Fixed assets as a percentage of Turnover for a period of five years before the 'sharp-bend', average figure.
Recovery Rate	Angle between the two OLS regression lines fitted for five years of decline and five years of recovery.

Discriminant analysis

Linear discriminant was used in an attempt to identify the most influential variables at each recovery stage. The results are contained in Table 7.A3. Clearly the limits pertaining to small sample sizes are approached with the use of multivariate techniques on this database. Hence two discriminating functions were specified – a full and a partial model. The partial model was constructed for parsimonious reasons and incorporated those variables that showed statistical significance on their group scores on their bivariate analysis. Moreover, we present the results merely as supportive evidence.

Table 7.A3 Linear discriminant analysis

| | Stage of recovery | | | | | |
| | Early | | Intermediate | | Late | |
Variable	Run 1	Run 2	Run 1	Run 2	Run 1	Run 2
Constant	−233.82	−16.88	−244.31	−18.16	−204.39	−16.68
Recovery rate	52.30		43.74		48.21	
Ext./int. causes[a]	2.57		17.20		1.12	
No. of causes	−7.43	0.62	−7.84	1.70	−5.01	2.14
Decline rate	29.53		29.01		−27.63	
No. of triggers	33.21		25.30		28.44	
Ext./int. triggers[a]	60.59	16.42	73.61	16.78	53.23	12.85
Decent/Central-isation[a]	−13.37	−2.41	−16.05	−1.16	−9.88	0.42
Size	46.30		55.50		44.28	
Mature/ decline stage[a]	36.60		50.24		33.24	
Market share	−41.78		−42.46		−38.50	
Ind. concentration	72.97	6.80	75.84	6.01	66.77	5.38
Ind/consumer buyers[a]	45.60	6.47	49.84	4.18	41.10	3.43
Exit barriers	6.37	2.34	11.84	2.54	7.46	2.84
No. of actions	4.38		0.44		3.92	

[a] Variables recoded into 0/1 dummies; zero score is first mentioned, i.e. Ext. = 0, Int. = 1.

Squared distance between groups:

| Run 1 | | | | | Run 2 | | |
	1	2	3			1	2	3
1	–	23.77	10.83			–	2.24	6.61
2	23.77	–	24.01			2.24	–	2.34
3	10.73	24.01	–			6.61	2.34	–

	Run 1	Run 2
N	27	27
N	Correct 27	19
	100%	70%

Groups
(1 = 75%
(2 = 73%
(3 = 67%

8 Currency risk management in multinational companies

A comparative study of performance evaluation[1]

Stephen G. Longden

The effective control of currency risk has become increasingly important due to the volatility of the currency markets and the increase in international trade. Though this chapter concentrates upon British and American multinationals and hence considers worldwide trade, trade within the EEC is becoming increasingly important to these companies and hence the exchange rate fluctuations between European currencies. Although 1992 will see the elimination of tariff barriers, the risk of exchange rate fluctuations presents an effective barrier to trade, particularly to small and medium-size companies, unless some form of exchange rate control is implemented.

This chapter presents the results of a case study based on analysis of currency risk management practice in large British and American multinational companies. The primary impetus for the study was to extend the methodology adopted by Collier and Davis (1985), to examine the management of transaction and translation risk, by matched pairs of British and American companies. Part of the study was focussed on the methods adopted by the companies to measure the performance of the currency risk management function, and it is this particular aspect which is discussed in this chapter.

The chapter considers what measures best identify the quality of performance of the currency risk management function and motivate staff to achieve the corporation's goals. One aspect of this is the establishing of criteria for evaluating performance together with related performance incentive programmes, in order to produce that set of treasury decisions which, given the operating assets and liabilities of the corporation, produce the best balance of cost and risk characteristics. The aspect of risk, in particular the company's attitude and policy to risk, is very important in this respect. The standard of performance must motivate the manager towards behaviour congruent with company policy. The current literature is surveyed to determine the methods recommended by both academic writers and practitioners. A critical analysis is then made as regards the motivational effect of each method and its practical application.

The case study analysis shows that of the twenty-three companies in the study the majority used some form of performance evaluation. Those companies which adopted a risk averse policy, seeking always to minimise the risk of loss, tended not to have any formal methods of performance evaluation. Methods which did exist were used to ensure that the company policy was being adhered to. Companies which actively managed their risk, seeking to optimise the opportunities for currency gains, used a variety of methods including the spot rate, forward rate, and the opportunity loss/gain. The paper highlights the use by the majority of companies of very basic methods of performance evaluation, with very few companies adopting a more sophisticated approach. For instance, very few of the companies operated their treasury function as a separate profit centre, and only one of the companies linked the performance of the currency risk function to a bonus scheme.

INTRODUCTION

Before considering the evaluation of the performance of the currency risk function we must first ask why performance needs to be evaluated. The two main reasons usually given in texts are goal congruence and employee motivation. The former refers to aligning the individuals goals with those of the company so that if the employee achieves his personal goals those of the company are also achieved. The latter refers to providing incentives to encourage employees to work towards the goals of the firm. Thus evaluation is often linked with reward. Linked with these is the use of performance measures to guide future decision-making and policy-making, e.g. significant exchange losses can make company policy more risk averse and, as discussed below, change the performance measure used to reflect this.

Much has been written on the motivational effects of performance evaluation. Emmanuel and Otley (1985), for example, state that the major impact lies in the extrinsic rewards, such as salary bonuses, enhanced promotion prospects or status that are associated with target attainment. The characteristics of a good performance evaluation system are typically quoted as (Dopuch *et al.* 1980).

1 Congruence of the evaluation measure with the firm's goal
2 Measurement error
3 Timeliness
4 Cost
5 Behavioural effects.

The performance indicator used should be such that if an individual seeks to maximise this indicator, he will also maximise the goals of the company. Any errors in measurement should be due to random effects and not due to any inherent bias in the measure, e.g. incentive to employees to over-book. Measures should be timely if they are to be effective, but this must be balanced with the cost of the reporting system. The system must provide a means of motivating better decision-making and provide a basis for learning and for improving decision-making in future periods.

A final point is whether a standard of performance should be set prior to the evaluation period. If such a standard is to be set, who should set it? Consideration has to be given to points such as:

1 Controllability – the evaluation should be confined to those aspects of performance which can be directly influenced by the manager.
2 Participation – the manager should be involved in the standard setting in order to motivate him towards its achievement.
3 Level – should the standard be set loose in order to be easily attainable or tight in order to spur the manager to a higher level of performance?

The reader is referred to the many texts on management control for a fuller discussion of this topic.

We now turn to the use of performance measures in the evaluation of the currency risk management function.

PERFORMANCE EVALUATION OF CURRENCY RISK MANAGEMENT

What measures best identify the quality of performance of the currency risk management section and motivate the staff to achieve the corporation's goals? In this section we review the current literature in this area before going on to evaluate the research findings in the case studies.

The *Statement of Management Accounting Practice – Study 2,*

Foreign Currency Exposure and Risk Management suggests that the performance measurements should be agreed at the outset by the Corporate Currency Committee. They should, among other things, set measurable and realistic objectives, and establish criteria for evaluating performance together with related performance incentive programmes. Cooper and Franks (1988) in their paper on treasury performance measurement state that 'The goal of a treasury management and performance appraisal system is to produce that set of treasury decisions which, given the operating assets and liabilities of the corporation, produces the "best" balance of cost and risk characteristics'. They go on to consider the governing principles of quantitative performance appraisal, these being:

1 Market value measurement – prices for transactions are available in the market.
2 Economic returns – the gain or loss to the corporation.
3 Opportunity gains and losses – incremental loss/gain of alternative strategies.
4 The benchmark – a benchmark is required to assess the alternatives.
5 Risk assessment – each decision involves a change in risk to the corporation. Assessment of this risk should be an integral part of the decision.

They conclude that the natural strategy for some commercial and industrial corporations is to fully hedge all foreign exchange exposure, using either the forward market or foreign currency borrowing. This is the benchmark strategy against which the management of foreign exchange risk by the corporate treasurer should be measured. A treasurer who chose not to fully cover would be viewed as speculating on the currency movement relative to the forward rate at the time the exposure was identified. Such a benchmark would naturally lead to a fully covered position.

PERFORMANCE EVALUATION OBJECTIVES

It is important that the objectives of currency management are incorporated in the measures used to evaluate the treasury function, and in particular the foreign exchange management function. The measures used must be consistent with the corporate objectives, the measurement of exposure, the perception of risk, and the allocation of responsibility. Poorly conceived or structured evaluation systems can create barriers to good management rather than enhancing performance.

As when allocating any responsibility it is important that the person held responsible has sufficient information upon which to make decisions and judgement, and has the authority to act. Frequently treasury is assigned responsibility for exchange gains and losses in situations over which it has no control.

Giannotti and Smith (1985) found that all too often corporate evaluation systems were inconsistent with the allocation of responsibility. The evaluation of financial managers tended to be subjective rather than quantitative. As a consequence, specific incentives or rewards for high-quality performance were rarely given. They considered that, as a matter of policy, the financial manager should be assigned specific performance goals by means of a budget.

In order to set such a budget there must be a consistent set of objectives for managing foreign exchange consistent with the company's perceived return on investment goals, and its attitude towards risk, i.e. cover nothing, cover everything, selectively hedge.

Giannotti and Smith found that few corporations systematically evaluated financial management performance with respect to exchange risk. Neither did they evaluate operating management since foreign exchange gains and losses were considered to be outside their control. Thus performance in this area is excluded from the evaluation measures in both areas. If, for example, foreign exchange gains and losses are not included in operational management's performance evaluation, treasury must be held accountable for them. Exchange transaction costs are segregated from local responsibility far too often without recognition of the very limited ability of others to manage them. The exchange risks are rarely fully reflected in operating decision-making or evaluation systems. Both have a detrimental effect on management decisions and actions.

ATTITUDE TO RISK IN THE SETTING OF STANDARDS

It is important that exchange management evaluation systems reflect the corporation's attitude and policy towards risk. If the standard of performance is against the fully hedged position then the manager will naturally move towards a fully hedged position in order to minimise his variance from the standard. He would only delay cover if he were very confident in his predictions of currency movements. If, on the other hand, the standard of performance is the spot rate at settlement, the manager will tend towards a fully open position. He would postpone cover at all times of uncertainty which could have expensive and unwelcome results. The method is also unsatisfactory since no exchange rate is available to the operating units to value costs or revenues until the transaction is completed. A third alternative is to set the standard as the best rate during the period. This will lead to a more aggressive policy, but with a possible loss of motivation because of the 'ideal' standard set. Perhaps a better solution is to set a range between the 'ideal' and the spot rate.

The selection of a standard is critical since, as noted above, a single hurdle rate, either forward rate at time of exposure or spot rate at maturity, leads to a hedge everything or hedge nothing approach, whereas a cost minimisation measure using the best rate in period, will lead to a selective hedging strategy. Which standard to select will depend upon not only the corporation's attitude to risk but also the time available and the skill of the treasury function. A cover everything or cover nothing approach will obviously take less time and can be performed by relatively unskilled personnel. On the other hand, a selective hedging strategy will consume more time and resources, and will require a higher level of expertise. Such an increase in cost must be justified by the savings.

THE ADOPTION OF SPECIFIC PERFORMANCE MEASURES

Certain practical difficulties also present themselves if the optimum rate is to be used for performance evaluation. In order to ascertain the optimum rate the market must be monitored constantly since the rate can vary minute by minute. In addition, different banks quote different rates, so no one standard is available. The only solution to this problem would be a real-time system which constantly monitors the market rates. One has to ask whether such a system is required anyway since we actually only require an approximate performance standard. An alternative, therefore, is to record the exchange rates at a point in time, perhaps daily or twice daily.

A further complication with these methods of performance evaluation arises because of the uniqueness of the actual transactions. It is usually impossible to combine transactions due to the variations in the period of exposure and the date of maturity. Each must be considered separately. To evaluate performance even on an approximate basis, therefore, requires some form of computer assistance. Again the cost of development and operation must be compared with the benefits, and it is likely that such a system would form part of an integrated system which records, processes and reports all the data required for exposure management purposes.

Harner and Roxan (1988) define a range of measures which could be used by management to assess the performance of the treasury function in its position-taking and hedging activities. They list exposure monitoring, risk control, retrospective opportunity evaluation, actual performance compared to no action scenario and the level of control of the dealing activities. Generally, they comment, they would expect the need for performance measures to arise in larger organisations, i.e. greater than £500 million turnover companies. One of the corporations already actively using performance measures interviewed by them emphasised 'the importance to the Treasury staff of performance measurement because of their profit related bonuses'. Another quoted its objectives as 'to measure the gains or losses that would have been made on foreign exchange contracts, if they had been covered on the day the exposure arose.'

THE ALLOCATION OF RESPONSIBILITY

The responsibility for exchange risk, exchange controls, and the level of sophistication of the particular management group all affect the structure of the performance evaluation system. For example, a profit centre manager can only be held responsible for transaction risk, since he is not responsible for the level of investment, whereas an investment centre manager can be held responsible for both transaction and translation risk. The problem with setting performance goals for currency management, e.g. minimise exchange costs, is that exchange risks are established by operating decisions and actions. There needs to be some form of shared responsibility so that operational decisions are taken in the light of their currency exposure implications. Currency management and operational management performance measures must reflect this.

Corporate treasury's advisory role is more difficult to evaluate objectively. If, for example, foreign exchange gains and losses are not included in operational management's performance evaluation, treasury must be held accountable for them. The difficulty arises in those situations where the hedging decision is vested with the subsidiary, subject to advice from the group centre. In particular, when disagreements arise between the parent and the subsidiary company on whether to cover or not. Since the gain or loss should be reflected in the responsible person's performance measure, it

Table 8.1 Performance evaluation: Separation of operating and exchange variances

Management group	Variance	Computation
Local	Local currency operating variance	(LC budget × budget rate) less (LC actual × budget rate)
International operations	Parent currency operating variance	(LC actual × budget rate) less (LC actual × actual rate)
Treasury	Foreign exchange variance from budget rate	(LC budget × budget rate) less (LC budget × actual rate)

LC = local currency.
Adapted from Giannotti and Smith (1985).

would seem wrong that the parent should disallow a hedging action without some form of compensation to the subsidiary. Some form of internal contracts would overcome this problem. The subsidiary would cover the exposure with the parent, leaving the parent to make the decision whether to cover or not. The main objection to this strategy is the additional administrative cost for no apparent benefit.

COST VERSUS PROFIT CENTRE APPROACHES

Giannotti and Smith (1985) state that one of the greatest short-falls of many budgeting and performance evaluation systems is the absence of targets and a quantitative evaluation for treasury staff. Treasury is considered a cost centre rather than a budget or profit centre. It should be evaluated on its ability to reduce exchange risks. Giannotti and Smith differentiate between treasury and operational management and allocate responsibility for variances according to Table 8.1.

In the example quoted, local managers are responsible for domestic operating results and are evaluated at the budgeted rate. International operations (treasury) are responsible for currency rate fluctuations applied to the actual results and treasury are responsible for the variance caused by currency rate fluctuations when applied to the budgeted results. Few companies in practice make this separation.

Gaunt (1988) stated that for his company group treasury was operated on a cost centre basis, whilst treasury operations were operated on a profit centre basis. Group treasury is responsible for advice on exposures and handling group translation exposure, whereas operational treasury is responsible for collating and centralising the management of group exposures to monetary risk, and advising units at transaction, level. Dealer performance is measured by comparing the spot and forward foreign exchange positions with the revaluation at closing rate in order to determine the contractual profit. The report analyses the profitability to allow the analysis of performance. The report shows the profit relative to new deals concluded that day, adjustment due to amendments and cancellations, profits due to spot movement and spread movement. If losses in excess of the dealer's limit are reported then serious questions are asked. Equally, if excessive profits are earned then the dealer is questioned as to the risk taken to achieve such results.

RESEARCH RESULTS

The case studies from this research are largely supportive of the above literature. Table 8.2 provides a summary of the case studies, with rough classification into whether the companies are neutral, conservative or averse in their attitude to risk.

Performance evaluation in risk averse companies

As can be seen from Table 8.2 those companies which adopt a risk averse policy, seeking always to minimise the risk of loss, tend not to have any formal performance measures. Measures which did exist were used to ensure that company policy was being adhered to. Company 9A's treasury were gauged on the cost of managing the multi-currency loan portfolio and the income received from investments. A similar measure was used by 7B, whose mission was to minimise overall financing costs to achieve where possible a negative financing cost. Company 10B paid attention to the cost effectiveness of individual hedging technique in order to minimise the cost of cover. Treasury performance in 2B was judged on the avoidance of losses in the income statement or equity in hyper-inflationary situations.

The currency management function of company 6B was operated as a separate profit centre with performance evaluated against the internal rate, which was based on the current forward rate. The normative literature suggests that such a performance measure will

Table 8.2 Performance measures used

Policy to risk Ref.		Profit /C.C.	Full cover	No cover	Oppor. L/G	Spot rate	Market aver'g	Other
1A	Neutral							Benchmark
2A	Neutral		Yes	Yes				Cash management
3A	Conserv							
4A	Averse							
5A	Averse							
6A	Neutral				Yes			Budget
7A	Conserv	Yes			Yes			
8A	Neutral				Yes			
9A	Averse							Cost
10A	Neutral							Internal
11A	Neutral					Yes		Average
1B	Averse							
2B	Neutral							No loss
3B	Averse					Yes		
4B	Conserv	Yes				Yes		
5B	Neutral							
6B	Neutral	Yes						No profit or loss
7B	Averse							Minimise finance
8B	Conserv							Committee
9B	Conserv							
10B	Averse							
11B	Neutral				Yes		Yes	Positive gain
12B	Neutral					Yes		Month end

lead to a fully covered position. The reason it does not in this case is due to the personality of the manager involved who seeks to maximise his profit. Also, although the company regards itself as risk averse, its policy is to minimise both risk and cost, cost being defined as both transaction cost and opportunity cost. This has led to the active use of options in order to maximise opportunities in currency movements whilst seeking to minimise potential losses.

None of these companies sought to evaluate the cost of their risk averse strategy by calculating the opportunity loss/gain had cover not been taken out. Company 3A considered it more important to give certainty as to the value in pounds sterling of future transactions. Where the corporate treasury acted as advisers to subsidiaries, no formal feedback systems were in operation. In the case of 4A an absence of feedback from subsidiaries was seen as a signal of success. Where cover was taken out on behalf of subsidiaries, the cost of cover and any surplus which arose was attributed to the operating unit (9A and 2B).

Performance evaluation in companies which actively manage transaction risk

Turning to those companies which actively manage their currency risk, a variety of methods were used. The spot rate compared with the actual rate was used by four of the companies (11A, 3B, 4B and 12B), but with some variations. Company 11A used the average of the previous month's daily rates rather than the actual spot rate, and company 12B used the end of month spot for closed and current positions. Related to this method is the opportunity loss/gain on transactions which was calculated by three of the companies (6A, 7A and 8A). This involves not only the comparison of the spot rate with the actual rate if cover is taken out, but also the comparison of the actual rate with the forward contract rate if no cover is taken out. Company 8A produce monthly reports covering:

1 the profits and losses on completed transactions;
2 the outcome of current open contracts if evaluated at the rates existing at the report date; and
3 the profit and loss on the net position comparing the rate at the report date with that when the exposure was notified to the treasury.

A variety of other methods were used, either alone or in conjunction with the above. Company 1A was actively engaged in currency dealings and operated a performance-related bonus scheme for its dealers. A balance was sought between making profits and avoiding undue risks. In an effort to obtain an independent view consultants were employed to set benchmarks based on the opportunities in the market during the period. The standard deviation around the mean was used as a measure of volatility and range of each currency.

Monthly monitoring was used by company 2A, comparing actual performance with the outcome if there had been either full or no cover during the period. A similar method was used to evaluate dealer performance on a daily basis.

Budget compared with actual exchange rates were used by company 6A, together with the opportunity loss/gain. Such a comparison is due, in part, to the company's better than average ability to forecast exchange rates. Company 11B also compared forecast and actual exchange rates with the planned rates on a quarterly basis in order to determine the effect on the annual plan. Comparison is also made with the market average rate for the period. Company 10A were expected to achieve breakeven or better against the internal rates quoted to subsidiaries. Monitoring was based around the complete revaluation of the book position on a monthly basis.

While company 8B did not have any formal system of performance evaluation the quality of its recommendations to the Foreign Exchange Committee were monitored. Two of the companies which were engaged in actively managing currency risk but which did not evaluate their performance were 5B and 9B. The reason given by 5B was that the company was sufficiently profitable for it not to be necessary to create another administrative unit with profit objectives. Company 9B gave the reason as the lack of scope for separate evaluation of decisions on currency risk between the corporate treasury and the subsidiaries, the impact of decisions taken by subsidiaries using advice from corporate being wholly reflected in the subsidiary's performance.

Performance evaluation of the treasury function

As can be seen from Table 8.2 very few of the treasury functions operated as a separate cost or profit centre. Company 2A did not view the currency risk management as a profit centre since, although the performance was evaluated in terms of gain or loss, the measure was notional and there was no opportunity for back judgement. Currency risk management in company 8A was not recognised as a profit centre even though profits and losses on foreign currency flows are taken centrally. The reason given for this was that the function of the department was to manage risk rather than to maximise profits from trading currencies. It was therefore considered unreasonable to evaluate performance when the freedom of action was curtailed. The treasurer of company 11A expressed the view that it was undesirable to have the treasury as a profit centre in any area where it gave advice, since there might well be conflicts between profit maximisation by treasury and the interests of the subsidiaries.

By contrast, however, the corporate treasury function of company 7A was organised as a separate limited company with its own performance criteria. These criteria tended to encourage a policy of limited exposure to risk as opposed to a full cover policy. The treasury function of company 4B was operated as a cost centre although it always dealt in the name of one of the major companies.

Company 6B had recently switched from a cost centre approach with no formal performance measure to that of a profit centre with its own trading statement with performance evaluated against the internal forward rate. This was due to a change in the company's policy from categorising currency movements as business risk, to isolating it and seeking to minimise the risk and opportunity cost.

Where the treasury acted in an advisory capacity to the operating subsidiaries no attempt was made to formally evaluate the effects of the advice given (8B, 9B). The analysis of variances between actual and planned rates and monetary flows was not attempted, and as a consequence responsibilities for variances were not determined.

CONCLUSION

In conclusion, the majority of the companies use some form of performance evaluation, a number using the opportunity loss/gain or spot rate as a measure. A number of other methods were used which best fitted the policy of the company and the information available. Generally, however, the standard of performance evaluation adopted was relatively basic, with only a very limited number of companies adopting a more sophisticated approach. In all cases there was a need to balance the benefits of evaluating performance against the increased administrative cost of determination.

NOTE

1 This chapter is based on research sponsored by the Institute of Chartered Accountants in England and Wales and conducted by J. B. Coates (Warwick), P. A. Collier (Exeter), E. W. Davies and S. G. Longden (Aston).

BIBLIOGRAPHY

Collier, P. A. and Davies, E. W. (1985) 'Currency risk management in UK multinational companies', *Accounting and Business Research*, Autumn 1985, pp. 327–35.

Dominiak, G. F. and Louderback, J. G. (1985) *Management Accounting*, Kent Publishing, pp. 413–17.

Donaldson, J. A. (1980) *Corporate Currency Risk*, The Financial Times Business Information, 41–72.

Dopuch, N., Birnberg, J. G. and Demski, J. S. (1982) *Cost Accounting – Accounting Data for Management's Decisions*, Harcourt Brace Jovanovich, pp. 177.

Eiteman, D. K. and Stonehill, A. I. (1986) *Multinational Business Finance*, Addison-Wesley, pp. 227–9.

Emmanuel, C. and Otley, D. (1985) *Accounting for Management Control*, Van Nostrand Reinhold, pp. 155–85.

Gaunt, K (1988) 'Dealer performance measurement', *Treasurer*, February 1988.

Giannotti, J. B. and Smith, R. W. (1985) *Treasury Management – A Practitioner's Handbook*, Wylie, pp. 391–411.

Harner, L and Roxan, J (1988) 'A review of treasury performance measurement software', *Treasurer*, February 1988.

Horngren, C. T. (1982) *Cost Accounting – A Managerial Emphasis*, Prentice-Hall, pp. 662, 687–9.

International Federation of Accountants (1986) *Statement on Management Accounting Practice – Study 2, Foreign Currency Exposure and Risk Management*, IFAC.

McRae. T. W. and Walker, D. P. (1980) *Foreign Exchange Management*, Prentice-Hall, pp. 72–84.

9   Analysing the performance of management planning systems

Val Brophy

This chapter introduces some of the issues concerning the analysis of the performance of management support systems at the short-run operational decision-making level. Secondly, it reviews the approach, pioneered by Demski, of using an 'ex post' optimum in performance analysis, and takes a critical view of its potential for managerial performance measurement. An extension of the 'ex post' system is then developed, and finally, we see how this may be useful in leading to improvements in the way that organisations manage their operations.

In 1985, Neil Dorward pointed out that most attention in the management accounting literature has focussed on the use of planning variances where change in material prices and labour wage rates frequently occur. This was seen as unsurprising as it was in this area that forecasting techniques had been developed to an advanced state. The traditional emphasis of management accounting on the manufacturing process can also be understood in terms of the relatively prescriptive nature of production as compared to the nature of more general management functions.

Conventionally, the analysis of overhead costs is perhaps more concerned with their allocation, based on some measure of production efficiency, than it is with the behaviour of the overhead costs themselves. As production becomes more efficient and more mechanised due to technological progress, a higher proportion of resources may be expected to be channelled away from direct manufacture and towards more indirect managerial activity. Also, we may see a shift in the more developed economies away from manufacturing and towards the provision of services. Both these trends support the view that the traditional approach of management accounting is becoming less relevant to the analysis of modern economic activity.

One of the general management functions alluded to above is that of finance. This is one of large and growing significance in terms of both its costs and the quality of its performance. According to Srinivasan and Kim (1986), the literature on cash management completely ignores the need to develop a set of control measures for continual evaluation of cash management decision-making. They have suggested that a simple and effective approach towards developing control measures would be to adopt the variance analysis approach from standard costing and develop a set of specific variances to serve as control measures in cash management.

The basis of the traditional application of standard costing to production and sales is that the variances can be broken down into distinct cost and conversion elements based on the unit costs of inputs and some desirable conversion ratios relating input units to output units. However, in the case of financial management, both the inputs and the outputs are sums of money or assets and liabilities quantified in monetary units, and the conversion is not from one type of unit to another, but from units at one point in time to essentially the same units at a different point in time. One could analyse a change in value of a monetary asset in terms of a price variance, in that one has 'bought' future cash with 'current' cash, for example. Alternatively, that same change in value could be analysed as a conversion, or efficiency, variance in that a current sum is being converted into a different future sum. It may not be obvious how the price and efficiency elements can be separated out in such financial applications.

In addition to the practical problem just described, another area of concern in trying to match, or adapt, the traditional standard costing system to the field of financial management emerges over the nature of the managerial processes to be monitored. In the traditional field of application, managerial objectives are closely associated with cost/quality/volume relationships. Here, the important issues are the acquisition of appropriate quality inputs at economic prices, the efficient conversion of inputs to outputs, the spreading of fixed costs over an appropriate volume of output, and the achievement of sales targets. The nature of the first three of these issues is largely bound up with the technology of the process being used to create the requisite goods. The nature of the fourth is closely allied to the characteristics of relevant marketing channels. On the other hand, forecasting and the control of risk (which also normally concern production and marketing managers), are not analysed by the traditional standard costing system. Forecasting and risk have become central concerns of financial management, and with the growing internationalisation of business in Europe, especially in the aftermath of 1992, they will undoubtedly assume even greater importance. Therefore, the potential of the traditional system as a basis from which a financial management performance appraisal system could be developed would appear to be increasingly limited.

In order to shift the focus of management accounting towards the overhead, or managerial, aspects of costs, we need to identify managerial activities germane to analysis. The most obvious requirement is that there should be quantitative data available that can be used as the basis for the analysis. The use of models for planning purposes might thus appear worthy of further investigation. One may take issue over the proportion of overhead costs amenable to the development and use of planning models, following the studies of Mintzberg (1971), for example. However, the collection of data for forecasting or estimating purposes, for instance, is clearly a significant expense of the typical modern business concern.

Dorward's paper reminds us of the danger, seen earlier by other authors, of incorporating planning errors into the traditional analysis of variance and goes on to highlight some of the pitfalls associated with the setting of ex post standards for manufacturing operations. Demski's (1967) approach necessitated the use of an optimising model for planning, and added two components to the traditional system. The first of these components was introduced as a 'rough indicator of the efficiency of the planning process', and was later shown as a set of forecasting variances. The second component, called the 'opportunity cost of non-optimal capacity utilisation', could be considered as a risk-related measure, as it values the range between observed performance and the theoretically best performance obtainable from hindsight. As ex post analysis promises us a way of evaluating forecasting and risk and focusses on the planning process, this approach, and the resulting criticism of it, are now summarised.

DEMSKI'S EX POST ANALYSIS FRAMEWORK

This approach takes the optimal solution of a planning model as the ex ante plan for the planning period using forecasts made for the start of the period, and the ex post net income is the optimised value from the model after the end of the period using observed data. Total net income for the planning period, NI, is expressed as:

$$NI = CX - F$$

where C is a vector of the contribution margins of the products, X is a vector of the output quantities of the products, and F is the total fixed cost. Ex ante or planned net income for the period is

$$NI^a = C^aX^a - F^a$$

observed net income is

$$NI^o = C^oX^o - F^o$$

and ex post net income is

$$NI^p = C^pX^p - F^p$$

The traditional comparison of ex ante and observed net income is extended by comparing each of those against the ex post income:

$$NI^a - NI^o = (NI^a - NI^p) + (NI^p - NI^o)$$

The first bracketed term, comparing ex ante and ex post optimum net income, focuses on the quality of forecasting used, as it compares what was thought to be possible from initial forecasts with what should have been possible given correct forecasts. The second term represents a 'hindsight' opportunity cost in that it shows what could have been achieved with perfect information over and above what was actually achieved.

Demski pointed out a number of assumptions on which his system was based. The first of these, that the system requires some kind of optimising model, was criticised by Cushing (1968) on the grounds that most variance analysis did not take place within the framework of such models. This issue should be less of a problem for current application as many optimising models have been described in the literature since 1968.

The second assumption was 'that management possesses the ability to distinguish between avoidable and unavoidable variances or deviations'. As managerial performance may be determined to a great extent by factors, such as market movements, outside the control of management, this assumption is clearly an important one.

Demski's model was concerned with providing feedback control information. He assumes that this information would be useful to the firm. Cushing was concerned about the problems of application in this respect. An important issue is whether or not the benefits from applying the system would exceed the costs. Therefore, it is essential that the potential benefits from such a system are clearly identified.

The fourth explicit assumption was that the firm's planning model would be capable of reflecting and measuring the complete set of opportunities available to the firm. Demski recognised the limitations of this assumption, whilst pointing out the need for a realistic approach towards 'synthesising opportunities'.

In Cushing's opinion, the assumption which most weakened Demski's system was 'that all deviations (unavoidable changes in model parameters) occur at the beginning of the period and persist throughout'. For control purposes, those whose performance was being appraised must have had every opportunity to adjust to the changes in model parameters. Cushing argued that if information on parameter deviations was available at the start of the planning period, then such information could be used to revise the ex ante budget, making it equivalent to the ex post budget. In reply, Demski (1968) emphasised that a need for intra-period revisions could be 'readily handled by introducing new products into the model and appropriately altering the constraint set'.

Amey (1973) dismissed the whole ex post approach with the words 'An ex post optimum can tell us nothing about current performance which is relevant to action'. He argued that a hindsight optimum excluded expectations and was thus totally unrealistic of the environment in which the firm operated. By introducing intra-period revisions, he was able to show that the term used by Demski to analyse forecasting performance could be broken down into elements which included a part of the traditional system.

An illustration of Demski's ex post analysis

Let us now consider the example of a simple choice between two alternatives, A and B. A has an expected payoff of £10,000 but is risky, whereas B has a certain payoff of £9,800. Following profit maximisation, one would choose alternative A. Let us now suppose that the payoff from A is actually £9,600. This situation can be analysed using Demski's ex post system, as shown in Table 9.1.

The traditional variance, assuming the ex ante optimum is taken as the standard,[1] is £400 U. The first point to emerge here is that the unfavourable traditional variance results directly from the forecast that led to the decision taken, and this forecast is also a key figure used in calculating the variance. The ex post analysis is interesting in showing that the best that could have been achieved given actual market conditions was an extra £200. It should be noted that even the best decision taken with hindsight here results in a traditional variance of £200 U, due to the erroneous forecast/expectations underpinning the ex ante payoff of A.

Let us now see the results from an identical ex ante situation, but where the outcome from that same alternative A is in fact £10,400, as shown in Table 9.2. In this case, the traditional variance (using the ex ante optimum as standard) is £400 F due to the erroneously low forecast. Clearly the traditional comparison (between ex ante optimum and observed result) is unsatisfactory in this situation as the sign of the variance can be positive or negative, depending on

Table 9.1 Example 1 of Demski analysis

	Ex ante (1)	*Ex post* (2)	*Observed* (3)
Payoff (A)	£10,000*	£9,600	£9,600
Payoff (B)	£9,800	£9,800*	£9,800
	< Forecasting variance> (1A) – (2B) £200 U^a	< Opportunity cost > (2B) – (3A) £200 U^a	

* Identifies an optimal solution/decision for the ex ante and ex post problems in turn.

^{a} Following Demski's definition of the traditional variance as $NI^a - NI^o$, the variances identified in the table are unfavourable when the relevant subtraction yields a positive number.

whether the forecast is low or high, and no assessment of the quality of decision-making is possible. The ex post analysis is more promising in this respect, but it is disturbing that although the absolute error of the forecast is the same, 4 per cent, in each example, the forecasting variances have quite different absolute values, i.e. £200 U and £400 F. This occurs because the forecasting variance accounts for both the error in the forecast itself and the subsequent influence that the forecast exerts on the decision. A forecast which is low in retrospect, contributes a favourable bias towards the forecasting variance.

In a more realistic situation where many alternative actions are available, where many forecasts are involved, and where there is a variety of policy constraints in operation, it will be much more difficult to break the ex post forecasting variance down into its more basic components of forecast error and faulty action choice.

In example 3, in Table 9.3, we see the effect of the disappointing payoff of £9,600 as in example 1 when alternative B is no longer riskless and, from hindsight, is seen to have a better than forecast payoff value of £10,000. This example illustrates how inaccurate forecasting can be totally masked in the ex post forecasting variance.

It could be argued that attempts to distinguish between errors in the forecasts and errors in actions taken solely as a result of those forecasts are irrelevant as the culpability of both types of error

Table 9.2 Example 2 of Demski analysis

	Ex ante (1)	Ex post (2)	Observed (3)
Payoff (A)	£10,000*	£10,400*	£10,400
Payoff (B)	£9,800	£9,800	£9,800
	< Forecasting variance >		< Opportunity cost >
	(1A) – (2A)		(2A) – (3A)
	£400 F		0

lies within the forecasting and modelling process. However, in a situation where forecasting forms a part of the decision-making process, monitoring of the accuracy of the forecasts themselves has a clear value in highlighting the potential for improvement, and in raising awareness of the limitations of the forecasts and the risks involved in their use.

One of the simplifying assumptions used in the above examples is that the ex ante plan is actually carried out in full. Generally, however, quantitative models will form no more than a part of the input into the planning process, and managers will be influenced by factors outside the scope of such models. Also, in a dynamic environment, where a multi-period model is being used, the expected values of some of the forecast parameters used to obtain the ex ante solution will change in the light of information received after the solution has begun to be put into effect. For both these reasons actions may well diverge from those indicated in the original ex ante plan, and such changes occurring during the implementation stage may be properly regarded as the responsibility of those making the changes.

For control purposes the ex ante standard is clearly unsatisfactory in that it is unachievable, and will thus tend to be a demotivating goal. The Demski analysis provides little to indicate what degree of shortfall in achieving this goal represents good or satisfactory planning or management, although it does have the virtue of identifying the opportunity cost.

By failing to separate the effects of forecasting errors from the erroneous courses of action that they cause, the Demski framework clearly limits its value in the analysis of the planning process. By obscuring the comparison of observed results and the ex ante plan it precludes the monitoring and evaluation of the subsequent management of the implementation process. Insofar as forecasting, planning and the monitoring and control of the implementation

Table 9.3 Example 3 of Demski analysis

	Ex ante (1)	Ex post (2)	Observed (3)
Payoffs (A)	£10,000*	£9,600	£9,600
Payoffs (B)	£9,600	£10,000*	£10,000
	< Forecasting variance > (1A) – (2B) 0	< Opportunity cost > (2B) – (3A) £400 U	

process in the light of up-to-date information are important responsibilities of management, it is clear that greater insight into the quality of their performance should be worthwhile. In the next section, we show how Demski's approach can be adapted to enable the separate evaluation of forecasting, planning and implementation.

A PROPOSED REVISION OF THE DEMSKI APPROACH

At the time when Demski proposed his analytical framework it would not have been unreasonable for practitioners to expect that, where a model were used for planning purposes, the main emphasis of management would have been to ensure that its solution were implemented as fully as possible. This framework of analysis is depicted in Figure 9.1.

It should be recognised that, in practice, it may not be possible to implement the solution exactly, because of errors in the forecast data. Nowadays, we may take a more enlightened view of the role of models in management operations. It may well be that the problem cannot be fully specified due to aspects that are not amenable to quantification, in which case the formal modelling of a complex problem may guide, rather than determine, the subsequent managerial action. In other words, we would wish to recognise that there is a role for managerial judgement and discretion outside the formal boundaries of the decision support model.

The failure to implement a solution through fate or fault may lead to a loss that we may properly regard as an implementation variance. However, the initiative shown by a manager in diverging from that solution may result in benefit or loss, and insofar as it is discretionary and under the manager's control, its effects could well be regarded as a suitable measure of the performance of the

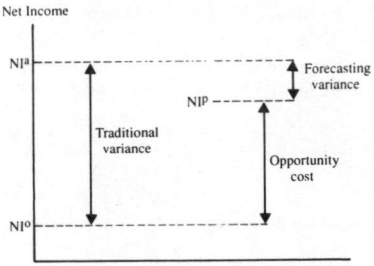

Figure 9.1 The Demski analysis

executive, and could be seen to be within his sphere of responsibility.

An objective measure of the above initiative may be made by comparing observed results (X^o) against the actions (X^a) proposed by the original plan. When this comparison is evaluated using observed rates (C^o), (i.e. in an ex post sense), the resulting variance is expressed as

$$C^oX^o - C^oX^a$$

or (more fully) as

$$NI^o - NI^{oa} = (C^oX^o - F^o) - (C^oX^a - F^o)$$

The new term (NI^{oa}), representing the (theoretically) realisable net income from the ex ante plan, thus replaces the speculative ex ante plan valuation (NI^a) used as a standard by Demski.

The revised analysis is shown in Fig. 9.2, where the 'managerial action variance' evaluates the observed divergence of actions from the ex ante plan. This variance is the measure of managerial effectiveness in implementing and/or overriding the original plan. It can be given some perspective through comparison with the planning variance shown in Figure 9.2.

The planning variance compares the realisable value of the ex ante plan with that of the ex post optimum (i.e. $NI^p - NI^{oa}$). It reflects the difference between the ex ante and ex post plans, both valued at observed costs, and could be interpreted as the effective cost of uncertainty. Insofar as it identifies the maximum theoretical cost of following the ex ante plan, it puts an absolute upper bound on the scope of the managerial action variance.

The revised forecasting variance now signals the difference between the expected value of the ex ante plan and its more objective value given hindsight. In measuring the effect of forecasting errors on

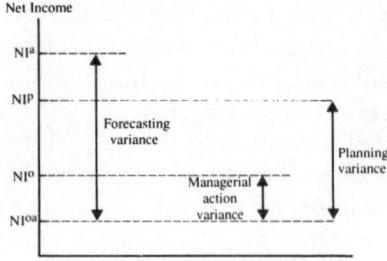

Figure 9.2 The revised approach

the value of the ex ante plan directly, it thus represents a less ambiguous measure of the forecasting error within the context of the planning process than does the Demski term, $NI^a - NI^p$. It can be expressed as:

Forecasting variance $= NI^{oa} - NI^a$

CONCLUDING REMARKS

In this chapter, we have recognised that the traditional approach of management accounting has not been widely and effectively employed to analyse the performance of managerial functions. In view of the tendency of resource utilisation to shift away from direct manufacturing in developed economies there is, perhaps, a growing need for a way of monitoring general managerial performance. In the areas of planning and decision-making, particularly where forecasting and the use of optimising models can form part of the process, ex post analysis looks promising insofar as it can measure the effectiveness of forecasting and the opportunity costs of achieved performance. Demski has pioneered the way, but his analysis of the forecasting component does not seem to go far enough in separating out the appropriate characteristics, and his opportunity cost fails to provide a realistic measure of performance.

The approach proposed here aims to provide an unambiguous measure of the accuracy of forecasts used in decision modelling, and to separate forecasting issues from the analysis of planning costs arising when actions proposed by an ex ante model differ from actions seen as more desirable from hindsight. Through the distinction between NI^a and NI^{oa}, we are able to see Demski's opportunity cost as the difference between the planning variance and a managerial action variance. In this way, a step is made to separate factors outside the manager's control from the results of actions within his control. The effectiveness of his contributions in implementing the ex ante solution and his initiative and judgement in overriding it in the light of intangible factors or new information should be recognisable in the managerial action variance.

The proposed framework introduces some perspective on risk in that the planning variance sets a scale within which the value of the implementation variance can be judged, but risk is such an important feature of managerial activity that more sophistication in its analysis may be desirable. Cooper and Franks (1987) recently made an interesting contribution in this area in showing how volatility can be used to calculate benchmarks for individual financial transactions, but that approach may be seen to lack some of the characteristics of an integrated optimising model where the interactions of the individual alternatives are taken into account.

The approach described here is sufficiently general to be applicable to a range of managerial functions, in particular where uncertainty looms large. With regard to the growing internationalisation of European business, uncertainty will surely be a prominent feature in the financial and marketing fields. In such areas, appropriate decision support models can provide guidance for the international executive, and the type of feedback provided by a suitable form of ex post analysis should be valuable in assisting him to develop his judgemental skills.

NOTE

1 Obviously the question of what is an appropriate ex ante standard here could be a controversial issue, but Demski does postulate the use of an optimising model as part of the firm's planning process.

REFERENCES

Amey, L. R. (1973) 'Hindsight versus expectations in performance measurement', in L. R. Amey (ed.) *Readings in Management Decision*, Chapter 12, pp. 258–72, London, Longman.

Cooper, I. and Franks, J. (1987) 'Treasury performance measurement', *Midland Corporate Finance Journal* 4, (4), 29–43.

Cushing, B. E. (1968) 'Some observations on Demski's ex post accounting system', *Accounting Review* 43 (4), 668–71.

Demski, J. S. (1967) 'An accounting system structured on a linear programming model', *Accounting Review* 42 (4), 701–12.

Demski, J. S. (1968). 'Some observations on Demski's ex post accounting system: A reply', *Accounting Review* 43 (4), 672–4.

Dorward, N. (1985) 'Variance analysis: pitfalls of present costing techniques', *Accountancy*, November, 204–6.

Mintzberg, H. (1971) 'Managerial work: Analysis from observation', *Management Science* 18 (2), B97–110.

Srinivasan, V. and Kim, Y. H. (1986) 'Deterministic cash flow management: Review and research directions', *Omega* 14 (2), 145–66.

10 In the eye of the gaze

The constitutive role of performance appraisal

Barbara Townley

INTRODUCTION

One of the expected impacts of 1992 is the need for increased productivity in the face of enhanced competition. Enterprise and effectiveness in the delivery of goods and services are highlighted as the key factors for the future. Managing high performance has been identified as requiring a framework which enables a systematic approach to problem-solving – one which aids policy formation and the identification of priorities, and thereafter facilitates their implementation and monitoring (Jackson 1988). This places a high onus on management, managerial control structures and information systems – effective decision-making and performance-orientated management requires data, as captured in the adage 'what you can't measure you can't manage'.

In particular, a strong emphasis is placed on the central component of this activity – systems of performance appraisal and evaluation. Performance information allows managers and staff to see how far targets and objectives are being met, and aids the setting of priorities for the future. Indeed high performance has been associated with a system in which managers work to clear objectives, with each person knowing what is expected of him or her and being given responsibility for specific results.

The UK has recently seen an increase in the introduction of performance appraisal systems, particularly at the individual level (Long 1986). Allied to the growth in performance- or merit-related pay, it reflects a changing managerial approach which emphasises 'productivity through people'. Generally portrayed in terms of organisational reform and improvement, performance appraisal is presented as the means by which an individual's and organisation's performance may be enhanced as procedures are changed, managerial and employee motivation are increased, and goals are achieved. As one more function in the technicist pantheon, it is essentially viewed as an aid or tool required for effective work organisation which no good organisation should be without. This chapter examines approaches adopted to the understanding of the role of appraisal within organisations, suggesting that it is more complex than this presentation of its acting as a facilitator of managerial decision making would suggest.

PERFORMANCE APPRAISAL

Whether called upon to function as a review of current performance, future potential or as a basis of a reward system, the appraisal process is generally presented as that of the acquisition of information to aid a process of rational decision-making and resource allocation. Performance appraisal in this sense constitutes a systematically developed data-handling system designed to facilitate management control. It operates to ensure that resources are used effectively and efficiently in the accomplishment of organisational objectives. As with other accounting procedures it gives the semblance of order and rationality in conditions of complexity and uncertainty, taking on simplification, rationalisation and legitimation roles in organisational decision-making (Earl 1983; Boland and Pondy 1983).

An assumption of this approach is that data are neutral. Performance appraisal, therefore, is a process by which 'an individual at work is given information as to how he is doing and what he should be doing differently' (Randell 1973: 222). Performance review becomes the 'neutral' process of 'observing, checking, receiving, and giving information about the behaviour of a person at work with the object of improving work performance' (Randell 1973: 222). Under this perspective appraisal is conceived of as being an essentially revelatory endeavour, a technical process which reflects what is 'out there' with the information gathered being used in the implementation of certain decisions – as the basis for recommendations on training, salary, etc. Concentrating on how information is used, however, singularly neglects how information is provided. It is also to make the assumption that 'organisation', 'work', and more broadly 'reality' are pregiven.

Dominated by a belief in a physical realism, the assumption of this traditional view of appraisal is that of a knowable and determinate nature or essence, in which, as part of this, individuals may also be described in an objective manner abstracted from their social context.

This view of the knowledge which decision-makers require as 'out there', independent of the person using it, the institutions in which they operate, is reflected in the following statement on the role of performance information:

> [P]erformance measures/indicators should not be thought of as a microscope which searches for the hidden elements within organisational life. Like invasive surgery such an approach is threatening . . . instead it is more useful to think of performance indicators as mirrors which reflect particular aspects of an organisation's activities. Each mirror (indicator) is set to reflect a particular facet of activity.
>
> (Jackson 1988: 11)

The role of the metaphor here is important; metaphors help structure ideas and knowledge. The impact of metaphor on theory construction has recently gained attention (Morgan 1980; Morgan and Smirchich 1980). As Morgan (1980: 607) notes 'different metaphors can constitute and capture the nature of organisational life in different ways, each generating powerful, distinctive but essentially partial kinds of insight'. This chapter takes issue with the 'mirror' as being the most appropriate metaphor for the role of appraisal, suggesting that an alternative metaphor, the gaze, might be more appropriate for understanding the role of performance appraisal systems and their effects in organisations.

Appraisal is essentially concerned with the presentation and representation of a complex, multi-faceted reality. It may be seen as a process whereby information is selected from everyday observation and participation, and through this process highlighted or privileged. As Pym (1973: 233) has noted:

> by a thousand intuitive observations and devices one learns how to relate and work with another . . . the dynamic of this relationship is bound up with its intangibility . . . the reduction of complex behaviour to mere words and numbers . . . cannot represent adequately [these] experiences.

The 'knowledge' which is created by this process is, by definition, partial. Appraisal operates first and foremost as a process by which a particular view of work and its organisation are made visible – some things are highlighted whilst others are excluded. Categories become established to impose coherence on chaotic organisational processes and in doing so define what is real, indicate that certain issues are important, relegating others to the insignificant or irrelevant.

What is involved, therefore, is not a matter of reproducing the visible but of rendering visible (Miller 1987). Implicit in the notion of visibility is the act of creation – in making something known, an object of knowledge is brought into being. 'Making visible is not shining a light on something there but hidden – visibility is invention' (Boland 1987: 271). This is illustrated in an unusual and humorous piece on critical accounting theory (Hines 1988), which takes issue with the frequently voiced demand that information should provide 'the full picture':

> but what is the full picture? There is no full picture. We make the picture that is what gives us our power: *people think and act on the basis of that picture!* . . . but we have not so much grasped reality, as created it, by thinking of it in a certain way and by treating it in that way.

> (Hines 1988: 254; italics in original)

From this perspective a crucial dimension in appraisal's operation is its constructivist activity. Appraisal serves to render visible certain aspects of the functioning of the enterprise but in doing so it constructs a particular field of visibility. What is involved in appraisal is the production of knowledge and through this the production of organisational reality. It is implicated in the construction of an organisational order rather than being independent, of it. Its exercise creates the dimensions of 'reality' it is assumed to reveal. From this perspective knowledge or information is not detached and independent, a source of illumination, it is implicated in, and integral to, the system of administration and governance which becomes established. Embedded within this constitutive role of constructing or creating the image which results is the operation of power. Under this perspective appraisal may be seen as the operation of power/knowledge (Gordon 1980). By ignoring the creation of knowledge which takes place in appraisal, the operation of power in that creation of knowledge is also denied. To treat data as self-contained facts ignores the production of knowledge, and concomitant with this, the operation of power in the creation of knowledge. The process of constitution is simultaneously an exercise of power and an exercise of knowledge, mutually reinforcing each other.

Rather than view appraisal as a neutral tool of observation, independent and merely reflective of the organisation, attention should be paid to the way in which appraisal, as an interactive and creative process contributes to the 'forming' of the organisation in making visible a particular order.

To take the view that appraisal does not provide a secure or accurate depiction of reality but offers a partial and socially created perspective is not, however, to relegate appraisal to being merely a product of organisational politics. Presenting it as an intersubjectively negotiated way of seeing would place an emphasis on the process of defining and interpreting of 'reality', and the management of meaning identified as a crucial aspect of political relations (Gowler and Legge 1983). Although these dimensions exist, this is not the intention here. Rather it is argued that the effect is deeper than this. Emphasis here will be placed on the relationship between rendering something visible and therefore knowable, and tracing how this relates to the operation of power. Rather than appraisal being a process in which 'an individual at work is given information (usually by a superior) as to how he is doing', it is argued that in its operation appraisal is constitutive of the individual (the industrial subject), the superior (management) and the work which is being done (the labour process).

THE METAPHOR OF THE GAZE

Having rejected the reflective role of appraisal encapsulated in the metaphor of the mirror, that which is offered in its place is the metaphor of the gaze – visibility highlighting that on which it alights, leaving in darkness that which lies outside its sphere. The latter is an essential aspect of the gaze – that which remains invisible serves to define the visible. Highlighted in the metaphor of the gaze, therefore, is the relation between the visible and the invisible. What gets left out is as relevant for consideration as that which the gaze falls upon. Appraisal as gaze emphasises the constitutive role of its operation. In addition it also emphasises the importance of agency, and the positive or creative effect of power.

Although the value of metaphor in organisational analysis has been questioned (Pinder and Bourgeois 1982), it is used as a leitmotif here because, as was argued earlier, of its ability to capture organisational life in a different way. The metaphor of the gaze in particular provides a useful entrée into the work of Michel Foucault, whose work offers a rich understanding of power relations and the effects of these processes on individuals and organisations.

The imagery of visibility and the metaphor of the gaze is strong in Foucault's work. Described as analyses of histories of the production of knowledge, Foucault's work on psychiatry (1971), medicine (1973), the human sciences (1972) and the penal system (1977), illustrate how 'sanity', 'health', 'knowledge' and 'punishment' once remaining below the threshold of visibility, become visible and therefore an object of knowledge. In his analysis of medical knowledge in *The Birth of the Clinic* Foucault illustrates how, what he terms, the 'medical gaze' was institutionalised, and became one of the central directing principles of hospitals. He describes the book as being about the act of seeing, the gaze, and how the medical gaze constituted medical knowledge (Gordon 1980). Equally his work on the asylum, *Madness and Civilisation*, illustrates how visible acts of madness would be made known to the madman whilst unobserved acts of the unconscious would later be the focus of observation and classification.

In such analyses the development of disciplines of knowledge become shaped by the gaze. Foucault has stated

> The historical embraces whatever, de facto or de jure, sooner or later, directly or indirectly may be offered to the gaze. Alone, the gaze dominates the entire field of possible knowledge. That which is not on the scale of the gaze falls outside the domain of possible knowledge.
>
> (Foucault 1973: 166)

This act of making visible indicates the intimate connection between power and knowledge. Visibility, or being made known, is intimately linked to control. Indeed for Jay (1986) the relevance of Foucault's work is the link established between vision (*voir*), knowledge (*savoir*) and power (*pouvoir*).

Operating by means of metaphor alone, however, is often criticised for being insufficiently concrete to relate to an individual's direct experience of organisations and specifically here the operation of managerial control systems. Again, from the work of Foucault (1977), it is possible to identify the institutional form which the operation of the gaze can take. It is exemplified in the panopticon. Designed by Bentham, the panopticon manifests the exercise of the gaze. It has been described as the very epitome of power–knowledge principles (Garland 1987). Originally designed for prison construction, although Bentham envisaged a wider application, the panopticon involved a central circular building around which were constructed the inmates' cells. Although the occupants were clearly visible to the central inspection tower, the reverse was not the case. The central tower served the dual function of the exercise of power and the registration of knowledge. The panopticon was thus an architectural form designed to subject individuals to the gaze and through this the knowledge and power of the central authorities. Determined by the distribution of places, each person is watched by another. It is an apparatus of total and circulating mistrust. The assumption was that by being exposed to constant visibility, the inmates would take it upon themselves to behave in the desired manner through the exercise of self-control.

For Bentham the panopticon was a system designed to enhance the easy and effective exercise of power operating through the mechanism of surveillance. This overseeing gaze constituted a new system of government achieved through the practice of total visibility. Recognising the inability of avoiding the observers' gaze, knowing that the individual is always in principle open to it, although with no way of knowing if this is actually the case, its operation becomes interiorised. Inexpensive to maintain, it is hoped the inspecting gaze will eventually inculcate a system of internalisation – the process by which the individual exercises surveillance over him or herself. In this sense the act of observation renders objects or subjects visible and is essentially a disciplinary act. Being constantly seen, or always able to be seen, produces a disciplined individual.

For Foucault the significance of the panopticon is the act not only of control but of knowing. His focus is on the simultaneous exercise of power and registration of knowledge. Whilst the operation of the gaze is an act of surveillance, essentially a negative act, the positive aspect of power, particularly the operation, through visibility, of the creation of knowledge is also recognised. Foucault's emphasis is those systems of codification, marking and classifying which visibility renders possible. In this sense the gaze has had great importance among the techniques of power developed in the modern era. It is this aspect of its workings which renders the panopticon a transferable technology and is identifiable operating in many domains – personal, technical, bureaucratic or legal.

Foucault identifies the panoptic principles of hierarchical observation and the normalising judgement which results, in attempts to increase control over individual's behaviour and dispositions precisely because they are organisational members, as features of the modern organisation. These principles are identified as influencing both organisational structures and the lived experience of organisational members, be they in prisons, schools, factories, barracks or hospitals. Although not specifically addressed by Foucault, the demands of production have been identified as using the same techniques in the operation of power. Fox (1989) identifies the hierarchical pyramid of modern large organisations as being based on panoptic principles, where members of headquarters, or the 'central tower' survey the organisation, able to sit in judgement on individual fates, through promotion, rewards and punishments, without being open to a reciprocal gaze. Organisational hierarchy and centralisation are reinforced as 'objectives', are channelled 'down' the organisation and their subsequent implementation is monitored.

As one mechanism in the cannon of managerial power appraisal operates as the paper equivalent of the panopticon – an 'information panopticon' (Zuboff 1988). As a mechanism of visibility, transparency is achieved through the architecture of the information system. In some cases, for example, where appraisal evaluations are not discussed with employees, it is the panopticon *par excellence* with its anonymous and continuous surveillance. In this informational form appraisal, through the gaze, offers the exercise of control at a distance both in terms of time and space. It operates as a technique of discipline for the organisation, overcoming central corridors (Boland 1987: 271).

THE NORMALISING GAZE

The gaze has implications for the individual. Through the detailed observation and articulation of work the gaze renders visible, and therefore potentially manageable, those on whom it falls. It renders visible those who are inside it, in doing so it provides the opportunity 'to act on those it shelters, to provide a hold on their conduct, to carry the effects of power right to them, to make it possible to know them, to alter them' (Foucault 1977: 172). As personalised control becomes more problematic with the increased specialisation of labour, control is operationalised either through programming behaviour, with expected behaviour specified in documentation, or through output regulation. In performance appraisal or assessment the two are often combined.

What is involved is the assessment of the individual in relation to the desired standard of conduct: a means of knowing how the individual performs, watching his or her movements, assessing his or her behaviour and measuring it against a rule – allowing incidents of non-conformity or departures from set standards to be recognised and dealt with. By referring individual actions to the 'population', a 'rule' or 'norm' becomes established. What is acceptable or normal, a conformity which must be achieved, comes into operation. Through observation, differentiation and assessment, the characteristics of the individual are recorded over time and in comparison with others.

For Foucault (1977: 184) it is part of a process which defines membership of a homogeneous social body: 'the norm introduces, as a useful imperative and as a result of measurement, all the shading of individual differences'.

Appraisal is the process of making a person known and visible. It is the activity by which the individual emerges as 'the object of positive knowledge' (Miller 1987: 157). From observation and examination a detailed and systematic knowledge of the individual emerges. It is the constitution of the 'individual as a describable, analysable object' (Foucault 1977: 149). The individual becomes visible, however, only in relation to an hypothesised essence, a norm, from which it is characterised. The kind of person that it is possible to know and the ways it is possible to know that person are created through a series of normative judgements. In this sense the individual is not a human essence that is waiting to be illuminated.

The procedures of observation, examination and measurement which allow this knowledge to develop are at the same time exercising power and control over the individuals within their gaze. 'It is the individual as he may be described, judged, measured, compared with others in his very individuality; and it is also the individual who has to be trained or corrected, classified, normalised, excluded' (Foucault 1977: 1971). Again it is a process which has the expectation that individuals will internalise discipline, attending to his or her own deficiencies.

Offe (1976) has identified a three-fold typology of 'norms' which become the focus of assessment and which identify those aspects of behaviour to become internalised: 'technical rules' are functional for the operation of work tasks; 'regulatory norms' facilitate the operation of cooperative work processes, for example, references to 'carefulness' or 'economy'; and 'extra-functional norms' which are functionally irrelevant for the work task but prop up the authority structure of the organisation, and check loyalty to the aims and interests of those in authority. He hypothesises that it is the latter which play an increasing role in assessment, a position which is supported by survey results of company appraisals (Bureau of National Affairs 1974; Lazer and Wikstrom 1977; Long 1986).

Although managerial jobs tend to be assessed in a results-orientated approach to performance, social criteria are used almost exclusively in non-managerial performance reviews where personality traits or characteristics are the main criteria for assessing employee performance. Criteria identified both in white collar and blue collar appraisals are work habits and personal characteristics rather than production achieved, and include: reliability, cooperation, adaptability, appearance, conduct, assertiveness, degree of self-discipline, diffidence and respect. 'The criteria identified by appraisals emphasise regulatory and extra-functional norms – readiness to adapt, avoidance of conflict, loyalty to dominant interests in the organisation, and the acceptance of the cultural pattern of the dominant groups' (Townley 1989: 104).

As a regulatory system appraisal seeks to promote a notion of subjectivity. As has been illustrated, however, normative judgements are essentially concerned with inducing conformity. The problem emerges when 'conformity' is encouraged at the expense of everything else.

DEFINING THE LABOUR PROCESS

Control of individuals is not just restricted to their behaviour, output is also important. Requiring knowledge of the expense of production processes places an emphasis on the measurement and recording at the point of production. Where appraisal systems are concerned with the supervision of activity, they may operate as an extension of this process by codifying and partitioning as closely as possible time, space and movement. The timetable becomes prominent and labour power is fragmented as each variable is observed, 'characterised, assessed, computed and related to the individual' (Foucault 1977: 145). Examples include the time within which phone calls are answered, turnaround time for letters, billing cycle etc. In operating in this way appraisal serves to 'inspect men, observe their presence and absence' (Foucault 1977: 148). It allows for comparisons to be made between individuals and encourages a view of individual capacities to be judged in a negative sense as departure from norms. In doing so the examinatory technique also serves to rank, placing individuals on a hierarchical grid, and distributes them along a scale in relation to one another (particularly seen in the case where overall performance ratings are subject to forced distributions). As with required behavioural characteristics the individual at work becomes surrounded by a series of norms and standards, a person's activities are judged according to prescribed standards and deviations from the norm.

However, in operating as a process by which certain aspects of everyday activity are rendered visible, appraisal also operates to articulate work. The labour process is 'created' in its exercise as certain aspects of work gain visibility and others are excluded. What is omitted may be as significant as that which is included. It may not be an exaggeration to say that the significance of appraisal lies in its silence. Viewed from this perspective, however, the questions arise: what aspects of activity become identified and graced with the term 'performance'; what aspects of behaviour are recognised and granted existence? In short, how does the labour process become identified and articulated, and in this process of formal articulation, redefined?

The overarching emphasis tends to be that of the numerical, reflecting the overriding belief that if something exists, it exists in a quantity and therefore must be measurable. Taken to be synonymous with 'objective' and 'value-free' data, the partial and numerical interpretation of organisational 'reality' takes precedence over other non-quantifiable aspects of work. However, some areas of performance do not lend themselves to quantification, and imposition of the latter becomes in danger of over-simplification. The preoccupation with quantifiable indicators of 'economy' and 'efficiency' may neglect less quantifiable but fundamental considerations of whether or not a service is effective in achieving its intended outcomes.

Equally emphasis tends to be very much on achievement, 'getting things done' – work becomes identified with action or activity. Again, performance can rarely be defined in terms of single outputs, there usually being a multiplicity. Although outputs can be identified and have some value in work control, they rarely serve as an adequate basis for assessing performance in isolation. Concentrating on activity or getting things done can also play an important role in the concept of time. Such systems serve to celebrate the present and the short term, with all the attendant, potentially detrimental impact of shortened time horizons on individual and organisational effectiveness, and the 'paralysis by analysis' which frequent 'accounting' procedures are in danger of instilling (Hopwood 1987). Concentrating on short-term results and short-term improvements in performance at the expense of long-term improvements in effectiveness is remediable only if senior management adopts a long-term planning horizon and judges individual performance in this light. This, however, makes contributions more difficult to measure.

The visibility and the allocation of responsibility in performance appraisal is usually attached to the individual. The underlying ethos of appraisal is what Offe (1976) has termed the 'achievement principle', that is, the reward of individual work, achievement or performance. However, the focus on the 'productivity' of the individual has the result of defining the individual, rather than the group or department, as the unit of work. The emphasis is placed on observation, supervision, invigilation – 'each actor is alone perfectly individualised and constantly visible' (Foucault 1977: 200). The individual becomes known according to his or her contribution to the efficiency of the enterprise, especially if this is an expression in numerical form. Also implicit within such an overview are assumptions of individuals' control over activity. The social or collective element of work remains obscure or hidden. This is despite the fact that 'the social organisation of work, the extent to which the parameters of work organisation are already defined, the reliance on at least a degree of "team cooperation" effectively render impossible the attempt to locate the success of any one individual' (Offe 1976: 81). In operating in this manner appraisal may in fact serve to mystify, rather than reveal, social relations which are involved in work.

The process of highlighting specific aspects of organisational activity illustrates another operation of the gaze. Most behaviour, and particularly most behaviour in organisations, is governed by performance programmes. By their very nature performance indicators are designed to motivate individuals, cause them to modify behaviour and meet targets. What is accounted for, however, can shape organisational participants' views of what is important. Performance appraisal may serve to shift perceptions of the nature and purpose of organisations and in doing so may mediate 'the recognition of problems and the options for their resolution' (Hopwood 1987: 228). Buchanan (1986) observes how practices of middle and junior managers are shaped by performance measures which encourage a parochial, low risk orientation to technical change. A police force judged by the number of arrests runs high risk of increasing the number of wrongful arrests – crime prevention presents a much less easily measurable and visible objective. The mechanical applications of performance measures may bring about similar unintended consequences in schools and hospitals.

The difficulties in defining performance and problems of measuring output both lead to difficulties in ensuring that appraisal measures do not produce undesirable outcomes, with targets and objectives pursued as ends in themselves: efficiency and short-term economising taking the place of effectiveness, and broader questions of purpose are neglected. As Garland (1987) notes, Bentham had an inadequate awareness of the degree of opacity and resistance panoptic principles might provoke. The unexpected or unintended consequences of performance monitoring, as people either resist or apply to the letter the system of surveillance, was neglected. When taken to their logical conclusion, these systems may bear little relation to the experience of organisational life. The pattern of visibility which is created by such systems, especially when used in conjunction with organisational rewards, reorientates participants' view of organisational function and purpose. Superficial aspects of performance become manipulated, producing what are perceived to be the desired measures of efficiency. Management techniques become ends in themselves – the triumph of technique over purpose.

REVERSING THE GAZE

The argument to date has been that appraisal operates as a gaze alighting on certain facets of organisational activity, denying other aspects. Generally it operates in a panoptic effect directed by a central observation tower, working to create desired behaviour in employees, defining the labour process and organisational reality. What are the implications if, in doing so, the constitutive role of appraisal functions in a manner which is ultimately detrimental to organisational effectiveness? How may this be countered? How may the organisation be reconstituted?

One mechanism which some organisations have experimented with is that of subordinate appraisal, where appraisal is conducted by subordinates on their superiors. It operates so as to reverse the effects of the gaze. Directed by those lower in the organisation, the gaze is not directed 'down' the organisation, but is reversed, looking 'up' to alight on the immediate managerial or supervisory tier. With the introduction of subordinate appraisal there is the potential for the organisation to be reconstituted.

Its introduction has been prompted by several considerations. For many organisations it represents the natural extension of employee commitment and involvement models of managing, concepts of teamwork demanding performance evaluations which are conducted in both directions. Here, however, it is generally seen as a supplement rather than a replacement of traditional appraisal methods. Other organisations, particularly where customer service is important, are beginning to recognise that employee opinion is of increasing importance, as the question for the future becomes: how is the manager able to help subordinates achieve better work performance? From such a perspective, subordinate appraisals become an essential component of evaluating managers' performance. They have been identified as an essential prerequisite of competitive survival and are seen as consistent with leadership models of the future. As a system of appraisal it also allows for those who are doing a task to define its dimensions, identify what is involved and what may facilitate task implementation rather than have these imposed by a higher authority.

Subordinate appraisal is justified on the grounds that it allows for improvement in the use of human resources, and provides a basis for personnel actions. There is an acknowledgement, however, that what constitutes 'effective' management or supervision is not really known, and that only by the gaze being directed at the issue from the subordinate position will the means of diagnosing management problems and improving performance become feasible. Although couched in terms of enhanced ability to observe and measure various job facets, in effect, what is happening is that dimensions of effective management become added to. Subordinates, often able to provide unique, that is, previously unknown or unacknowledged dimensions of management performance, are in a better position to evaluate dimensions which might be omitted from other sources of assessment. Multiple gazes, as several subordinates highlight aspects of one manager's performance, are able to discover more and different dimensions of managerial effectiveness than just one gaze.

Subordinate gazes, however, tend to be restricted, directed by the use of structured questionnaires. Questions focus on managerial style and attitudes: behaviour under stress, ability to provide feedback, the conduct of meetings, accessibility and being open to employee suggestions, communication, using recognition and praise, and maintaining work standards (Levinson 1987). Sometimes criteria identify issues which may be of direct relevance for organisational effectiveness, as for example, whether managers provide a climate conducive to innovation. Non-directed prompting highlights other aspects of desired management performance, including listening to and taking subordinate concerns seriously and acting upon them (Carew 1989). It can be seen that employee criteria of managerial effectiveness may deviate radically from senior management/organisational definitions of the same qualities. These 'new' dimensions are then incorporated into decisions affecting managerial merit pay, promotions and transfers, again serving to reconstitute what is defined as important by the organisation, and what is recognised as such by its participants.

The direction of the gaze is often obscured in the process of its implementation. '*De luxe*' versions of subordinate appraisals suggest that interviews with subordinates are conducted through the offices of an intermediary a consultant, who then integrates comments into a general statement. Another, less expensive, aspect of their administration is that subordinates remain anonymous when giving their appraisals – often justified in terms of their fear of reprisals (McEvoy 1988; Balzo *et al.* 1989; Kiechel 1989). This anonymous surveillance, however, only increases the panoptic effect on managers. When used in organisations having minimal communications their introduction has only served to feed paranoia (Kiechel 1989).

Managerial resistance is the greatest barrier to the implementation of subordinate appraisals, with reports of shock or disbelief at negative feedback (Nelson-Horchler 1988). Many managers and supervisors do not normally receive such views for a variety of reasons: the illusion that they already know how they are perceived; isolation; a domineering or abrasive demeanour which implies a negative approach to criticism; their being in positions of power and the inherent hierarchical assumptions of management. Employee response, however, is generally positive, given the opportunity to break out of the alienation of lack of confidence and support represented by bureaucratic managerial controls. The reconstitutive role of appraisal is compromised, however, as subordinate appraisal is used in conjunction with other methods – the gaze is multiplied rather than redirected, being used by senior management to increase their gaze on subordinates. It does, however, provide some opportunity for the potentially adverse consequences of appraisal to be modified.

CONCLUSION

Appraisal constitutes one system in a plethora of information processing procedures for social and economic calculation, one which is increasingly featured in organisations desirous of introducing effective management control and information systems. The danger lies, however, in its constitutive and mobilising role being overlooked or denied and its being perceived solely as a technical exercise, a value-free aid for organisational decision-making. What has been presented here is not appraisal as a technical exercise, reflecting organisational 'reality' but operating as an incidence of the gaze and, as such, serving to create or constitute perceptions of the organisation in which it operates. Like accounting, it is involved in the construction of ways of seeing (Hines 1988). The data which emerge are not pre-given or external to the process which accesses them, but are constructed in that process. It helps create particular patterns of organisational visibility and articulate forms of management structure and in doing so helps to constitute the organisation. As such the appraisal process has implications for the subjective experience of the individual as an object of knowledge, the operation of management, and the degree of control exercised over the labour process. Rather than being a passive instrument of technical administration revealing organisational functioning appraisal is implicated in the creation of a specific organisational order. It facilitates the exercise of particular conceptions of power and becomes implicated in the construction of prevailing conceptions of organisation. Appraisal under this purview is embedded in the organisational fabric, both reflective and creative.

Necessarily, therefore, appraisal is also implicated in the process of change. Patterns of visibility affect changes – the organisation becomes 'mobilised in the name of what is known of it' (Hopwood 1987: 224). Aspects of the organisation which are rendered visible influence organisational processes and actions, becoming used to guide future decisions. Particular patterns of visibility may, therefore, preclude other ways of viewing the organisation. The demands of a changing economic climate require that patterns of visibility in organisations be examined more closely to see what is highlighted, what excluded, and what the consequences of these practices are. By changing these patterns, how they reflect on and articulate the nature of employee behaviour, managerial roles and the labour process, appraisal can function so as to influence and eventually change the nature of the organisation.

REFERENCES

Balzo, D., Joseph, M. and Miller, A. (1989) 'A new organisational flight pattern', *Training and Development Journal*, March, 40–4.
Bernadin, J. and Beatty, R. (1987) 'Can subordinate appraisals enhance managerial productivity?', *Sloan Management Review*, Summer, 63–73.
Boland, R. (1987) 'Discussion of "Accounting and the construction of the governable person"', *Accounting Organisations and Society* 12 (3), 267–72.
Boland, R. and Pondy, L. (1983) 'Accounting in organisations: a union of natural and rational perspectives', *Accounting Organisations and Society* 221–35.
Buchanan, D. A. (1986) 'Management objectives in technical change', in D. Knights and H. Willmott (eds) *Managing the Labour Process*, Aldershot, Gower.
Bureau of National Affairs (1974) 'Survey no. 104', *Management Performance Appraisal Programme*. Washington, DC, Bureau of National Affairs.
Carew, J. (1989) 'When salespeople evaluate their manager', *Sales and Marketing Management*, March, 24–7.
Earl, M. (1983) 'Accounting and management', in M. Earl (ed.) *Perspectives on Management: A Multidisciplinary Analysis*, Oxford, OUP.

Foucault, M. (1971) *Madness and Civilisation*, London, Tavistock.

Foucault, M. (1972) *The Order of Things*, London, Tavistock.

Foucault, M. (1973) *The Birth of the Clinic*, London, Tavistock.

Foucault, M. (1977) *Discipline and Punish*, London, Penguin.

Fox, S. (1989) 'The Panopticon: from Bentham's obsession to the revolution in management learning', *Human Relations* 42 (8), 717–39.

Garland, D. (1987) 'Foucault's *Discipline and Punish*: An exposition and critique', *American Bar Foundation Research Journal* 4, 847–80.

Gordon, C. (1980) *Power/Knowledge: Selected Interviews and Other Writings by Michel Foucault*, New York, Pantheon Books.

Gowler, D. and Legge, K. (1983) 'The meaning of management and the management of meaning: a view from social anthropology' in M. Earl (ed.) *Perspectives on Management: A Multidisciplinary Analysis* Oxford, OUP.

Hines, R. (1988) 'Financial accounting: In communicating reality, we construct reality', *Accounting, Organisations and Society* 13, 251–61.

Hopwood, A. (1987) 'The archeology of accounting systems', *Accounting Organisations and Society* 16, 220–44.

Jackson, P. (1988) 'The management of performance in the public sector', *Public Money and Management*, Winter, 11–15.

Jay, M. (1986) 'In the empire of the gaze: Foucault, and the denigration of vision in twentieth century French thought' in D. Hoy (ed.) *Foucault: A Critical Reader*, Oxford, Blackwell.

Kiechel, W. (1989) 'When subordinates evaluate the boss', *Fortune*, June, 201–2.

Lazer, R. and Wikstrom, W. (1977) *Appraising Management Performance: Current Practices and Future Directions*, Washington, DC, The Conference Board.

Levinson, H. (1987) 'How they rate the boss', *Across the Board*, June, 53–7.

Long, P. (1986) *Performance Appraisal Revisited*, London, IPM.

McEvoy, G. (1988) 'Evaluating the boss', *Personnel Administrator*, September, 115–20.

Miller, P. (1987) *Power and Domination*, London, Routledge & Kegan Paul.

Miller, P. and Rose. N. (1990) 'Governing economic life', *Economy and Society* 19, 1–31.

Morgan, G. (1980) 'Paradigms, metaphors and puzzle solving in organisational theory', *Administrative Science Quarterly* 25, 605–22.

Morgan, G. and Smirchich, L. (1980) 'The case for qualitative research', *Academy of Management Review* 5, 491–500.

Nelson-Horchler, J. (1988) 'Performance appraisals', *Industry Week*, September, 61–3.

Offe, C. (1976) *Industry and Inequality*, London, Edward Arnold.

Pinder, C. and Bourgeois, V. (1982) 'Controlling tropes in administrative science', *Administrative Science Quarterly* 27, 641–52.

Pym, D. (1973) 'The politics and ritual of appraisals', *Occupational Psychology* 47, 231–5.

Randell, G. (1973) 'Performance appraisal: purposes, practices and conflicts', *Occupational Psychology* 47, 221–4.

Townley, B. (1989) 'Selection and appraisal: reconstituting "social relations?"' in J. Storey (ed.) *New Perspectives in Human Resource Management*, London, Routledge & Kegan Paul.

Zuboff, S. (1988) *In the age of the Smart Machine: The Future of Work and Power*, New York, Basic Books.

11 Different gender – different rules

Assessment of women in management

*Beverly Alimo-Metcalfe

With the approaching dramatic decline in the number of skilled young people in the workforce, large organisations in Europe are taking urgent steps to recruit more women, and to develop the largely untapped reservoir of potential among their female staff. Recent research in Britain conducted by the Henley Centre for Forecasting (Stewart 1989) predicts that by the year 2000, half the workforce will be female and three-quarters of new jobs created in the 1990s will be filled by women. The question that begs to be asked is, which jobs will they fill? Stewart (*op. cit.*) predicts that the proportion of women in full-time professional occupations or senior management will increase from its present 5 per cent (though in 1986 the Institute of Directors reported that in the last decade there was a *decrease* of women in management from 9.7 per cent to 6.2 per cent (*The Sunday Times* 1986). The figures across Western Europe may be more depressing if little has changed since 1982, when a survey conducted by the Management Centre Europe found that of 420 companies in nine Western European countries, fewer than half (49 per cent) had ever employed a female manager. Worse still, of the remaining 51 per cent, 15 per cent stated that they would never promote a woman into management.

Those concerned with women's career development, and who fear that the increasing female workforce will be used largely to fill the gaps in low level positions, warn that true equality of opportunity for women will only be possible if organisations are persuaded to review their personnel procedures, socialisation processes and culture, which currently operate in the main to the detriment of women, to prevent tokenism and merely temporary access.

This chapter identifies some of the factors that have contributed to

---

* Formerly Beverly Alban Metcalfe

the current situation in which female employees are either covertly or overtly impeded in their career development, with the result that their numbers tend to be greater in lower level or lower status jobs, and conspicuously small in high level or high status positions. It will include references to the literature on organisational socialisation processes, and assessment techniques in particular, and relate these to the possible dangers of current assessment practices in organisations, and offer warnings for the future.

ORGANISATIONAL SOCIALISATION

Organisational socialisation is the process by which individuals are inducted in the norms, values, standards and procedures of the organisational culture. It takes place as a result of the individual crossing a variety of boundaries. In order to achieve a senior management position in an organisation one has to make several boundary passages, each of which is marked by some process of assessment. These include the assessment procedure for initial selection into the organisation and the subsequent assessment practices, formal and informal, located in specific events and ongoing, and they are the subject of this chapter. They are viewed from the perspective of research on gender in organisational socialisation.

Acker and Van Houten as long ago as 1974 maintained that gender differences in organisational participation are related to:

1 differential recruitment of women into jobs requiring dependence and passivity;
2 selective recruitment of particularly compliant women into these jobs; and
3 control mechanisms for women used in organisations which reinforce control mechanisms to which they are subjected to in other areas of society (Acher and Van Houten 1974: 161).

Despite the passage of time and the introduction of equal opportunities legislation, there is little evidence that any real progress has been made at either the organisational or individual level, to lead women to expect to be able to receive equitable treatment to that of male colleagues. Moreover, there may be signs that discrimination may be becoming subtler and less amenable to initial scrutiny.

However, there are hopeful signs that change might be around the corner, at least in Europe. Herriot (1989) identifies three major factors that will directly influence the practice of assessment in organisations in member states of the European Community. These are: (1) the enactment of stricter employment legislation with respect to discrimination; (2) greater concern for safeguards to protect individuals' privacy and their rights of access and ownership of data produced in assessment procedures; and (3) the implications of increased labour mobility across national boundaries.

Given the increased competition for highly educated and skilled individuals, organisations are greatly concerned with the need to attract and retain such people, and in particular those with potential for the most senior positions. As a consequence, interest in techniques for assessing potential has grown dramatically in Europe, as witnessed by the plethora of texts published in the last five or so years, and accelerated by the British government's own involvement in the field through its Management Competences initiatives (Training Agency 1988). Interest in the assessment centre method in particular, has also been marked, evidenced by the instigation in 1987 of the first *European Congress on the Assessment Centre Method*, which in November 1990 included contributions from Eastern Europe.

ASSESSMENT OF POTENTIAL

The assessment of potential is a particularly complex and often controversial procedure. Since by definition it is concerned with prediction, it inevitably involves risk taking, and to those unfamiliar with the complex technicalities and processes involved, there exists a range of potential pitfalls.

The three major aspects of assessment that should be scrutinised to ensure that there is no gender bias in any procedure are, (1) the criteria or dimensions on which assessments are based; (2) the techniques or predictors chosen as methods of assessment; and (3) the judges or assessors who make the final decisions with respect to the suitability of candidates undergoing the processes.

The first boundary passage at which the individual is assessed is, of course, selection into the organisation. There exists a wealth of data on the practice of discrimination against women for posts which are typically male-gender stereotyped. Examples abound for preference for male candidates over equally well-qualified females in academic, managerial, scientific, and semi-skilled positions, (e.g. Rosen and Jerdee 1974; Haefner 1977; Gutek and Stevens 1979; McKenna and Johnson 1981).

Despite its renowned reputation for poor reliability and validity the selection interview remains the most commonly used procedure in most organisations (Robertson and Makin 1986). Suitability for a job depends very largely on the selector's stereotype of the 'ideal' candidate, amongst other things. By employing a selection procedure which is so vulnerable to the influence of subjective opinion with respect to appearance, interpersonal perception and social judgements, it is far from surprising that the selection interview has been found to be biased against females applying for 'out-of-role' jobs (e.g. engineering, computing, management, etc.). Type of dress, that is 'masculine' as opposed to 'feminine', has been shown to affect one's chances of 'success', and even the wearing of lipstick was found to influence the judgements that male assessors made of female candidates. Whilst the effects of perceived attractiveness might increase the chances of acceptance of male candidates for managerial jobs, it has been found to jeopardise the chances of females (Iles and Robertson 1988), and it is worth remembering that it is frequently males who occupy powerful gatekeeping positions to entry to organisations (Stewart 1978: 336).

Some organisations recognise the problems endemic to the social process of the selection interview and have introduced more standardised procedures for gathering information for their selection decisions. The use of biodata – that is information from a candidate's past career, including academic qualifications and positions of responsibility – is becoming increasingly popular in Britain (Robertson and Makin 1986). Whilst one might be inclined to welcome this initiative as a means of reducing the effects of bias there is a danger that unintentional hidden bias is overlooked. Scoring individual's previous achievements and responsibilities as in the case of biodata, might inadvertently prejudice women, who as a result of historical factors and current pervasive societal expectations of parenting, have followed paths other than 'the golden pathway'. Davies and Rosser (1986) described the golden pathway as the yellow brick road that leads towards a successful senior management position. Their particular study referred to the British NHS which is one of the largest employers of females in the country. To remain on it, mobility is essential, with the optimum length of time in one post being around two years. The years before the thirty year milestone are particularly crucial and the acquisition of additional professional educational qualifications very important. Stepping off the pathway seriously jeopardises one's chances of being seen as a potential senior manager. For women the obvious obstacles are domestic commitments and the expectation of having to move to accommodate a male partner's career development.

There is little evidence to suggest that attitudes in the 1980s have changed significantly. Gutek and Larwood (1987) starkly state that textbook models of careers ignore the most important factors influencing women's careers. Gilligan (1982) says it all in the title to her paper 'Adult development and women's development: Arrangements for a marriage'. Not only is the combination of being married and holding a demanding career viewed as providing no conflict for a man, it is frequently regarded as an asset suggesting stability and a sense of responsibility (Bryson *et al.* 1978; Bronstein *et al.* 1987), whereas for women it is frequently seen as a liability (Laws 1979; Valdez and Gutek 1987).

Standardised psychological tests are becoming increasingly used by organisations in Britain (Robertson and Makin 1986). Whilst one might welcome this initiative as another way of eliminating potential bias, we need to be particularly wary that it does not in fact hide a more deeply rooted and hence less easily challenged prejudice. Gender bias may be due to the construct and content validity of the instrument as a result of the composition of the original sample on which the dimensions were derived, and the norms on which the interpretations are based (Mottram 1987; Rose and Rose 1979; Webb 1987).

The most recent popular advance in assessment technique is the assessment centre methodology (Thornton and Byham 1982). Although its origin dates back to the 1940s (Moses and Byham 1982; Thornton and Byham, 1982), its growth in usage is a relatively recent phenomenon (Robertson and Makin 1986 *op.cit.*). One again needs to be wary of potential problems for women's career development.

The assessment centre covers all stages of the assessment process from the identification of criteria for success in a job, through the design of exercises and simulations and the selection of standardised tests, and the subsequent assessment by trained observers of candidates who perform the tasks. The final stage is the production of a feedback report to each candidate of her/his performance. The assessment centre is probably regarded as the most advanced and sophisticated assessment method and is increasingly adopted by organisations for recruitment, selection, promotion, and the identification of individual development needs. As a relatively expensive methodology its use is usually restricted to graduate entrants into management jobs and fast-track career development programmes, and for spotting talented individuals to be groomed for senior management positions. It therefore provides entry into the most senior positions in the organisation and identifies the cadre of most talented staff. A recent study evaluating the use of assessment centres in a large public sector organisation (Alban Metcalfe 1989b) identified some potential concerns. Some of these have implications for women's career development.

The first stage of assessment centre design is the identification of criteria for job success and is typically undertaken by gathering data from existing job encumbents and their bosses, using most commonly the repertory grid (Kelly 1955) and the critical incident interview (Flanagan 1954). Standardised job analysis questionnaires might also be employed. The issue for those concerned with women's career development is that the sample from whom the criteria are identified tend to be solely or at least predominantly male since they are considerably more likely to occupy senior organisational positions. There is an obvious potential bias that people will reflect the espoused views of the characteristics of successful managers and these are undoubtedly gender-based. For example, Broverman *et al.* (1975) and O'Leary's (1974) studies of the opinions managers hold of the characteristics of successful managers concluded that traits identified, such as emotional stability, aggression, leadership ability, self-reliance, lack of uncertainty, vigour, desiring responsibility, objectivity, etc. are more characteristically associated with men than with women. V. E. Schein's early studies (1973, 1975) showed that these beliefs were held equally strongly by female and male managers. A recent repeat study (Schein 1989) of the attitudes of US female and male managers showed that whilst women's attitudes have changed, the males' had not. To ascertain whether attitudes had changed over time and to assess how widespread these changes may be Schein conducted a cross-cultural study (Schein and Mueller 1990) of female and male business students in the UK, US and Germany. She and her co-auther found that whilst for the male students there was a large and significant resemblance between the ratings of men and managers, a near zero or insignificant resemblance was obtained for ratings of women and managers. It would appear, therefore, that nothing has changed with respect to men's attitudes. Amongst the females in the British and German sample, there was a significant resemblance between their ratings of women and managers, however, it was significantly less strong than the coefficient between men and managers. So women also perceived characteristics of managers to be those more closely ascribed to men than women. Only the US females obtained equally strong coefficients between ratings of men and managers and women and managers. Given that such students were likely to become the senior managers of the future the data are particularly worrying, since not only then is there the danger of inherent gender bias as a result of the composition of the sample, but also because of the societal stereotypes of characteristics of successful managers that still appear to be all pervasive. Schein describes this as 'think manager, think male' (Schein 1989: 12). However, whilst this may appear on the surface to be somewhat depressing, there can be an alternative interpretation. It may well be that Schein's data are in fact 'covering' the fact that European women see different characteristics as important for management and that they not only do not see a similarity in female characteristics and pervasive characteristics of male-dominated management, but that they want to offer an alternative. More research needs to be conducted around this question, and in fact the author is currently engaged in such an investigation.

That new and different constructs of managerial effectiveness, which may in fact be more characteristic of females, are emerging may be reflected in some recent studies. John Kotter (1982), for example, conducted a detailed analysis of what twenty general managers actually did in their jobs, i.e. how they spent their time. He compared the data he obtained with the textbook or 'popular view'.

The data substantiated previous findings of Mintzberg in the USA (1975) and Stewart in the UK (1979) that managers' work is largely reactive rather than pro-active, and that it is characterised by variety, fragmentation and frequent interruptions. The data emphasise the fact that successful managers spend time establishing informal networks inside the organisation, creating and being involved in many cooperative relationships with people inside the organisation and in the business; and that they asked questions more frequently than they issued instructions. Peters and Waterman (1982) stressed the 'walk around style of management'. One suspects that few, if any, of these characteristics can be assessed in an assessment centre. How exactly these points relate to potential gender bias is unclear but what might be concluded is that: (1) assessment centre criteria appear to achieve face validity, but that could be due to their close resemblance to textbook definitions of management; (2) despite well-established studies of management work (Mintzberg, Stewart, Kotter) which emphasised frenetic, disjointed activity, the emphasis on using informal methods of disseminating and collecting information, and an increasing realisation of the paramount importance of people skill, these are difficult to simulate in the typical assessment centre format. Yet certainly the latter characteristics, namely 'a concern for people' has characterised a quality commonly attributed to women.

A recent paper (Granleese and Murray 1990), re-examining an earlier US study of female and male managers' decision style (Boulgarides 1984), concluded that the female managers scored significantly higher on the behavioural decision style, which incorporated traits such as 'supportive, empathy, warmth'. A British study (Vinnicombe 1987) provides similar evidence.

Bias in assessors' ratings of candidates has been investigated in several studies but results have been equivocal (Arvey 1979; Landy and Farr 1980; Nieva and Gutek 1980). Recent studies (Mobey 1982; Wexley and Pulakos 1982; Peters *et al.* 1984) which have examined a possible interaction effect between the sex of the rater and the sex of the ratee found no evidence for such an effect, although this might be due to the explicit investigative nature of the research. Walsh *et al.* (1987) in fact found a significant interaction effect between the sex composition of the assessor group and the assessees' sex, which favoured females over males when the assessor group was male. The researchers offer several possible interpretations of the results, namely that the females were accurately evaluated, or that the all-male group may have been over-lenient in their evaluation. These latter conclusions are similar to those drawn by Abramson *et al.* (1977), who found that when women were perceived as having achieved unexpected success (in traditional male occupations), their achievement was magnified. Abramson *et al.* (1977) refers to this as 'the talking platypus phenomenon', adding 'it matters little what the platypus says, the wonder is that it can say anything at all'. One wonders whether such findings would be obtained in British organisations. This is not simply a cynical view of the research but the question is posed because considerable research evidence exists which suggests that gender affects the evaluation of behaviour (Nieva and Gutek 1980 for a review; Thomas 1987). Anecdotal evidence which emerged from a recent research study in which the author was involved (Alban Metcalfe 1989b) included feedback from assessors. Some of the assessors stated that on occasions at assessor conferences, reference was made to the personal appearance and personality characteristics of female candidates, despite the fact that they were not included in the assessment centre criteria. Is this common place? Unfortunately, there appears to be no research on the subject. Until such data are collected one can only urge great care with respect to ensuring: (a) that at the stage of criteria identification as many females as male job encumbents and bosses are included in the sampling population; (b) that criteria are scrutinised as to whether they merely reflect 'espoused' theories of management or what managers *actually* do;

(c) that the assessor panel is composed of female and male assessors in equal proportions; (d) that assessor training promotes rigorous guidelines as to non-sexist assessment language to be adopted in the assessor conference; and (e) that groups of candidates include equal proportions of females and males.

This last point is an important one not to be overlooked, because there is substantial evidence from the study of group dynamics that being a minority member of a group imposes pressures on the individual which inhibit her/his potential contribution (Rosenberg *et al.* 1955). Eskilson and Wiley (1976) found in an experimental situation that the sex ratio (i.e. proportion of females to males, or vice versa) of problem-solving groups significantly affects the rate of leadership activity performed by males and females. Female and male leaders exhibited similar and high rates of leadership when in groups comprised exclusively of members of their own sex. However, female leadership activity dropped drastically in male-dominant groups even in those cases where the female was the formal leader of the group.

A recent field study which attempted to directly test Kanter's theory that being in a numerical minority in an unbalanced sex-ratio group (i.e. unequal numbers of females and males) would inhibit performance in a group (Finigan 1982), found that the results confirmed the hypothesis for three sex-ratio situations: male-dominant groups, female-dominant groups, and those in which there were equal numbers of both sexes. However, underachievement was particularly pronounced for females in male-dominant groups. The reasons suggested for this state might be due to what has been called the 'feminine modesty' effect identified by Gould and Stone (1982). Finigan (1982) offers three possible reasons why individuals in a minority group appeared to be inhibited from contributing to group discussion:

1 Members of the majority sex may inhibit contributions of the token by restricting opportunities for input. Males tend to ask fewer, and only specific kinds of questions of females. Also they most frequently asked women for information rather than opinions. Consequently, the majority sex may be seen to direct the nature of the minority response.
2 A second source of inhibition might stem from the minority's perception of the illegitimacy of their contribution; thus, feeling that they are 'outside' may result in self-imposed inhibitions by the females. An extension of the 'modesty effect' (Gould and Stone 1982) may also be exacerbating the situation.

3 Inhibition may be due to cultural gender role norms. This relates to the experiences of females in male-dominant groups of not being valued for their contributions as highly as the male members.

Male members of female-dominant groups contributed actively to the leadership roles in the group and their contributions were valued as highly as those of females members. Finigan interprets this as being due to the high status attributed to males overcoming any stigma associated with being a minority member. This is virtually the same explanation as that put forward by Fairhurst and Snavely (1980, 1981, 1983) in which males did not appear to suffer from token dynamics when in a position of minority membership, by virtue of their higher societal status.

If there is such support for the influence of group dynamics on females' performance then how are we to create conditions of equal proportions of females and males in assessment centre exercises, when assessors and candidates for senior management assessment centres are still highly likely to be predominantly male?

JOB PLACEMENT

Once selected, the issue of initial job placement can determine the pace of progression and the explicit expectations that the organisation has of the individual's career path. These in turn will determine to a large extent the opportunities afforded to the individual to enhance their career development. There is substantial evidence of inequality with respect to the treatment of females at the point of entry and at later stages of career development for a wide range of occupations (e.g. Terborg and Ilgen 1975; Ashridge 1980; Hunt 1981; Corby 1982, 1983; Spencer and Podmore 1987).

PERCEPTIONS OF MOTIVATORS FOR WOMEN AND MEN

Clearly, beliefs as to what motivates people at work affect the opportunities and encouragement offered to individuals. Anecdotal and more objectively gathered research evidence of personal characteristics, including attitudinal data, have concluded that 'the professional literature is replete with theoretical examples explaining women's 'lesser work commitment'. Women are assumed to be less assertive, less ambitious, and less career orientated than men (Kaufman and Fetters 1980: 251). Motivation is a significant determinant of performance, and the expectations significant others have of employees will affect what career development opportunities they are offered, irrespective of whether they are accurate or not. A study of nearly 800 female and 1500 male managers and professionals in Britain concerned with career development issues sought data on what they believed to be important in a job (Alban Metcalfe and Nicholson 1984). The seventeen items of the attitudes to work scale were derived from existing literature on motivation and hence based substantially on male populations; however, the results obtained challenged widely held myths as to the differences in motivators for females and males. In brief, taking the sample as a whole, the top five motivators for women were identical to the top five for men and whilst not identical in relative ordering, the females obtained significantly higher mean scores than did the males (controlling for age). These were a desire for: 'challenge', 'an opportunity to improve knowledge and skills', 'being appreciated', 'good quality senior management', and 'autonomy'.

The belief that senior managers, who are predominantly male, appear to hold in regard to what women want in a job would seem to directly contradict these data. Doubtless these attitudes will affect the opportunities offered to women with respect to career development and promotion.

APPRAISAL

Organisations' appraisal systems vary considerably; nonetheless, irrespective of whether they are primarily evaluative or developmental, since they are concerned with reviewing performance they contain an element of assessment. They are also considered to be an important method for ensuring the creation of personal development plans and ensuring that they are monitored (e.g. Fletcher and Williams 1985). Research by Corby (1982) highlighted the different quality of appraisals for women and men in the British Civil Service. Whilst the men, generally speaking, received critical feedback, the women were far more likely to receive innocuous non-specific criticism if indeed they received any. This suggested the discomfort male bosses felt in relation to female subordinates. Since the quality of information exchanged in the appraisal was crucial for development purposes, and indeed is used either intentionally or unintentionally for the purposes of making recommendations for promotion, it is a procedure not to be overlooked when investigating organisational procedures in women's career development. Corby's (1982) study of promotion in the Civil Service drew attention to the relationship between such practices and her findings that women were far less likely to be identified and placed in highly visible mainstream general management positions. A recent survey of appraisal in the British NHS found significant differences with aspect to gender. Women found the discussion more difficult and were rated significantly lower than men (Alimo-Metcalfe 1991).

A study by Thomas (1987) of anonymous narrative accounts of appraisals of the job performance of female and male US naval officers investigated whether gender influences judgements of the job behaviour of individuals. Her results demonstrated that different words were used to evaluate the performance of female and male line officers. The differences were with respect to both the content of the evaluations and also the accuracy of information imparted, and suggested among other things that women were 'less competent, logical, and mature', and their performance appeared to 'warrant fewer recommendations and only nebulous praise'. She concludes:

> This research focused on women in a single organization, but there are implications for all women who compete with men in the professions, particularly those dominated by men. Schein (1978) identified several probable consequences of stereotyping on women's careers in management. First, if women are viewed as being more sensitive to the needs of others than are men, they are likely to be placed in staff versus line positions. As a result, they are less likely to acquire the skills and knowledge of the upwardly mobile. Second, if supervisors feel they lack the traits valued among managers and leaders (i.e., ambition, competitiveness, aggressiveness), women will be denied developmental tasks and their promotional potential will suffer. Third, women will be excluded from the organizational power network and thus be limited in their ability to function as effective managers.
>
> (Thomas 1987: 107)

CAREER PATHS AND PROMOTION

There have been several studies comparing female and male upward mobility (Corby 1982; Di Prete and Soule 1988; Cannings 1988) and salary (Strober 1982; Olson and Frieze 1985; Dixon and Shaw 1986), most of which conclude that differences clearly exist. A recent study (Cox and Harquail 1990) following the career paths and career success in the early career stage of male and female MBA graduates in the US, perhaps unsurprisingly, found that the females experience lower levels of salary progression, and fewer management promotions, and achieve lower management positions than do comparable male managers, even when controlling for career path variables. The authors conclude that their findings

> support the notion of 'pacification by promotion', advanced by Flanders and Anderson (1973). They hypothesised that women are given promotions in order to create the appearance of increasing responsibility and opportunity, but that these promotions are essentially hollow. Non-managerial promotions do not move women into hierarchical positions of greater authority, leadership and responsibility.
>
> (Cox and Harquail 1990: 10)

CHANGES IN ORGANISATIONS – THE FUTURE

Modern organisational theorists such as Handy (1989) and Kanter (1989) maintain that large organisations will have to undergo metamorphosis to meet the considerable pace of change. They will become smaller, flatter and decentralised, relying on people working across functions in project teams, and they will require different styles of management where emphasis is on informal open communication. Managers will no longer be able to rely on the authority of status and position but will have to establish personal credibility by results, much of which will depend on their interpersonal and team-building skills. This is not simply a vision of the future, it is already a reality. Ashridge Management Centre and the Foundation for Management Education (Barnham *et.al.* 1988) undertook a survey of leading edge companies in Europe. Their findings paint a picture of managers as developers encouraging openness and trust in the workplace, encouraging informal communication and adopting a participative style. Chief executives need to be visionaries encouraging change and challenge to the status quo, transforming cultures where past emphasis has been on 'doing' to 'being' values such as cooperation, belonging, caring and receptivity. Few would not acknowledge that these were qualities more closely associated with women than men and indeed this has been found to be the case in a British study (Vinnicombe 1987). It remains to be seen whether women will be encouraged to offer such resources to the organisations that desperately need them.

CONCLUSION

In conclusion, this chapter has intended, at a time of apparent growth of opportunities for women, to draw attention to some of the possible hidden obstacles to the realisation of their potential. It has drawn on examples of research relating to assessment and other human resource management procedures such as job placement and appraisal, and linked these findings with data from the wider field of managerial attitudes. There is little evidence that despite more than a decade of equal opportunities legislation significant barriers to women's career development have been removed. Moreover, concern is expressed that even at a time of considerable opportunity for women, given the well-recognised skills shortage in the economy, unless organisations – which ultimately implies male senior managers in the main – are prepared to scrutinise established attitudes and practices which operate to a large extent against women's progress, little will change.

Perhaps more disturbingly, it suggests that with increased enthusiasm in organisations for more rigorous assessment techniques, with little or no attention paid to potential bias against women, less obvious sources of discrimination may become deeply entrenched and consequently go unnoticed and unchallenged.

Finally, it tentatively proposes that women may bring new qualities of effectiveness to management which may both enrich organisational life and provide crucially important resources to deal with the dramatic demands of the future.

REFERENCES

Abramson, P. R., Goldberg, P. A., Greenberg, J. H. and Abramson, L. M. (1977) 'The talking platypus phenomenon: Competency ratings as a function of sex and professional status', *Psychology of Women-Quarterly* 2(2), 114–24.

Acker, J. and Van Houten, D. R. (1974) 'Differential recruitment and control: the sex structuring of organisations', *Administrative Science Quarterly* 19, 152–63.

Alban Metcalfe, B. (1989a) 'What motivates managers: An investigation by gender & sector of employment', *Public Administration* 67, Spring, 95–108.

Alban Metcalfe, B. (1989b) *The Use of Assessment Centres in the NHS*, report published by the NHS Training Authority.

Alban Metcalfe, B. and Nicholson, N. (1984) *The Career Development of British Managers*, London, British Institute of Management Foundation.

Alimo-Metcalfe, B. (1991) Paper submitted to the Institute of Health Service's Management for a Report entitled *Individual Performance Review in the NHS*, London: IHSM.

Arvey, R. D. (1979) 'Unfair discrimination in the employment interview: Legal and psychological aspects', *Psychological Bulletin*, 86, 736–65.

Ashridge Study (1980) *Employee Potential: Issues in the Development of Women*, London, IPM, Ashridge Management College.

Barnham, K., Fraser, J. and Heath, L. (1988) *Management For the Future*, Ashridge Management Research Group and the Foundation for Management Education.

Boulgarides, J. D. (1984) 'A comparison of male and female business managers', *Leadership and Organisation Development Journal* 5(5), 27–31.

Bronstein, P., Black, L., Pfennig, J. L. and White, A. (1987) 'Stepping onto the academic career ladder: How are women doing?' in B. A. Gutek and L. Larwood (eds) *Women's Career Development*, London, Sage.

Broverman, I. K., Vogel, R., Broverman, D. M., Clarkson, F. E. and Rosenkrantz, P. S. (1975) 'Sex-role stereotypes: A current appraisal', in M. T. Schuch Mednick, S. S. Tangri and L. W. Hoffman (eds) *Women and Achievement: Social and Motivational Analyses*, New York, Hemisphere Publishing.

Bryson, R., Bryson, J. B. and Johnson, M. F. (1978) 'Family size, satisfaction, and productivity in dual-career couples', *Psychology of Women Quarterly* 3, 67–77.

Cannings, K. (1988) 'Managerial position: The effects of socialization, specialization, and gender', *Industrial and Labor Relations Review* 42, 77–88.

Corby, S. (1982) *Equal Opportunities for Women in the Civil Service*, London, HMSO.

Corby, S. (1983) 'Women in the civil Service: Looking back or held back?' *Personnel Management*, February, 28–31.

Cox, T. and Harquail, C. V. (1990) 'Career paths and career success in the early career stages of male and female MBAs', paper presented at the Academy of Management Conference, San Francisco, USA, 12–15 August.

Davies, C. and Rosser, J. (1986) *Processes of Discrimination: A Study of Women Working in the NHS*, London, DHSS.

Dixon, M. and Shaw, C. (1986) *Maximising Management Investment in the NHS*, London, Kings Fund.

Di Prete, T. A. and Soule, W. T. (1988) 'Gender and promotion in segmented job ladder systems', *American Sociological Review* 53, 26–40.

Eskilson, M. G. and Wiley, A. (1976) 'Sex composition and leadership in small groups', *Sociometry* 39, 183–94.

Fairhurst, G. T. and Snavely, B. K. (1980) 'The effects of numerical imbalance and gender on tokens: an examination of Kanters theory', paper presented at Annual Convention of the International Communication Association, Acapulco.

Fairhurst, G. T. and Snavely, B. K. (1981) 'An examination of the communication between high status tokens and their dominant colleagues: Kanter's theory re-examined', paper presented at the Annual Convention of the International Communication Association, Minneapolis.

Fairhurst, G., T. and Snavely, B. K. (1983) 'Majority and token minority group relationships: Power acquisition and communication', *Academy of Management Review* 8 (2), 292–300.

Finigan, M. (1982) 'The effects of token representation on participants in small decision-making groups', *Economic and Industrial Democracy* 3, 531–50.

Flanders, D. P. and Anderson, P. E. (1973) 'Sex discrimination in employment: Theory and practice', *Industrial and Labor Relations Review* 26, 938–55.

Flanagan, J. C. (1954) 'The critical incident technique', *Psychological Bulletin* 51, 327–58.

Fletcher, C. and Williams, R. (1985) *Performance Appraisal and Career Development*, London, Hutchinson.

Gilligan, C. (1982) 'Adult development and women's development: Arrangements for a marriage', in J. Giele (ed.) *Women in the Middle Years: Current Knowledge and Directions for Research and Policy*, New York, Wiley.

Gould, R. J. and Stone, C. G. (1982) 'The "Feminine Modesty" Effect: A self-presentational interpretation of sex differences in causal attribution', *Personality and Social Psychology Bulletin* 8 (3), 477–85.

Grandjean, B. D. (1981) 'History and career in a bureaucratic labor market', *American Journal of Sociology* 86, 1057–92.

Granleese, J. and Murray, M. (1990) 'Managerial decision styles: A behavioural gender difference', paper presented to Annual Occupational Psychological Conference, Bowness on Windermere, 3–5 January.

Gutek, B. A. and Larwood, L. (eds) (1987) *Women's Career Development*, London, Sage.

Gutek, B. A. and Stevens, D. A. (1979) 'Differential responses of males and females to work situations which evoke sex-role stereotypes', *Journal of Vocational Behavior* 14, 23–32.

Haefner, J. E. (1977) 'Sources of discrimination among employees: A survey investigation', *Journal of Applied Psychology* 62, 265–70.

Handy, C. (1989) *The Age of Unreason*, London, Century Hutchinson.

Herriot, P. (ed.) (1989) *Assessment and Selection in Organisations*, Chichester, John Wiley.

Hunt, A. (1981) *Women and Underachievement at Work*, EOC Research Bulletin No. 5 Spring.

Iles, P. A. and Robertson, I. T. (1988) 'Getting in, getting on, and looking good: Physical attractiveness, gender and selection decisions', *Guidance and Assessment Review* 4 (3), 6–8.

Kanter, R. M. (1989) *When Giants Learn to Dance*, London, Simon & Schuster.

Kaufman, D. and Fetters, M. (1980) 'Work motivation and job values among professional men and women: a new accounting', *Journal of Vocational Behaviour* 17, 251–62.

Kelly, G. A. (1955) *The Psychology of Personal Constructs*, vols I and II, New York, Norton.

Kotter, J. P. (1982) *The General Managers*, London, The Free Press.

Landy, F. J. and Farr, J. L. (1980) 'Performance rating', *Psychological Bulletin* 87, 72–107.

Laws, J. L. (1979) *The Second X: Sex Role and Social Role*, New York, Elsevier.

Lewin, A. Y. and Duchan, L. (1970) 'Women in academia; A study of the hiring decision in departments of physical science', paper presented at the meeting of the American Association for the Advancement of Science, Chicago, December.

McKenna, D. J. and Johnson, D. A. (1981) 'Selection risk, sex-role stereotyping, and sex discrimination in employment decision', *Journal of Occupational Behaviour* 2, 223–8.

Mintzberg, H. (1975) *The Nature of Managerial Work*, New York, Harper & Row.

Mobey, W. H. (1982) 'Supervision and employee race and sex effects on performance appraisals: a field study of adverse impact and generalizability', *Academy of Management Journal* 25, 598–606.

Moses, J. L. and Byham, W. C. (eds) (1982) *Applying the Assessment Center Method*, Oxford, Pergamon Press.

Mottram, R. (1987) 'Problems for the test user in avoiding sex bias', *The Occupational Psychologist, Special issue: Gender Issues in Occupational Psychology* 3, 6–7.

Nieva, V. F. and Gutek, B. A. (1980) 'Sex effects on evaluation', *Academy of Management Review* 5 (2), 267–76.

O'Leary, V. E. (1974) 'Some attitudinal barriers to occupational aspirations in women', *Psychological Bulletin* 81, 809–26.

Olson, J. E. and Frieze, I. H. (1985) 'Women MBA's in accounting: Are they earning as much as men?', Working paper series WPNo.623, Pittsburgh, University of Pittsburgh, Graduate School of Business.

Peters, L. H., O'Connor, E. J., Weekley, J., Pooyan, A., Frank, B. and Erenkrantz, B. (1984), 'Sex bias and managerial evaluations: A replication and extension', *Journal of Applied Psychology* 69, 349–52.

Peters, T. and Waterman, R. H. (1982) *In Search of Excellence*, London, Harper & Row.

Robertson, I. and Makin, P. J. (1986) 'Management selection in Britain: A survey and critique', *Journal of Occupational Psychology* 59, (1), 45–58.

Rose, S. and Rose, H. (1979) *The Political Economy of Science*, Basingstoke, Macmillan.

Rosen, B. and Jerdee, T. H. (1974) 'Influence of sex-role stereotypes on personnel decisions', *Journal of Applied Psychology* 59, 9–14.

Rosenberg, S., Erlich, D. E. and Berkowitz, L. (1955) 'Some effects of varying combinations of group members on groups' performance measures and leadership behavior', *Journal of Abnormal and Social Psychology* 51, 195–213.

Schein, E. H. (1973) 'Personal change through interpersonal relationships', in W. C. T. Bennis, D. E. Berlew, E. H. Schein and F. I. Steel (eds) *Interpersonal Dynamics*, 3rd edn, Homewood, Illinois, Dorsey.

Schein, V. E. (1973) 'The relationship between sex-role stereotypes and requisite management characteristics', *Journal of Applied Psychology* 57 (2), 95–100.

Schein, V. E. (1975) 'Relationships between sex role stereotypes and requisite management characteristics among female managers', *Journal of Applied Psychology* 60 (3), 340–4.

Schein, V. E. (1978) 'Sex role stereotyping, ability and performance: Prior research and new directions', *Personnel Psychology* 31, 259–68.

Schein, V. E. (1989) 'Sex role stereotypes and requisite management characteristics past, present and future', paper presented at the Current Research on Women in Management. Conference, Queen's University, Ontario, Canada, 24–26 September.

Schein, V. E. and Mueller, R. (1990) 'Sex role stereotyping and requisite management characteristics: A cross cultural look, paper presented at the 22nd International Congress of Applied Psychology, Kyoto, Japan, 22–27 July.

Spencer, A. and Podmore, D. (eds) (1987) *In a Man's World*, London, Tavistock.

Stewart, F. (ed.) (1989) *Family Futures*. Report of the Henley Management Centre for Forecasting.

Stewart, J. (1978) 'Understanding women in organizations: Toward a re-construction of organizational theory', *Administrative Science Quarterly* 23, 336–50.

Stewart, R. (1979) *Managers and their Jobs*, London, Macmillan.

The Sunday Times (1986) 'New welcome for women', 29 January.

Terborg, J. R. and Ilgen, D. R. (1975) 'A theoretical approach to sex discrimination in traditionally masculine occupations', *Organisational Behaviour and Human Performance* 13, 352–76.

Thomas, P. J. (1987) 'Appraising the performance of women: Gender and the naval officer', in B. A. Gutek and L. Larwood (eds) *Women's Career Development*, London, Sage.

Thornton, G. C. and Byham, W. C. (1982) *Assessment Centers and Managerial Performance*, London, Academic Press.

Training Agency (1988) *Classifying the Components of Management Competence*, a report by the occupational standards branch of the Training Agency, September.

Valdez, R. L. and Gutek, B. A. (1987) 'Family roles: A help or a hindrance for working women?', in B. A. Gutek and L. Larwood (eds) *Women's Career Development*, London, Sage.

Vinnicombe, S. (1987) 'What exactly are the differences in male and female working styles?' *Women in Management Review* 3 (1), 13–21.

Walsh, J. P., Weinberg, R. M. and Fairfield, M. L. (1987) 'The effects of gender on assessment centre evaluations', *Journal of Occupational Psychology* 60, 305–9.

Webb, J. (1987) 'Gendering selection psychology', *The Occupational Psychologist, Special issue: Gender Issues in Occupational Psychology* 3, December, 4–5.

Wexley, K. N. and Pulakos, E. D. (1982) 'Sex effects on performance rating in manager-subordinate dyads: A field study', *Journal of Applied Psychology* 67, 433–9.

12 Knowledge is not enough

Developing the capacity for self-regulation in health and safety at work

Sandra Dawson

INTRODUCTION

Occupational safety is an area of concern for managers and politicians in the UK and also a subject of interest for those both in Brussels and in member states of the EC who are concerned with effectively completing the creation of a single European market. Each member country has its own distinct legislative and regulatory context for occupational safety (European Foundation 1988). These differences create enormous difficulties for direct comparisons but there is a common theme in that improvements in standards are assumed to follow at least to some extent from local initiatives or 'self-regulation' in the workplace.

This chapter concentrates on an analysis of the UK experience and in particular addresses the question of what, at workplace level, is required for effective self-regulation and what are its limits. The findings in relation to the UK will then be used to make some preliminary observations about the state of the task which any common European initiative would face.

THE SCALE OF THE PROBLEM IN THE UK

Recent major disasters, like Piper Alpha and Kings Cross, and less dramatic but nonetheless chilling reports of incidents associated with well-known installations, like the Sellafield Reprocessing Plant and the Channel Tunnel, arouse public interest. But such incidents are only the tip of the iceberg when compared with the trends revealed by a study of accident statistics. Problems in using accident statistics as a measure of safety performance are manifold (Dawson *et al.* 1988: 27–30). Particularly notable are the problems of achieving a common base line given changes in reporting requirements, and consequently one cannot make direct comparisons between the figures for 1973–80 and those for 1981–5 in the UK. However, a comparison between the trends revealed in each period is startling. In the period 1973–8 there was a 40 per cent decrease in the incidence of fatal accidents in construction and a 36 per cent decrease in the incidence of fatal accidents in manufacturing, whereas the period 1981–5 saw a 31 per cent increase in the combined rates of fatal and major accidents in manufacturing and a 45 per cent increase in construction. The rise in the same incidence rates for the same period for all industries is a less dramatic 8 per cent and there is a slight decrease in the fatal rate overall. However, these overall rates reflect national shifts in employment from manufacturing to service industries which generally present less hazardous working conditions. Thus in the UK in the late 1980s, it appears that instead of seriously injuring a decreasing proportion of our workforce the opposite is the case. (Dawson *et al.* 1988: 30–42).

THE UK LEGISLATIVE CONTEXT

The legislative framework for occupational safety and health in the UK is enshrined in the 1974 Health & Safety at Work Act (HASAWA) which in turn reflected the major conclusions of the Robens Committee of Inquiry which reported in 1972. The Act, in contrast to previous attempts to improve occupational safety and health, sought to establish a new approach by encouraging workplace and enterprise self-regulation within minimum statutory requirements. The legal obligation was firmly placed on employers, employees, suppliers and other people involved in the design, production and distribution of goods and services through work, to secure, 'as far as is reasonably practicable', the health, safety and welfare of themselves and other people at work. General requirements were supported by the specific requirement on employers in enterprises employing more than five people to produce a written safety policy, including information on the organisation and arrangements for its achievement. Additional specific requirements and suggestions are contained in Regulations (for example, covering the reporting of accidents, the appointment of safety representatives and the control of substances hazardous to health), Codes of Practice (for example, for reducing the exposure of employed persons to noise or working with asbestos) and Guidance Notes (for example, on storing liquid petroleum gas or transporting dangerous substances).

These Regulations, Codes of Practice and Guidance Notes are published by the Health and Safety Commission (HSC), the tri-partite quango with policy responsibility for occupational health and safety. The HSC is advised by the Health and Safety Executive (HSE), the national inspection and enforcement agency which has powers to enter and inspect workplaces, to serve improvement and prohibition notices and to prosecute. The relationship between national policy and enforcement agencies and local institutions of self-regulation is determined within a context in which the HSC and HSE share a preference, based on limited resources and long traditions, to work through education and advice and only to prosecute persistent or flagrant offenders (Dawson *et al.* 1988: 223–42).

A model of managing occupational safety in which employers, managers, employees and suppliers only have to do what the national agencies tell them to do or else risk punitive consequences, is inappropriate, for the UK and indeed for the rest of the EC. The number of visits by HSE and HSC agency inspectors declined from 481,000 in 1976, to 246,000 in 1985. The number of inspectors, having risen during the 1970s began to decline in 1979. The Robens Report recorded that inspectors went to factories on average once every four years (Robens 1972: 684–5). In 1982 it was reported that the average expectation of a visit was once every seven years (House of Commons 1982: 92) although any premises identified as posing a higher risk, or where serious or fatal accidents or dangerous occurrences had been reported could expect more frequent visits. The number of notices related to health and safety at work served by HSE and HSC agencies did not show much variation in the period 1980–5, but there has recently been an increase in notices with 9,480 being served in 1986–7 and 11,139 in 1987–8. This last figure reflects a major enforcement initiative with small construction sites (HSC 1988: 51, 86). The number of prosecutions has declined somewhat since a peak of 1,671 in 1978 to 1,265 in 1985.

Given this inspection and enforcement regime, it is likely that many who are less effective in managing their occupational safety will never be identified, and even if identified, are unlikely to be the subject of formal proceedings. Should flagrant abusers of the law be successfully prosecuted, the fines they are likely to suffer are very small (Table 12.1). Furthermore, even though the HASWA carries with it the liability for guilty parties to be imprisoned, in the fifteen years since its enactment there have only been two

Table 12.1 Average fine per conviction on prosecutions brought by HSE and HSC agencies

Average fines at 1975 prices (1975–83)[a]		Average fine per conviction (1983–7/8)[b]	
Year	£	Year	£
1975	75	1983	252
1976	77.3	1984	313
1977	76.7	1985	436
1978	87.2	1986/7	410
1979	112.8	1987/8	794
1980	90.1		
1981	97.4		
1982	109.4		
1983	107.3		

[a]From HSE Statistics 1975–83, based on all prosecutions completed in Factories Acts premises during year, average for all offences, deflated by December 1975 RPI (retail price index).
[b]From HSC/HSE Annual Report 1987/8 table 6.

cases which have ended in custodial sentences. One person in 1985 was given a one month sentence suspended and another person in 1987 was given two sentences, each of nine months to run concurrently, which were also suspended. If executives and managers at work are reluctant to do anything constructive about occupational health they are extremely unlikely to be dragooned into doing it by the enforcement agencies. Both the letter of the law and its practice depend crucially on effective self-regulation if industry is to stem the tide of a growing rate of serious and fatal accidents and to cut down on the losses arising from associated absenteeism, loss of production and compensation. What then does effective self-regulation require of people in workplaces? Is it a realistic aim?

THE ORGANISATIONAL DYNAMICS OF SELF-REGULATION

This chapter draws on the findings of two research projects on industrial safety. The first focussed on the chemicals industry, the second on the construction and retail sectors. These two projects provide a set of thirty-six case studies of establishments together with an analysis of the policies and practices of the HSC and HSE. The case studies are the main source material here.

Understanding the hazard process

To understand self-regulation, one needs to get a grip on what one is regulating or controlling, which for occupational safety is the hazard process. Hazards – defined as potential for loss or harm – exist in all workplaces. Figure 12.1 shows four critical stages of hazard control beginning with the identification of the hazard by people in the workplace. It is not enough for it to be generally known that falls from heights are common killers in the construction industry or that eye injuries are often suffered by chemical workers or hearing damage is an occupational disease for disc jockeys. The critical issue is: are these hazards identified and acknowledged by the people working with them? If identified, some form of assessment whether implicitly or explicitly, will follow and some form of decision made either to accept them or to attempt to take some action. If action is the determined route, choices relate to three approaches. First, whether to seek to eliminate the hazard, for example by changing materials or removing people from the hazard scene. Secondly, whether to seek to contain the risk of the hazard being realised, perhaps through design solutions, and lastly whether to prepare to mitigate the possible consequences, for example through issuing protective clothing or training workpeople in evacuation procedures. If action is prescribed and implemented it may subsequently be monitored and adapted. Whether action is, or is not, being taken, the hazard, for example the liability to lung disease or to fracturing an arm or to death, is likely to continue as part of working life, unless total elimination, which is rarely possible, is achieved.

Knowledge of the hazard process

The title of this chapter 'Knowledge is not enough', refers to the fact that although it is a necessary condition that people are aware of hazards, can identify them and know about alternative actions which may be taken to deal with them, knowledge alone will not ensure self-regulation or improved safety standards. Insofar as hazard and control information is generated, it enters an organisational context illustrated in Figure 12.2 in which all the actors have a variety of other objectives and interests and in which there is inevitably competition for scarce resources and differing opinions on what is 'acceptable' and 'desirable'. No student of organisations would expect that 'knowledge', backed by the legislative requirement to self-regulate, would ensure that there was sustained pressure to generate

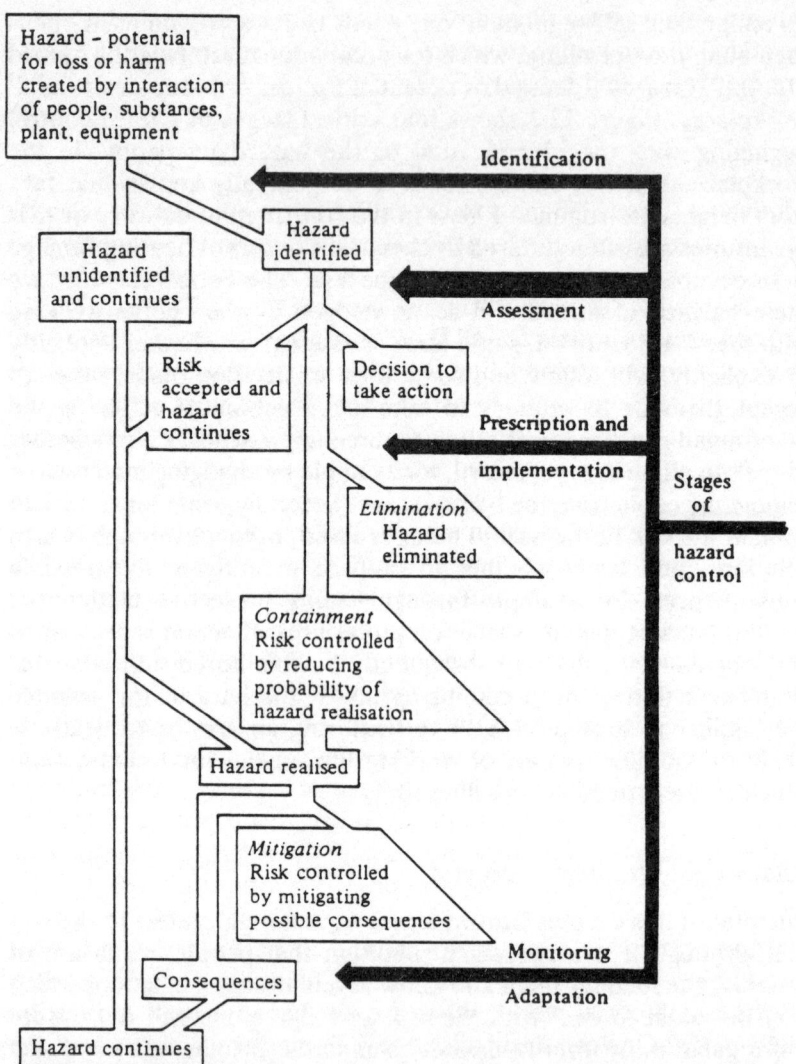

Figure 12.1 Controlling the hazard sequence. (Adapted from Dawson *et al*. 1988: 158.)

and use the knowledge to ensure health, safety and welfare – *unless* other ingredients were present in the organisation. The conclusion of our research was that there are two other vital ingredients which must be added to knowledge to secure the basis for self-regulation. These are motivation and capacity.

Motivation

Motivation, the willingness to expend effort in the cause of securing increased standards of occupational health and safety, requires that the following question is addressed. Why should safety and good health at work succeed in winning a place amongst an existing list of competing priorities for all those involved? At a very basic level there is a common motivation: even accepting that assumptions are dangerous, it seems safe to assume that few, if any, actually want an accident or ill health to occur – least of all to themselves. However, other pressures and priorities interfere with this 'natural' motivation. For the employer and manager there is the need to maintain efficient production and distribution of goods and services. For the employee there may be the need to achieve work targets which will determine incentive payments or promotion possibilities or the need to maintain social relationships at work, for example through 'macho' forms of behaviour. In unionised workplaces the shop steward and full-time trade union officials may be preoccupied with representing members' interests in job security, terms and conditions of employment and so on. Only the specially designated safety officer or safety specialist and trade union safety representatives where they exist, are specifically enjoined to put safety at the top of their agenda. But acting alone each of these 'specially designated groups' lacks power within the workplace (Dawson *et al.* 1988: 167–71, 174–6).

Concentrating just on employers and managers let us ask why, given competing pressures, they should maintain or increase their efforts for safety at work? What are the bases of their motivation likely to be? One can distinguish between punitive factors where the mainspring of motivation is fear of failure and more positive aspects where motivation is geared to achieving success. The distinction is somewhat arbitrary because each side implies the other and both need feedback between behaviour and outcome. Nonetheless the analytical distinction may be useful, since a dominance of 'fear of failure' motivations is likely to lead to meeting minimum standards, whereas striving for success may encourage rising standards

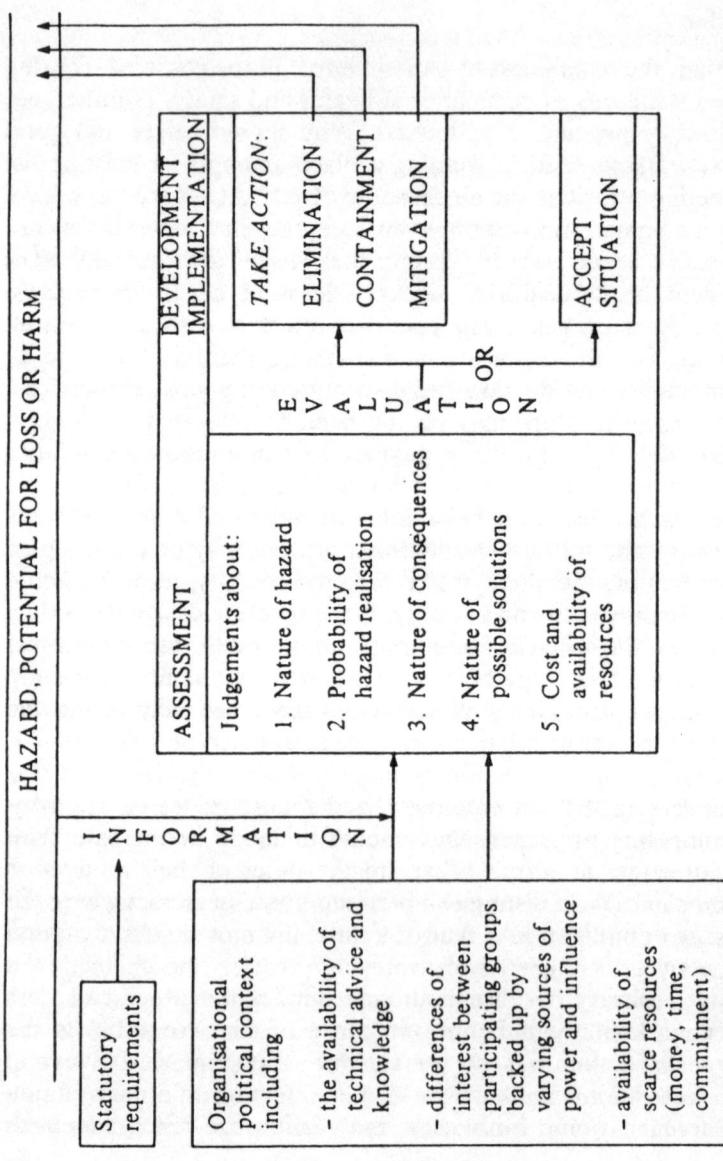

Figure 12.2 Formulating strategies to control hazards at work. (Adapted from Dawson *et al.* 1988: 161.)

Figure 12.3 Sources of motivation for employers and executives

Fearing Consequence of Non-compliance
* Involvement in formal external proceedings,
  resulting in   – criminal record
                       – fines
                       – imprisonment

* Involvement with trade union representatives
  resulting in   – forced expenditure
                       – loss of face/prerogative

Avoiding Costs
* avoid litigation and compensation costs
* avoid costs of   – lost production
                       – lower morale
                       – problems of recruiting and retaining personnel
* avoid increasing insurance premiums

Demonstrating 'acceptable face of capitalism'
* demonstate effective self-regulation
  to avoid greater imposed regulation

* demonstrate social responsibility
  in relation to wider environmental management

Developing 'total management' approach
* developing 'total management' approach
  to cover safety as well as quality etc.

through reviewing what is acceptable and desirable rather than just acknowledging what may be forcefully required. Figure 12.3 summarises the main sources of motivation which were identified in the research.

The first set of motivational forces derives from fears of the consequences of non-compliance. In the post-1974 period, managers were very apprehensive about the threat posed from two main sources. One was the possibility of individuals as well as their companies being subject to criminal prosecution as a result of violations of HASAWA. And yet we know now that prosecution of companies is comparatively rare and that of individuals even rarer. Fines are relatively small and custodial sentences more or less non-existent. Even the threat of a visit from an inspector is only occasionally realised. Another fear was that the safety representatives and safety committee regulations would open a flood gate of trade union demands which would both challenge managerial prerogative and require heavy expenditure. Our research suggested that apart from odd instances, this scenario was actually rarely realised. Undoubtedly the presence of safety representatives, their rights to inspection, their opportunities for training under the auspices of the TUC and their increasing confidence and knowledge about occupational safety were important contextual factors which, with others, can be used to explain the decreasing accident rate and improved safety performance for British industry in the late 1970s. However, we encountered very few myths, let alone verifiable instances, where it was felt that managers had actually been subject to pressures they felt were 'unreasonable'.

In the event, therefore, fears for the consequences of non-compliance, although giving the odd individual sleepless nights, did not retain major significance as sources of motivation. As the political and economic climate in the UK has changed in the 1980s, as the banners of de-regulation of industry and reduction in union power have been raised, so motivational forces dependent on the fears of externally imposed consequences, particularly those associated with state intervention or trade union involvement, have lessened (Dawson *et al.* 1988: 251–7).

With less pressure from these two external influences the three other sets of motivational forces listed in Figure 12.2 may assume more significance for managers. One of them, avoiding costs, still focusses managerial attention on avoiding a form of punishment whereas the other two, demonstrating the acceptable face of capitalism and a 'total management approach', have more positive foundations.

As regards cost reduction there is an increasing awareness of the heavy costs that can result from civil litigation and claims for damages. Requirements to report occupational disease under the Reporting of Injuries, Diseases and Dangerous Occurrences Regulations, 1985 and an awareness of the chronic disability that can result from some occupational diseases, as well as claims in respect of widely reported major accidents, have indicated to executives something of the scope of damage claims for which they may be liable. Industrial injury compensation has always been a feature of occupational safety programmes and indeed a major concern for trade union representatives. However, a national trend, detectable in other areas as well as this one, to resort to litigation and the increasingly large awards of damages by the courts probably makes the desire to avoid liability in the civil courts a more significant and certainly more sustained source of motivation than avoiding the consequences of criminal proceedings, although one should note that civil liability may be contingent on criminal liability. In this context there is a growing industry of occupational safety and health consultants who sell their services to companies with the promise of significant savings and cost reduction, not just in compensation claims but in terms of avoiding costly losses in production, increases in insurance premiums, or a decline in employee attendance and morale. In-house safety specialists are also learning that these are powerful and essential forms of argument which they must use if their advice is to be heeded (St John Holt 1987). The foundation of this motivational force depends on quite sophisticated cost-benefit analysis and we should note that its apparent attractiveness hides, as anyone conversant with such techniques knows, major debates about determining cost and benefit criteria and in particular how one accounts for, and who bears, the costs.

Moving on to the remaining sources of motivation in Figure 12.3, we can note that demonstrating the 'acceptable face of capitalism', a theme of Conservative governments in the early 1980s, is now assuming wider political importance with increasing support for a 'green agenda' of environmental issues. If one is considering the emission of toxic fumes, or of fires or explosions, it is the people in the workplace who are in the front line of danger and hence concern to make the environment safer is likely to focus attention and effort inside, as well as outside, the boundaries of the workplace. Similarly, concern for consumer rights, for example, to unadulterated food, invites investigation of standards of hygiene in the workplace. In public pronouncements and in the institutional interfaces between government and industry one notes strong pressures for industry to demonstrate that it can effectively put and maintain its house in order. Large organisations are increasingly concerned with their corporate image and its importance on their relationship with shareholders, customers and employees (Olins 1989). To be associated with a reported major hazard or disaster incurs costs which few board members would willingly incur.

The third source of motivation has a resonance with other developments in contemporary management practice in which it is argued that managers need to be developed to perceive their responsibilities in the round and hence to be principally concerned with adjunct aspects of their task, like quality and safety, as well as with production and service (Hendry *et al.* 1988).

Figure 12.3 identifies a range of reasons why managers may decide to put effort into seeking to improve standards of occupational safety. It also implies the obverse, that is the reasons why occupational safety may be disregarded. Patterns of individual motivation are highly contextually based. Specific features of both the external political and economic climate and the internal strategy and culture of any one organisation will influence the significance which any manager accords each of these reasons. Is a 'total management approach' encouraged? Have insurance premiums rocketed? Who is responsible for processes which embody serious health hazards and how is their job defined – to whom and for what are they responsible? If within industry something is not done about controlling hazards will there be increased external and imposed regulation? In the political context of Norway, offshore operators responded to the Ekofisk disaster with improved internal arrangements in part because of fears that if they did not respond positively, external regulation would be increased (Qvale 1985). Thus, we come to the third ingredient to effective self-regulation, that is the capacity of the organisation to use the knowledge and harness and maintain the motivation.

Capacity

The concept of organisational capacity refers to the managerial structures and processes which must be developed, instituted and above all, adapted and maintained as appropriate, if self-regulation is actually going to take a firm hold in the workplace. The line manager's role is crucial in developing this capacity. Every fatality from a routine hazard, like falling off a scaffolding on a building site, and all the prolonged suffering which results from contracting already identified occupational diseases, demonstrate that considerations of individual safety and health are not naturally uppermost in people's minds when at work. Most of the people who are killed or seriously injured at work, suffer as a result of well understood hazards which could be contained using state-of-the-art technology or well accepted management practices. We do not have the political or cultural basis for strong, comprehensive external enforcement – which in any case would only spring into action when activated by information on failure when the harm has actually occurred. Hence it is essential to graft safety management into mainstream managerial responsibilities just as it was decided some years ago that if you wanted to make quality a priority you had to graft that onto the line. Accidents and ill-health are largely created in the central production and distribution core and those who are responsible for these core activities must be responsible for controlling the hazards associated with them.

Figure 12.4 Elements of organisational capacity

Divisions and definitions of responsibility
Reporting relationships
Coordinating relationships
Procedures and protocols governing actions
Systems of communication
Systems of appraisal, definitions and
    measures of performance
Systems of resource allocation
Systems for raising and maintaining safety
    awareness throughout the workforce
Developing modes of thought which encourage
    creativity and insight as well as the
    ability to develop and follow rational
    systems

This all sounds very reminiscent of the Robens report and in intention it is. The difference is that in the early 1970s, it was somehow assumed that the development of this capacity would follow naturally once the legislative framework was enacted. Our research and the trends in accident statistics show that whilst capacity to act may be developed in some work situations on the basis of that framework alone, it does not necessarily follow. The question remains: how does one develop employers and managers to perceive and enact their self-regulating role – assuming of course that the prior question of motivation has been answered and that a combination of forces identified in Figure 12.3 encourages them to put effort into this activity.

Figure 12.4 identifies the elements of organisational capacity. It covers formal structural and procedural arrangements and the way these arrangements are actually put into practice so as to make them real. There is nothing in Figure 12.4 to startle delegates at the British Academy of Management conference for we see here a fairly routine list of structure and process variables. The innovation is that we are thinking of how to apply and develop them in terms of occupational safety and health objectives, and how, in doing this they will mesh with the pursuit of more acknowledged regular business objectives.

Developing capacity in hierarchical organisations

Given a hierarchial organisation, developing the capacity for self-regulation of safety involves clear designation of responsibilities, including some agreement on objectives which are considered achievable within specified time spans. Information on performance and achievements implies some measures of success and failure and this is an area where there is room for considerable practical developments if the capacity for self-regulation is to be realised.

Insofar as safety performance has ever been measured, the measures have related to failure of control systems in terms of accidents and ill-health. Figure 12.5 shows four groups of activities and outcomes which can provide the basis of performance measures. The first group concerns the actual hazard outcomes, the incidence and frequency rates for accidents, ill-health, incidents and material loss or damage. The second group, called 'control outcomes', relates to information on the actual physical conditions and behaviour displayed in the workplace. The third group concerns data on the extent and effectiveness of technical control activity in the workplace and arises from investigations of, for example, the extent to which a manager is ensuring that relevant information is available and s/he is actually using it in making operational judgements. Lastly motivational activity can be monitored; questions can be asked, for example, about the extent to which occupational safety features in people's job descriptions, the extent to which newly appointed people are made aware of their safety responsibilities and the methods by which safety is incorporated into training. Even though fixing line responsibility for safety is crucial, this does not mean that only the line is involved. There are critical roles for information providers on hazard identification, means of prevention, likely consequences of accepting a risk and on the four groups of outcomes and activities identified in Figure 12.5. Safety advisers or specialists are usually very important in developing and enacting the coordinating and communicating activities identified in Figure 12.4.

Developing capacity for safety also involves paying attention to the ways in which line management responsibilities are sustained and supported. Two very important aspects are highlighted in Figure 12.4. One is the need for systems of informal and formal appraisal in which safety performance is reviewed. Unless senior support for safety is reinforced through mechanism of appraisal and accountability, capacity for self-regulation will not be developed. Here it is notable that we found it rare for managers, even those for whom safety features

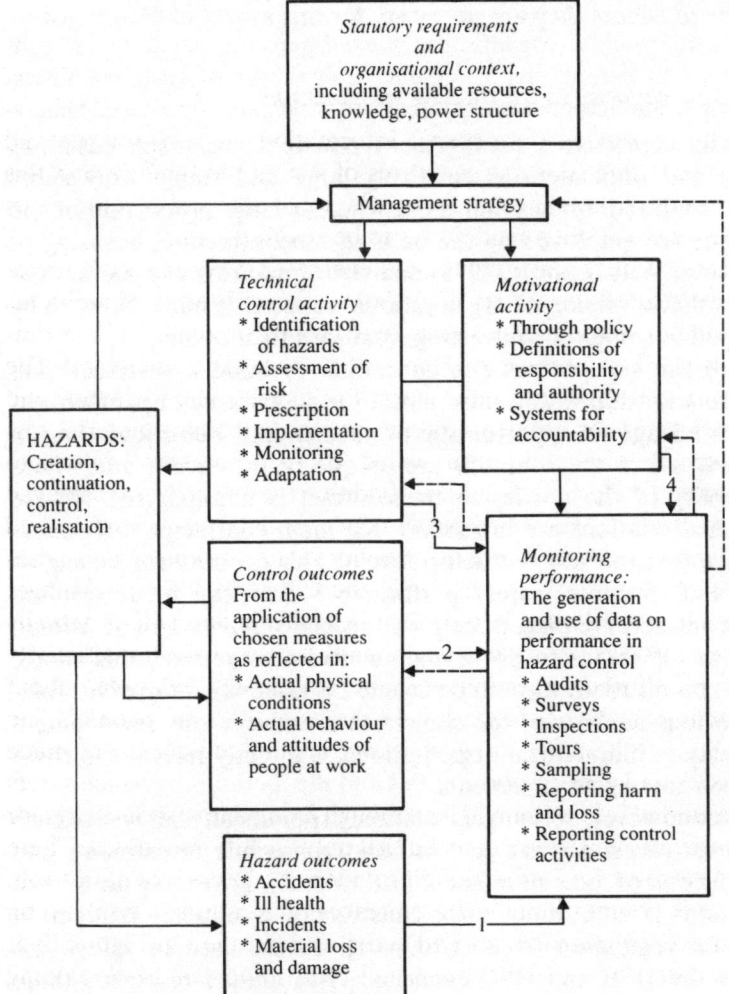

Figure 12.5 Monitoring performance. Numbered arrows: sources of performance data; dashed arrows: feedback from monitoring. (Adapted from Dawson *et al*. 1988: 163.)

in their job description, to report being asked at appraisals to review their past performance and set future objectives in this aspect of their work. Du Pont, with their scheme of safety management is one of the few companies to have developed ways for systematically fixing and maintaining management accountability for safety. Another form of vital support identified in Figure 12.4 is systems for the allocation of the provision of resources when as a matter of judgement the line manager considers they are necessary for this aspect of his/her job.

Developing capacity in contracting relationships

The basis of effective management practices are much easier to identify and implement in relatively large and stable workplaces than in small enterprises and those where a large proportion of the workforce are employed on the basis of subcontracting, licensing or franchising. Williamson's (1975) analysis of markets and hierarchies suggests that a version of organisational capacity is more likely to be developed in some subcontracting situations than others.

Where the subcontractor is concerned to build a sustained and strong relationship with a third party, the subcontractor is much less likely to engage in opportunistic or substandard behaviour than in situations where the contracts are unique or infrequent and where the identity of the parties to the contract is unimportant. Where established relations are important, the main contractor can *choose* to ensure that the subcontractor develops his capacity for managing safety. For example, safety performance data can be scrutinised before contracts are placed, help and specialist advice can be offered and so on. Whether or not a main contractor exercises this choice depends on his motivation to do so and his understanding of his role. The previous analysis of the choices that underlie the development of capacity in hierarchical organisations, is directly relevant to these stable contracting arrangements.

Where, however, exchanges occur only sporadically but where each party must invest a great deal in non-transferable investments and where the cost of some permanent institution for governing occasional transactions is high, as in some construction contracts, Williamson argues for regulation by a third party. In the case of safety this must be the HSE and HSC agencies. With limited resources there can be no doubt that external inspection and enforcement should be concentrated on the smaller enterprises and the network of self-employed people who are shifting parts of complex contracting relationships. It is here that there is least likelihood of effective self-regulation developing and yet in the past they have been part of the group which is least rather than most likely to be the subject of inspection and enforcement.

There are, however, signs of change. For example in the construction sector, the HSE, increasingly concerned about the rise in the incidence of major and fatal accidents amongst employees and the self-employed, launched a major enforcement initiative in 1987–8 aimed at small sites. Some 5,000 sites and 6,000 contractors were visited. Conditions were found to be so bad on 1,000 sites that the inspectors levied prohibition notices on them all, stopping work until remedial action was taken (HSC/HSE 1988: 51). This sort of 'blitz' was a new venture for the HSE and represents an acknowledgement of the particular problems posed with a market rather than a hierarchical base for self-regulation.

The place for workforce involvement

The development of managerial capacity in hierarchical and market organisations is crucial to self-regulation. But as Figure 12.4 indicates, the organisation's capacity to deal effectively with occupational health and safety also depends on systems for raising and maintaining awareness of occupational safety and health throughout the workforce.

Robens acknowledged the importance of workforce involvement although left open the best means for its achievement. In the spirit of the early 1970s – a very different political and economic context to the late 1980s – the decision was made to restrict the right to workforce involvement in safety matters to members of recognised trade unions. Only these institutions had the right to appoint safety representatives, who in turn were alone in possessing the right to request the formation of a safety committee. The concept of a recognised trade union is now redundant with the passing of the Employment Act 1980 since there is now no mechanism to request recognition. Trade union organisation, collective bargaining and representational structures built on this model of industrial relations must take their place amongst a range of what can be called styles of employee relations or human resource management, which include anti-union 'macho management' and non-union consultative styles (Purcell 1987).

The present model of workforce involvement in safety can be used to raise awareness but only in those organisations with a strong trade union presence, and even so there are sometimes difficulties in recruiting and retaining safety representatives (Leopold and Beaumont 1984). What are the prospects for workforce involvement in the two other employee relations styles cited above? The macho management model has no role for workforce involvement in this or any other matter. Standards of occupational safety will rise, stand or fall entirely with management. There is, however, scope for workforce involvement in occupational safety through non-union consultative institutions, such as quality circles and briefing groups. They can make no pretence to independence and so they lack the possibility of developing the 'forceful policeman' role which some people thought would be the strength of safety representatives and safety committees. However, consultative structures may facilitate the flow of information between levels in a workplace on experience of hazards and on attempts at their control as well as the flow of suggestions for all stages of the hazard control process (Figure 12.1). Furthermore, they contain the possibility for people at different levels in the organisation to influence the nature of the agenda of and the outcomes of discussions on safety.

One advantage of a consultative system is that it places safety as a major consideration for all – alongside their other concerns. It used to be thought that safety had to be dealt with independently of other concerns, otherwise it would always become a subordinate concern. This was the basis of the argument that line managers should not be directly involved in decisions about safety since there was a 'prima-facie' case that they would be more interested in other things. However, this 'independence' – in the absence of any strong power base for 'the safety people' – meant a marginalisation and complete subordination of the issues, at least until senior executives were shocked by a major disaster or alarming statistical trends to begin to consider real as well as rhetorical responsibilities. Issues such as these are highlighted in the Fennell Report on the King's Cross fire in which a discussion of safety management – as a central concern of all managers and supervisors – is raised (Fennell 1988).

The last aspect of capacity I want to raise in this chapter is also relevant to reflections on the Fennell Report. In managing safety one must stress the formal, pre-programmed aspects of control; the rational planning of actions which should be followed in the event of an emergency is an important part of risk management. Required actions must be identified, accepted, understood and rehearsed or else the rationality of pre-planned organisation will be threatened and plans will simply not be routinely followed. But although such rational aspects must be stressed, they must not be overstressed. Routine procedures must be seen as significant, be encouraged and monitored but people at all levels should also be developed to be alert to take initiative and to think laterally. Emergencies on a large or small scale – although amenable to *post hoc* rational explanation – require that people both follow procedures and yet exercise independent judgement. The final trick in developing capacity is to develop awareness in the workplace of both sorts of working models, as well as developing the basis of judgement to know when each model is appropriate. This combination of creativity and insight on the one hand and ability to manage and maintain formal rational systems is indeed a major challenge for management, and not just in the area of safety.

Generating an understanding that one must develop an organisational capacity for managing safety in order to utilise knowledge and maintain motivation is perhaps the most important message to executives from our research. One can conclude that as far as large and medium-sized hierarchical organisations and some workplaces with extremely stable subcontracting arrangements are concerned, self-regulation of safety is possible but it will not happen naturally. It has to be created and our research has revealed some performance indicators which can be applied to see whether it has been created and is being sustained. Where industrial sectors are experiencing instability or relatively high levels of casual or subcontract labour one must be much more cautious about the feasibility of a self-regulatory system. In such contexts improved standards of health and safety will be heavily dependent upon the maintenance of obvious external pressures.

IMPLICATIONS OF THE UK SCENE FOR EUROPEAN INITIATIVES

This analysis of the feasibility and limits of self-regulation in the UK is relevant to contemporary considerations within the European Commission about the harmonisation of policy and practice for occupational health and safety throughout the Community. It is a tenet of Commission policy that all workers should be protected by health and safety legislation. Although there are major differences between the law in each member state, there is a common theme which is that somehow appropriate arrangements of a self-regulatory kind should be encouraged with those directly engaged in work taking major responsibility for securing adequate standards of occupational safety and health. Just as in the UK the implication for the European Commission is that direct intervention needs to be targeted to those sectors and types of establishments where self-regulation is least likely to flourish.

Hence there is a fundamental need for comparative statistics in order to seek to establish if there are significant differences between groups of workers in the degree of protection they are afforded. However, whilst of critical importance to a common European policy, comparative statistics, as past reports testify, are extremely difficult to achieve (Brancoli 1982). Should the European Commission be successful in this enormous task, their achievement will be a significant step towards wider harmonisation beyond Europe, a state of being which the ILO, OECD and WHO would welcome.

Thus, before one can begin to take a truly European perspective, we need to know a lot more about indices of relative performance, otherwise there is no basis from which to develop both policy and targeted action plans. Sufficient harmonisation of data collection and analysis will not, however, be easily achieved.

We have seen that even in the UK there are problems with the collection and interpretation of statistical data which derive from interrupted time series, changing databases and uneven rates of underreporting between sectors and types of enterprise. These problems are multiplied if one attempts to look at performance across member states.

A recent review of reporting requirements and practices in member states (European Foundation 1988) reveals that whilst many states have in the last decade made changes to their reporting requirements, these changes have in no way been geared towards harmonisation. There is variation concerning the accidents which need reporting, for example, legislation requires all accidents which have caused injury to be reported in Belgium and France, whereas in the UK and Netherlands only accidents which have caused worker incapacity for a specified number of days are reportable. There are significant discrepancies, for example, the time elapsed between the accident and subsequent death, for the accident to be deemed a fatal accident. There are great national and regional differences in rates of reporting as well as in the categories of persons who are covered (e.g. trainees, self-employed, etc. are sometimes included and sometimes excluded). The receivers of the reports also vary. In some countries, e.g. Italy and Portugal, accidents are reported to private or state-run insurance bodies; their collection and use therefore reflects a major concern with compensation. In other countries, e.g. the UK and Ireland, accident reports are the concern of the equivalent of the labour inspectorate with an associated greater interest in determining the causes of accidents. Nonetheless, in December 1982, the European Council formally resolved to harmonise accident statistics, thus in theory at least the debate is not whether but how harmonisation can be achieved. The Statistical Office of the European Communities and the

Directorate General for Employment Industrial Relations and Social Affairs are currently engaged in a joint project on European statistics on accidents at work and they are hoping to formulate proposals for the harmonisation of statistics on accidents at work. It is essential that they address the central issues of the definition of what is reportable, by whom and in what form, together with recommendations on the infrastructure to secure that harmonisation is really achieved.

Seeking to establish a common basis for the analysis of occupational health across member states is even more difficult than with the subject of accidents. The UK experience of the struggle to get agreement on how to require the reporting of occupational health statistics which eventually resulted in the Reporting of Injuries, Diseases and Dangerous Ocurrences Regulations (1985) reveals something of the state of the problem. A European Market initiative would require agreement between all interested parties on categories of industrial sectors and disease to be represented. The task facing the European Commission is thus enormous if they are even to get to first base in their attempt to establish a system which will enable them to look at performance and problems across sectors, types of establishment and national and linguistic groupings, on a Community-wide system.

This chapter also shows that it is important that consideration is given to the particular social, economic and managerial contexts for work in different parts of the Community, since one of the conclusions from our UK work is that unless local capacity as well as knowledge and motivation is encouraged, self-regulation will not be effectively sustained. The elements of capacity are such that they cannot be externally dictated but have to develop appropriate forms within given contexts. Furthermore, there are some contexts in which capacity will never be developed. We need the statistical analysis to identify these 'blackspots' and then develop some European-wide initiatives to compliment – or to precipitate – local governmental initiatives to tackle them with strong external inspection and enforcement.

CONCLUSION

The market mechanism is an increasingly powerful concept in our understanding of organisations in the late twentieth century – markets for labour, markets for capital, markets for goods and services – and many of us spend a lot of our time in showing how our various management disciplines can contribute to maximising returns for organisations from these markets. But where is the market place for safety? Who is to pay (not simply in terms of financial costs) for better or worse safety at work?

This chapter shows that if we wish to reduce the proportion of people who are killed or suffer serious injury or ill-health at work we need to develop a conception of excellent management to include safety and health. It may be – and I hope it is – that 'safety does pay' and shows good balance sheet returns. But if it doesn't, at least in the short term, is it not the case that organisational capacity for safety must be developed if we are to reduce the daily toll of death and injury? Established hierarchies and market relationships contain within them the basis for managing safety effectively. It is up to their participants to decide whether they wish to develop in this way. The choices which are made will, as the paper has indicated, be highly influenced by perceptions of both the external political and internal organisational environments.

The chapter also explains that it is difficult to find the basis of a capacity for self-regulating safety in temporary and transient market relationships. Consideration needs to be given at national and European levels to the question of whether this is an area which should consume proportionately more of the limited resources of external regulation and enforcement. However, before this issue can really be effectively tackled or even analysed on a European basis, there is a prior requirement for the harmonisation of statistical collection and analysis, and this is an enormous and as yet unfilled task.

REFERENCES

Brancoli, M. (1982) *Standardisation of Occupational Statitics in the European Community: Present Possibilities, Prospects and Proposals*, Geneva, International Social Security Association.

Dawson, S. Willman, P. Clinton, A. and Bamford, M. (1988) *Safety at Work: The Limits of Self Regulation*, Cambridge, Cambridge University Press.

European Foundation for the Improvement of Living and Working Conditions (1988) *How Occupational Accidents and Diseases are Reported in the European Community*, Luxembourg, Office of Official Publications of the European Community.

Fennell, D. (1988) *Report of Investigation into the Kings Cross Underground Fire* CM499, London, HMSO.

Hendry, C., Pettigrew, A. and Sparrow, P. (1988) 'Changing patterns of human resource management', *Personnel Management* 20(11), 37–41.

House of Commons (1982) *Sixth Report from the Employment Committee: The Working of the HSC*, London, HMSO.

HSC/HSE (1988) *Annual Report, 1987–8*, London, HMSO.

Leopold, J. W. and Beaumont, P.B. (1984), 'The turnover and continuity of safety representatives', *Industrial Relations Journal* 15(4), 74–82.

Olins, W. (1989) *Corporate Identity*, London, Thames & Hudson.

Purcell, J. (1987), 'Mapping managment style in employee relations', *Journal of Management Studies* 24(5), 533–48.

Qvale, T. U. (1985) *Safety and Offshore Working Conditions*, Oslo, Universitets for laget.

Robens (1972) *Safety and Health at Work*, Report of the Committee 1970–72, Cmnd 5034, London, HMSO.

St. John Holt, A. (1987) *Health & Safety – Towards the Millenium*, A collection of articles on the future of the Safety Professions, Leicester, IOSH Publishing.

Williamson, O. E. (1975) *Markets and Hierarchies*, Glencoe, Free Press.

Part III

Decision-making and implementation

13 Problem finding, idea finding and implementation

An exploratory model for investigating small-group problem-solving

Tudor Rickards and Gerard Puccio

INTRODUCTION

According to Sternberg (1988), research into creativity as an academic subject was stagnant for some time, received a new lease of life following J. P. Guilford's presidential address to the American Psychological Society in 1950, languished again in the 1970s, and received another boost in the middle 1980s. Sternberg was able to assemble the work of an authoritative group of American and European researchers to illustrate this proposition. Further evidence to support Sternberg can be found in Isaksen (1987), and Grønhaug and Kaufmann (1988), two substantial collections of review articles, and from Barron and Harrington (1981) who were granted the first ten year review of the topic in the *Annual Review of Psychology*.

From these recent reviews we can trace the impact of the pioneers in the field: Maslow (1959), Rogers (1959) and Koestler (1964) building a philosophical framework; Guilford's (1981) attempts to identify emprical support for his three-dimensional 'Structure of Intellect' model; Osborn's (1963) 'invention' of brainstorming; Parnes and Noller's (1972) work on the identification of measurable learning gains from creative training programmes; Torrance's establishment of his tests of divergent thinking (1974) and his longitudinal studies of the impact of creativity training (1981); MacKinnon's (1978) studies of the creative individual.

We can also see the recent emergence of new directions of research, notably Kirton (1976, 1987, 1989), and his timely distinction between creative problem-solving abilities ('level'), and the cognitive processing of information ('style'); Amabile (1983) and her work on intrinsic motivation; Simonton (1988), and his mathematical modelling of aspects of exceptionally gifted individuals; Schank, (1988) and his human information-processing model.

The overall impression left from citations in these reviews is that creativity as a field has been dominated by North American researchers, with primary interests in individual psychology and education. Rickards (1988) suggests this may be misleading, partly because European work on creativity has tended to be more eclectic, and has failed to fit into a well-established body of knowledge. He also suggests that European material (especially from non-English sources) finds difficulty in diffusing into American research publications. This view has found support in the far wider range of practitioners and researchers who contributed to a pan-European networking conference on the subjects of creativity and innovation recently, indicating a broad interest base, and great deal of important work in various languages which had received poor international circulation (Colemont *et al.* 1988).

Overall, there seems to be burgeoning interest in creativity internationally. Furthermore, the subject is now attracting attention beyond the fields of education and cognitive psychology, and is gaining interest in core subjects of managerial behaviour, such as coping in turbulent environments (Gryskiewicz 1980; Kanter 1985, 1989; Peters 1987); management of innovation (Carson and Rickards, 1979; Buijs 1984; Drucker 1985; Nyström 1988); complex problem-solving (Schank 1982; Talbot 1982; Simon 1984; Kaufmann 1988); and the climate for creative performance and leadership (Amabile 1983; Ekvall 1987; Wesenberg 1986–7); and Burnstein (1987).

Another notable area of applied research is the study of how creativity might be stimulated. Early work was reviewed by Stein (1974/1975) who noted the emerging evidence of the effectiveness of the so-called creative problem-solving techniques in assisting idea generation in laboratory conditions. However, Stein pointed out the paucity of reliable data from actual experiments in industrial contexts. Recent researchers have added some evidence that new product development teams have made extensive use of idea stimulating methods in their work (see Carson and Rickards 1979; Gryskiewicz 1980; Geschka 1983; Buijs 1988). It can safely be concluded that studies of creativity, while attracting interest from organisational change agents of various kinds, remain poorly diffused in the management literature. In what follows we attempt to integrate these two overlapping fields.

TOWARDS AN INTEGRATION OF CREATIVITY AND MAINSTREAM MANAGEMENT STUDIES

The search for a competitive edge has brought an increase in references to creativity and innovation in the practitioner-oriented literature. Drucker (1969, 1985) might be seen as a harbinger of the post-industrial writers. The global commercial success of Peters and Waterman (1982) emphasised the dominance of North American management thinking internationally. Other influential figures include Kanter (1985, 1989 and Porter (1980).

Research addressing innovation issues in Europe includes recent reports from Sweden (Nyström and Edvardsson 1982; Nyström 1988); Norway (Elden 1988; Trolle and Graverson 1989); Germany, Switzerland and Austria (Geschka 1983, 1988); the Netherlands (Buijs 1984, 1988; During 1986); France (Jaoui 1979), and the UK (Bessant 1982, 1991; Johne 1985). The EC is also sponsoring a wide range of programmes for stimulating innovation across the Community and is active in building a communications network to disseminate information (Rickards and Moger 1989). Other cross-cultural studies of innovations in work practices are emerging from the European Foundation for the Improvement of Living and Working Conditions (Frohlich *et al.* 1989).

The managerial work cited above may mention creativity and innovation as 'good things'. The dominant tendancy is to avoid offering definitions, or to offer a definition created to suit the author's purpose. It has recently been suggested that mainstream management science researchers have ignored the accumulating body of knowledge concerning the creative process (Rickards 1990a, b).

It is possible, however, to find much common ground, albeit hardly remarked upon in the texts. Morgan (1980, 1986), for example, has presented a powerful and widely recognised view that organisations can be regarded in various different ways, each captured within a dominant metaphor. The interpretive and problem-solving importance of metaphor has been widely studied within the creativity literature (Gordon 1961; Prince 1970; Neçka and Kubiak 1989); as has the concept of simultaneous validity of multiple perspectives within any complex problem investigation (Stein 1975).

Another bridge between the fields of management science and creativity research may be built using soft systems theory (Ackoff and Vergara 1981; Ainsworth-Land 1982; Rickards and Puccio 1989). Brainstorming has been modelled in cybernetic terms of variety production and reduction (Rickards and Freedman 1979). Rickards (1985) later pointed out the benefits of treating the innovation process to a systems approach and subsequently demonstrated how creative problem-solving techniques could be represented as a sequence of variety-generating and variety-reducing components with feedback loops (Rickards 1988). Isaksen and Treffinger (1985) also drew attention to what they called the 'dynamic balance' between the convergent and divergent states in creative problem-solving.

In their introduction to a seminar at the International Institute of Applied Systems Analysis at the start of this decade, Kindler and Kiss (1984) made a case that could easily have emerged from a gathering of creativity practitioners: 'All positivist approaches to science . . . are deficient in their capacity for generating knowledge for use by members of organisations for solving problems they face.' Summarising the seminar, Tomlinson (1984) proposed that systems enquiry has to accept that to formulate a problem requires understanding of the possibly conflicting needs of various problem-owners. He goes on to state that in investigational work 'the most important element is often in finding a way of breaking away from the shackles of conventional thought'. These points again would be consistent with the views of workers in the field of creative problem-solving. (Osborn 1963; de Bono 1971; Adams 1980; Getzels and Csikszentmihalyi 1976; Isaksen and Treffinger 1985; Kaufmann 1988).

CREATIVE PROBLEM-SOLVING: THE EXPERIMENTAL DESIGN

For several years researchers at Manchester Business School have been examining the nature of small-group problem-solving on realistic industrial problems. One source of more controlled environmental conditions is the MBA programme within which there are assorted team projects. To prepare the graduates for working in teams, an introductory project has been designed which involves the participants in various creative problem-solving tasks. Earlier papers reported that the outputs can be enhanced by electronic communication networks which assist in monitoring and giving feedback to the groups (Rickards 1987); and that the characteristics of more, and less, successful teams can be discriminated by measures of team climate (Rickards *et. al.*) Prior to the 1988 introductory project, an attempt was made to model the problem-solving process in systems terms which would permit examination of variables involved when small groups engage in realistic managerial tasks. Three dimensions were considered worthy of initial attention (Figure 13.1):

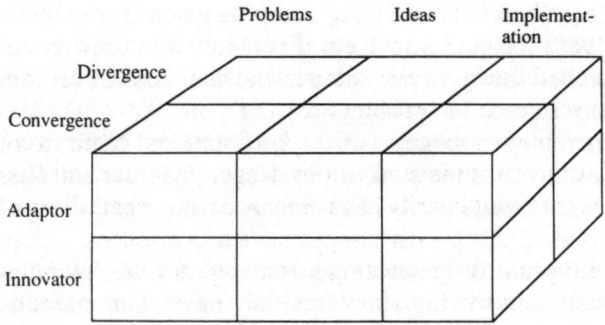

Figure 13.1 Three-dimensional model for studying small-group problem-solving processes

1 The stages found in the creative problem-solving literature: the problem stage, the ideas stage and the implementation stage.
2 A divergent and a convergent component within each stage.
3 Differing contributions to the creative problem-solving process from individuals with differing creative problem-solving capabilities and preferences.

METHOD

Subjects

The subjects were 120 full-time MBA students (104 male, 16 female) from the Manchester Business School. Ages ranged from 21 to 44, with a mean age of 26.9. All students were in their first year of the graduate programme, and they represented a diverse array of educational backgrounds and work experiences.

Procedure

To explore the problem-solving process using the model we considered means of assessing individual perceptions of preferences and performance, within each stage, and across the stages. (For technical reasons we have postponed attempts to collect data on group performance from expert observers, although we hope to report such results in a later publication.) This model was used to design a Problem-Solving Preference and Performance Questionnaire

(PSPPQ). The PSPPQ included two biographic items (Q1 and Q2) and seven other items probing personal views of competence at the different stages of problem-solving (Q3); learning gains at the differing stages (Q4); personal preference for divergence or convergence (Q5); personal contribution at the different stages (Q6); personal contribution at divergence or convergence components (regardless of stage in the problem-solving) (Q7). Additionally, there were questions on group performance stage by stage (Q8) and at convergent and divergent components of problem-solving, regardless of stage (Q9).

To examine individual differences we selected a well-validated instrument capturing individual problem-solving styles, namely, the Kirton Adaption–Innovation Inventory (Kirton 1976, 1987). This inventory ('the KAI') indicates the subject's preference for either an adaptive or innovative style of problem-solving. Scores on this inventory range from 32 to 160, with a theoretical mean of 96. Scores below this mean indicate a preference for the adaptive style of creativity, and scores which fall above the theoretical mean indicate a preference for the innovative style of creativity.

The measure ('KAI') has attracted considerable research attention, recently summarised in Kirton (1989) and purports to distinguish individual differences in cognitive style specifically as these influence preferred problem-solving styles. A high KAI score reflects an 'innovative' style characterised by interest in large numbers of ideas, but with low concern for problem-solving detail, or for rule conformity. A low KAI score reflects a bias towards fewer ideas, together with a greater concern for detail, and for rule conformity. For our exploratory purposes we concentrated on aggregate scores, permitting comparisons with a wealth of previous data (Kirton 1987, 1989). We recognise arguments for extending the analysis to the three KAI subscales (Payne 1987). Such refinement fell outside the scope of this preliminary study.

Data on the PSPPQ and KAI were collected during a week-long introductory project for the first-year MBA students. The first two days of this project focussed on the development of creativity-relevant skills. The first morning of the creativity session examined mind sets and how they can inhibit creative performance. The remainder of the creativity sessions focussed on the use and application of various creative problem-solving techniques in small groups.

Table 13.1 Descriptive statistics for the Kirton Adaption–Innovation inventory

	Entire sample			Males			Females		
	M	(N)	SD	M	(N)	SD	M	(N)	SD
Rickards and Puccio (1989, MBAs)	107.71	(120)	15.15	107.69	(104)	15.37	107.81	(16)	14.10
Foxall (1986, MBAs)	110.02	(146)	15.52	109.49	(129)	15.57	114.05	(17)	14.88
Goldsmith (1984, Undergrads)	100.14	(106)	11.70	NR		NR	NR		NR
Goldsmith (1987, Undergrads)	100.37	(96)	11.88	NR		NR	NR		NR
Isaksen and Puccio (1988, Undergrads)	100.12	(184)	14.23	104.67		13.68	97.69		14.27
Puccio (1987, Undergrads)	100.28	(146)	14.83	104.24		NR	98.29		NR

RESULTS

Kirton Adaption–Innovation Inventory

The mean scores and standard deviations for the KAI are found in Table 13.1. This table also provides a comparison with another sample of MBA students (Foxall 1986), as well as several undergraduate samples (Goldsmith 1984, 1987; Isaksen and Puccio 1988; Puccio 1987). No significant difference was observed in the mean scores of male and female sub-groups in this study, a result which contrasts with Foxall's MBA results (1986) in which the females had more innovative mean scores; and Isaksen and Puccio's (1988) and Puccio's (1987) undergraduate results, in which the females had lower scores. More consistent is the pattern of MBA students reporting mean results significantly above the population mean towards the innovative end of the KAI scale.

Problem-Solving Preference and Performance Questionnaire

Table 13.2 presents the frequencies of responses for the PSPPQ broken down by sex and score for Kirton's measure. Using the standard deviation for the KAI, the subjects were divided into three groups (Relative Adaptors, KAI < 101; Middles, KAI = 101–114; and Innovators; KAI > 114). A chi-square was carried

Table 13.2 Frequency distribution for the problem-solving Preference and Performance Questionnaire

| | Gender | | | | KAI groups | | | | | |
| | Male (104) | | Female (16) | | Adaptors (36) | | Middles (44) | | Innovators (36) | |
Question no.	(Freq.)	(%)	(Freq.)	(%)	(Freq.)	(%)	(Freq.)	(%)	(Freq.)	(%)
3. Individual preferences for:										
Problems	38	38.0	8	50.0	16	45.7	16	37.2	13	38.2
Ideas	42	42.0	7	43.8	12	34.3	21	48.8	14	41.2
Solutions	20*	20.0	1	6.2	7	20.0	6*	14.0	7	20.6
Missing	4		1		1		1		2	
4. Training added most value in:										
Problems	32	31.7	3	18.8	8	22.9	14	32.6	11	31.4
Ideas	39	38.6	4	25.0	14	40.0	17	39.5	12	34.3
Solutions	30	29.7	9	56.2	13	37.1	12	27.9	12	34.3
Missing	3				1		1		1	
5. Individual's best performance came in:										
Divergent	47	47.0	6	37.5	9**	26.5	21	48.8	20	57.1
Convergent	53	53.0	10	62.5	25**	73.5	22	51.2	15	42.9
Missing	4				2		1		1	
6. Individual contributed most to group in:										
Problems	25	25.2	10*	62.5	8	23.5	15	34.9	11	32.4
Ideas	47*	47.5	5	31.3	17	50.0	20	46.5	13	38.2
Solutions	27	27.3	1	6.2	9	26.5	8	18.6	10	29.4
Missing	5		1		2		1		2	

	n	%	n	%	n	%	n	%	n	%
7. Individual contributed most to group in:										
Divergent	62*	60.8	11	68.7	20	55.6	26	60.5	24*	68.6
Convergent	40	39.2	5	31.3	16	44.4	17	39.5	11	31.4
Missing	2						1		1	
8. Individual's perception of group's best performance in:										
Problems	29	28.4	7	43.8	11	30.6	16	37.2	8	22.9
Ideas	61**	59.8	7	43.8	21**	58.3	23**	53.5	21**	60.0
Solutions	12	11.8	2	12.4	4	11.1	4	9.3	6	17.1
Missing	2						1		1	
9. Individual's perception of group's best performance in:										
Divergent	86**	84.3	13*	81.2	31**	86.1	35**	81.4	30**	85.7
Convergent	16	15.7	3	18.8	5	13.9	8	18.6	5	14.3
Missing	2						1		1	

*p<0.05; **p<0.01.

out to determine if these frequency distributions occurred by chance. The following statements provide a summary of this analysis for each of the questions on the PSPPQ:

Q3   *Individual preference.* All groups showed a preference for the first two stages (problems and ideas) over the third stage of idea development or implementation. (This was particularly strong in the responses of females.)

Q4   *Added value of training.* Females showed a clearer pattern of more reported 'added value' at the third, solution-finding, stage of the training.

Q5   *Preferences for convergence over divergence.* The *ab initio* assumption was that preferences would reflect Kirton scores. Some support was found for this proposition. Table 13.2 shows that as preferences moved from an adaptive style to an innovative one there was a corresponding increase in the percentage of subjects reporting that their greatest contribution to performance occurred at the divergence stage of the process. The adaptive sub-group reported their best performance in the convergent phase, a result statistically significant (chi-square $p < 0.01$).

Q6   *Personal contribution at differing stages.* Respondents felt they contributed more at the problem and idea stages. This is consistent with perceived preferences for these stages (Q3).

Q7   *Personal contribution for convergence or divergence.* Here, the similarities of responses between contribution and preference were again found (innovators were the only KAI group which significantly favoured the divergence stages, see Q3).

Q8   *Assessment of group performance by stage.* The responses, across all groups, indicated that the subjects felt that the group's best performance came at the idea generation stage.

Q9   *Group performance at convergence and divergence.* Here, the reports were strongly biased towards greater perceived competences at divergent activities over convergent activities. Interestingly, this held for all three KAI sub-samples.

Further analysis of the responses to the PSPPQ involved parametric statistics. Using problem-solving stages (problem, ideas and solutions) and components within stages (divergence and convergence) as grouping variables, one-way analysis of variances and *t*-tests were used to identify significant differences in KAI scores. The only significant difference amongst KAI scores was found for the responses to the question on individuals' best performance for the components within stages. The mean KAI score for divergent responders was 111.64 and for the convergent responders the mean was 104.47 ($t114 = 2.54$, $p < 0.05$).

DISCUSSION

Issues emerging from the MBA study

The modelling of the process led to an elegant means of exploring perceived group preferences and behaviours. Even with a preliminary questionnaire the patterns and differences were highly suggestive. Thus, from the results we can see how cognitive style (as measured by the KAI) appears to be associated with preferences for convergence (KAI adaptors) or divergence (KAI innovators).

There is some evidence for differences in attitudes and self-perception between male and female respondents. Several interpretations of the differences are possible and the relatively small female sample makes us cautious about reading too much into the results. Nevertheless, further work is called for to investigate possible male/female differences in behaviours in problem-solving groups.

Management decision-making and the role of decision-support

This preliminary experiment provides us with some cautious optimism for further work aimed at connecting creative problem-solving to mainstream management science. Specifically it encourages us to address the important practical issues of individual differences, and implications for decision-support systems. Churchman and Schainblatt (1965) have already provided one powerful conceptual framework for modelling implementation. This work indicated an inherent communications problem between people seeking to introduce change, and people with power and/or responsibility for accepting change. Our own study reveals a discrimination made by those involved in a simulation of a complex managerial problem-solving situation between (perceived) behaviours and competence at the pre-implementation stages and implementation stage (as we have defined them). One interpretation of this is that problem-solving groups are better able to appreciate the potential value in new ideas at earlier stages in problem-solving, and more powerfully constrained by perceived difficulties at the implementation stage.

Furthermore, we found evidence that supports Kirton's theory of cognitive style (1989) which proposes individual differences in cognitive style which are stable over time, and which are strongly related to problem-solving preferences, and decision bias. We have interpreted the differences as pointing to a bias by some individuals toward seeking large numbers of ideas, during problem-solving, and a bias towards conservatism in other individuals. In practical decision-making terms these findings have implications for decision-support systems.

Broader implications for 1992 and beyond

The results appear consistent with growing recognition that decision-support systems have to account for individual differences in user behaviours. The design of effective support systems will require understanding of such differences (Polding and Lockett 1982). Already workers are examining the relationship between creativity and decision-making, using computer systems for modelling and support purposes (Schank 1982, 1988; Proctor 1988). The next steps might explore the differing needs according to individual user and situation. At stages requiring divergence, behavioural support would help overcome impulses for premature evaluation; at stages requiring selection, extensions of existing approaches for multi-criteria analysis will assist in clarifying differences arising from perceptual differences and communication distortions. Our work suggests that individuals with high KAI scores (innovative style) will continue to challenge boundaries during this stage, when individuals of lower KAI scores (adaptive style) will be impatient to achieve closure.

In her most recent work Kanter (1989) argues that organisationally there has been a swing away from bureaucratic conservatism towards an appreciation of the importance of entrepreneurial behaviours. She further argues that we now need to find a balance between the two modes of behaviour. Achieving a balance is critical at the stage of implementation of business ideas, strategies and innovations. It is the arena where creative problem-solving and decision-support systems may have the most to offer for practical and theoretical advances.

The turbulence of the managerial environment is hardly likely to be reduced as organisations form themselves into increasingly multinational alliances to meet the European challenges of 1992 and beyond. This will be particularly important for the UK whose organisations lead the EC in cross-border acquisitions in a recent survey (Mole 1990: 11). One leading industrialist quoted in Mole stated it as follows: 'Within the European Single Market, working with other European Managers will be increasingly common. It is crucial that we should be able to create effective working releationships rapidly' (Mole 1990: ix). Although multinationals have considerable experience of such teams, there may be an increase in demand for information and technology to assist in overcoming the interpersonal issues which will arise (Rickards 1990c). As Van Gundy noted, 'organisational growth and survival can be tied directly to an organisation's ability to produce (or adapt) and implement new services, products, and processes' (Van Gundy 1987: 358).

We suggest that the study and application of creative problem-solving procedures will provide a framework in which all members of teams may collaborate. Furthermore, the effectiveness of such teams may be influenced by person-environment matches or mismatches (Puccio 1990). The proposed three-dimensional model suggests itself as a framework for such studies, in conjunction with data on individual differences, including problem-solving styles and preferences.

REFERENCES

Ackoff, R. and Vergara, E., (1981) 'Creativity and planning: a review', *European Journal of Operational Research* 7, 1–12.

Adams, J. (1980) *Conceptual Blockbusting*, 2nd edn, New York, Norton.

Ainsworth-Land, G. and V. (1982) *Forward to Basics*, Buffalo, DOK.

Amabile, T. M. (1983) *The Social Psychology of Creativity*, New York, Springer-Verlag.

Barron, F. and Harrington, D. (1981) 'Creativity, intelligence and personality', *Annual Review of Psychology* 32.

Bessant, J. (1982) 'Influential factors in manufacturing innovation', *Research Policy* 11(2), 117–32.

Bessant, J. (1991) *Fifth Wave Manufacturing: Management Implications of New Manufacturing Technology*, Oxford, Blackwells.

Buijs, J. (1984) *Innovation en Interventie*, Deventer, the Netherlands, Kluwer.

Buijs, J. (1988) 'Innovation and vision', in P. Colemont, P. Grøholt, T. Rickards and H. Smeekes (eds) *Creativity and Innovation: Towards a European Network*, Deventer the Netherlands, Kluwer.

Burnstein, R. (1987) 'Improving corporate climates for creativity; learning from four interventions', paper presented at *First European Conference on Creativity and Innovation*, Noordwijk, the Netherlands, 13–16 December.

Carson, J. and Rickards, T. (1979) *Industrial New-Product Development*, Epping, Gower.

Churchman, W. and Schainblatt, A. H. (1965) 'The researcher and the

manager: a dialectic of implementation', *Management Science* 11(4), B69–B87.
Colemont, P., Grøholt, P., Rickards, T. and Smeekes, H. (eds) (1988) *Creativity and Innovation: Towards a European Network*, Deventer, the Netherlands, Kluwer.
de Bono, E. (1971) *Lateral Thinking for Management*, London, McGraw-Hill.
Drucker, P. (1969) *The Age of Discontinuity*, London, Heinemann.
Drucker, P. (1985) *Innovation and Entrepreneurship*, London, Heinemann.
During, W. (1986) *Innovatieproblematiek in kleine industriele bedrijven*, the Netherlands, Van Gorcum.
Ekvall, G. (1987) 'The climate metaphor in organization theory', in B. M. Bass and P. J. D. Drenth (eds) *Advances in Organizational Psychology*, Beverly Hills, Sage.
Elden, M. (1988) 'Innovation can be learned – some issues in designing a large scale Norwegian innovation program', in P. Colemont, P. Groholt, T. Rickards, and H. Smeekes (eds) *Creativity and Innovation: Towards a European Network*, Deventer, the Netherlands, Kluwer.
Foxall, G. R. (1986) 'Managers in transition: an empirical test of Krton's Adaption–Innovation Theory and its implications for the mid-career MBA', *Technovation* 4, 219–32.
Frohlich, D., Fuchs, D. and Kreiger, H., (1989) 'New Information technology and participation in Europe; the potential for social dialogue', in T. Rickards and S. Moger (eds) *Creativity and Innovation Yearbook*, Manchester, Manchester Business School, Vol. 2, pp. 85–94.
Geschka, H. (1983) 'Creativity techniques in product planning and development, a view from West Germany', *R & D Management* 13(3), 169–83.
Geschka, H. (1986) 'Creativity workshops in product innovation', *Journal of Product Innovation Management* 3(1), pp. 48–56.
Geschka, H. (1988) 'Generation of ideas by managers in Germany, Switzerland and Austria', in P. Colemont, P. Grøholt, T. Rickards and H. Smeekes (eds) *Creativity and Innovation: Towards a European Network* Deventer, the Netherlands, Kluwer.
Getzels, J. W. and Csikszentmihalyi, M. (1976) *The Creative Vision: a Longitudinal Study of Problem Finding in Art*, New York, Wiley.
Goldsmith, R. E. (1984) 'Personality characteristics associated with adaption-innovation', *Journal of Psychology*, 117, 159–65.
Goldsmith, R. E. (1987) 'Creative level and style', *British Journal of Social Psychology* 26, 317–23.
Gordon, W. J. J. (1961) *Synectics – the Development of Creative Capacity*, New York, Harper & Row.
Grønhaug, K. and Kaufmann, G. (eds) (1988) *Innovation: a Cross-Disciplinary Perspective*, Oslo, Norwegian University Press.
Gryskiewicz, S. S. (1980) 'Targeted innovation: a situational approach', *Creativity Week Proceedings*, Center for Creative Leadership, Greensboro, USA.
Guilford, J. P., (1981) 'Higher-order structure-of-intellect abilities', *Multivariate Behavioral Research* 16.
Isaksen, S. G. (ed.) (1987) *Creativity Research: Beyond the Basics*, New York, Bearly.

Isaksen, S. G. and Puccio, G. J. (1988) 'Adaption–innovation and the Torrance Tests of Creative thinking: the level-style issue revisited', *Psychological Reports* 63, 659–70.

Isaksen, S. G. and Treffinger, D. J. (1985) *Creative Problem-Solving: the Basic Course*, Buffalo, Bearly.

Jaoui, H. (1979) *Crea Prat*, Paris, Epi.

Johne, E. A. (1985) *Industrial Product Innovation*, London, Croom Helm.

Kanter, R. M. (1985) *The Change Masters*, London, Unwin.

Kanter, R. M. (1989) *When Giants Learn to Dance*, London and New York, Simon & Schuster.

Kaufmann, G. (1988) 'Problem-solving and creativity', in K. Grønhaug and G. Kaufmann (eds) *Innovation: a Cross-Disciplinary Perspective*, Oslo, Norwegian University Press.

Kindler, J. and Kiss, I. (1984) 'Future methodology based on past assumptions', in R. Tomlinson and I. Kiss, *Rethinking the Process of Operational Research and Systems Analysis*, Oxford, Pergamon.

Kirton, M. J. (1976) 'Adaptors and innovators: a description and measure', *Journal of Applied Psychology* 61, 622–9.

Kirton, M. J. (1987) *Kirton Adaption–Innovation Inventory Manual* 2nd edn, Hatfield, Occupational Research Centre.

Kirton, M. J. (ed.) (1989) *Adapters and Innovators: Styles of Creativity and Problem-Solving*, London, Routledge.

Koestler, A. (1964) *The Act of Creation*, London, Hutchison.

Kuhn, T. (1970) *Structure of Scientific Revolutions*, Chicago, University of Chicago Press.

MacKinnon, D. W. (1978) *In Search of Human Effectiveness*, Buffalo, New York, Bearly.

Maslow, A. (1959) 'Creativity in self-actualising people', in H. H. Anderson (ed.) *Creativity and its Cultivation*, New York, Harper and Brothers.

Mole, J. (1990) *Mind Your Manners: Culture Clash in the European Single Market*, London, Industrial Society Press.

Morgan, G. (1980) 'Paradigms, metaphors, and problem-solving in organization theory', *Administrative Science Quarterly* 25(1).

Morgan, G. (1986) *Images of Organization*, London and Beverley Hills, Sage.

Nȩcka, E. and Kubiak, M. (1989) 'Can training influence metaphorical thinking, creativity and level of dogmatism?', *Creativity and Innovation Yearbook*, Manchester, Manchester Business School, Vol. 2, pp. 95–110.

Nyström, H. (1988) 'Company creativity and innovation', in P. Colemont, P. Groholt, T. Rickards and H. Smeekes (eds) *Creativity and Innovation: Towards a European Network*, Deventer, the Netherlands, Kluwer.

Nyström, H. and Edvardsson, B. (1982) 'Product innovation in food processing', *R & D Management* 12, 67–72.

Osborn, A. F. (1963) *Applied Imagination* 3rd edn, New York, Scribner's Sons.

Parnes, S. J. and Noller, R. B. (1972) 'Applied creativity: the creative studies project – part 2: results of the two year programme', *Journal of Creative Behavior* 6, 164–86.

Parnes, S. J., Noller, R. B. and Biondi, A. M. (1977) *Guide to Creative Action*, New York, Scribner's Sons.

Payne, R. L. (1987) 'Individual differences and performance amongst R & D personnel: some implications for management development', *R & D Development Journal* 17, 153–61.

Peters, T. (1987) *Thriving on Chaos*, London, Macmillan.

Peters, T. and Waterman, R. (1982) *In Search of Excellence*, New York, Harper & Row.

Polding. E and Lockett, G. (1982) 'Attitudes and perceptions relating to implementation and success in operational research', *Journal of the Operational Research Society* 33, 733.

Porter, M. E. (1980) *Competitive Strategy: Techniques for Analysing Industries and Competitors*, New York, Free Press.

Prince, G. (1970) *The Practice of Creativity*, New York, Harper & Row.

Proctor, A. (1988) 'Creative aspects of problem-solving: a critical analysis and explanation of the attribution of meaning during interactive problem-solving sessions, sequences, and simulations', unpublished PhD dissertation, Victoria University of Manchester, UK.

Puccio, G. J. (1987) 'The effect of cognitive style upon problem-defining behaviour', unpublished Master's thesis, State University College at Buffalo, USA.

Puccio, G. J. (1990) 'Person-environment fit: using Kirton's Adapter–Innovator Theory to determine the effect of stylistic fit upon stress, job satisfaction, and effective performance', unpublished PhD dissertation, Victoria University of Manchester, UK.

Rickards, T. (1985) *Stimulating Innovation*, London, Pinter.

Rickards, T. (1987) 'Can computers help stimulate creativity?', *Management Education and Development* 18, (2), 129–39.

Rickards, T. (1988) *Creativity at Work*, Farnborough, Gower.

Rickards, T. (1990a) 'Innovation and creativity, woods, trees, and pathways', keynote speech, R & D Research Unit 25th anniversary conference, Manchester Business School, Manchester, 9–11 July.

Rickards, T. (1990b) 'The creative product: a review of twenty years practical experiences and theoretical implications in industrial contexts', *International Research Conference on Creativity*, Buffalo, 14–18 August.

Rickards, T. (1990c) 'The KAI as a survey-feedback instrument', *Journal of European Industrial Management* 14 (6), 3–7.

Rickards, T. and Freedman, B. L. (1979) 'A reappraisal of creativity techniques', *Journal of European Industrial Training* 3, 3–8.

Rickards, T. and Moger, S. (1989) 'EEC notes: the council decides on seven community research and technological development programmes', *Creativity and Innovation Yearbook*, Manchester Business School, Manchester, Vol. 2, pp. 160–170.

Rickards, T. and Puccio, G. (1989) 'Creative problem-solving and general systems theories: towards an integration of two paradigms', 33rd Annual Meeting, International Society for General Systems Research, Edinburgh, August.

Rickards, T., Aldridge, S. and Gaston, K. (1988) 'Factors affecting brainstorming: towards the development of diagnostic tools for assessment of creative performance', *R & D Management Journal* 18 (4), 309–320.

Rogers, C. (1959) 'Towards a theory of creativity', in H. H. Anderson (ed.) *Creativity and its Cultivation*, New York. Harper & Brothers.

Schank, R. C. (1982) *Dynamic Memory: a Theory of Learning in Computers and People*, Cambridge, Cambridge University Press.

Schank, R. C. (1988) 'Creativity as a mechanical process', in R. J. Sternberg (ed.) *The Nature of Creativity*, Cambridge, Cambridge University Press.

Schank, R. C. and Abelson, R. (1977) *Scripts, Plans, Goals and Understanding*, Hillsdale, Laurence Erlbaum.

Simon, H. (1984) 'What we know about the creative process', in R. L. Kuhn (ed.) *Frontiers in Creative and Innovative Management*, Cambridge, Mass., Ballinger.

Simonton, D. (1988) *Scientific Genius: a Psychology of Science*, Cambridge, Cambridge University Press.

Smyth, D. S. and Checkland, P. B. (1976) 'Using a systems approach: the structure of root definitions', *Journal of Applied Systems Analysis*, 5(1).

Stein, M. (1974/1975) *Stimulating Creativity*, Vols. 1–2, New York, Academic Press.

Sternberg, R. J. (ed.) (1988) *The Nature of Creativity*, Cambridge, Cambridge University Press.

Talbot, R. (1982) 'Creativity', in M. Smith *et al.* (eds) *Introducing Organisational Behaviour*, London, Macmillan.

Tomlinson, R. (1984) 'Rethinking the process of systems analysis and operational research: from practice to precept – and back again', in R. Tomlinson and I. Kiss (eds) *Rethinking the Process of Operational Research and Systems Analysis*, Oxford, Pergamon.

Torrance, E. P. (1974) *Torrance Tests of Creative Thinking*, Lexington, Mass., Personnel Press.

Torrance, E. P. (1981) 'Predicting the creativity of elementary school children (1958–1980)', *Gifted Child Quarterly*, 25, 55–62.

Trolle, H. and Graversen, H. (1989) 'Making product development more creative', *Creativity and Innovation Yearbook* 2, 146–9.

Van Gundy, A. (1987) 'Organizational creativity and innovation,' in S. G. Isaksen (ed.) *Frontiers of Creativity Research: Beyond the Basics* Buffalo, Bearly.

Wesenberg, P. (1986/7) 'Creativity in organisations – a contradiction in terms?', *Creativity and Innovation Network* 12(3/4) 62–8.

14 Getting decisions to work

Analysing successful implementation

Susan Miller

DECISION-MAKING AND AFTER

The process of organisational decision-making has received much attention from researchers in recent years, with particular interest being paid to the making of strategic decisions. These are the larger, more important decisions which occur less frequently in organisations. They are usually 'non-programmed' (Simon 1960) or 'unstructured' (Mintzberg *et al.* 1976), which means they are more difficult to make, as they do not follow tried and tested decision-making routines. Such decisions are normally made by senior management.

Research has tended to concentrate on how such decisions are made. In other words, how the matter for decision is formulated, how information is gathered and processed and who is involved (or left out) of decision-making. The general purpose has often been to categorise or in some way classify different types of decision-making process. Hence, Mintzberg and his colleagues (1976) studied twenty-five decisions and discovered seven kinds of process; Nutt (1984) looked at seventy-eight cases and distinguished five types of process; while the most recent, large-scale project, the 'Bradford Studies' (Hickson *et al.* 1986) investigated 150 decisions in thirty organisations and came up with three distinct types of process. One might be tempted to suggest an inverse relationship between the amount of cases studied and the number of process categories here!

So, we know something about how strategic issues are decided, what we do not know is what happens when such decisions are put into effect. To begin with, are they put into effect, do they get implemented? If so, are they implemented completely, or only in part? Do these decisions have the results which the decision-makers expected? Are they successful, or do they fail? Do organisational members all share the same opinion about the answers to the above questions?

These issues are not often addressed in studies of decision-making. Researchers do not usually ask such questions. Their research interest generally stops once the decision has been arrived at. Few stay in the organisation long enough to see what happens next.

But what happens next should be of interest, not only to researchers but also to the decision-makers and others in the organisation. It has been suggested by Cohen *et al.* (1972) that sometimes people are more interested in participating in decision-making than in the actual outcome. They argue that what is important is to be part of the process and that the final decision and its enactment are of secondary consideration. Even if this is true for some decision-makers in some cases, the implementation of decisions may be of concern to others in the organisation. For example, to those required to put the decision into operation (the 'implementors') and those affected by it (the 'implementees'). For these reasons alone, the study of strategic decisions needs to be expanded in order to encompass the implementation stage. Furthermore, it is in the interest of organisational members and researchers alike to examine the outcomes of decisions, and to find out whether the costs and time expended in decision-making are worth all the effort.

POTENTIAL PROBLEMS IN RESEARCH ON IMPLEMENTATION

It is argued that research into implementation is clearly desirable. But is it possible? There are two potential difficulties here. They concern the identification of the implementation process and its delineation. And they revolve around the questions: 'how can you analyse an implementation process?' and 'where does decision-making end and implementation begin?'.

First, the problem of identifying implementation. Social processes in organisations are sometimes hard to pin down. They are ephemeral and intangible. As Hickson and Miller (1991: 2) note: 'The conceptualization of something so elusive as a decision making process is not an easy task. For it is not "some-thing" at all. It is a movement of events through time.' It is likely that the conceptualisation of implementation will share some of the difficulties which are encountered in the analysis of decision-making. So, decision-making and implementation processes may be less than clear-cut. This is the case with many organisational activities. What helps analysis is the formation of concepts which can be used to make descriptions of process more precise. The Bradford Studies (Hickson *et al.* 1986) attempted this in terms of decision-making processes. The research discussed in this chapter attempts to do the same for processes of implementation.

Then there is the issue of separating what happens 'pre-decision' from what happens 'post-decision'. Heller *et al.* (1988) see implementation as being part of the total decision process. They break down the complete process into four phases, implementation being the fourth and final phase, covering 'the period between finalization and the final operation of the decision or its failure' (Heller *et al.* 1988: 4). So whilst they see implementation as just a phase in a larger process, it is distinguishable. According to Heller *et al.* (1988), implementation starts when the decision has been made, and finishes when the decision is either working or is seen to be unworkable for whatever reasons.

It is acknowledged that decision-making and implementation processes may be hard to separate out. There may be some overlap between the two; nevertheless it is felt that distinction is possible. This research is a verification of this view. Research in other fields of enquiry also bears this out, and is briefly summarised below.

IMPLEMENTATION RESEARCH IN POLICY ANALYSIS

Some of the research on implementation has been carried out by writers in the fields of policy studies and analysis. Using examples taken mainly from public administration organisations researchers have highlighted the 'implementation gap' – the fact that there are significant problems in realising some decisions. Pressman and Wildavsky (1973) were among the first to document these in their description of the difficulties faced by local government agencies in the US when trying to implement federal policy.

Barrett and Hill (1984), Barrett and Fudge (1981), Bardach (1977) and others studying public administration in Britain have similarly drawn attention to these problems. But these are conclusions based primarily on studies of local authorities, and the question is, how far can such results be applicable to the implementation of strategic decisions in other organisations. Hjern and Porter (1981) have demonstrated the complex network of relationships which are necessarily built up between local authorities and other organisations when implementing policy decisions. Does this perhaps render such implementations more problematic? If so, decisions made and implemented largely within the boundary of a unitary organisation may follow a different path.

So, research in this area is a useful guide to the potential problems of implementation but further work in a variety of organisations is still required. In addition, policy research tends to be descriptive, rather than analytical. That is, particular cases of implementation are discussed, but as yet there has been little attempt to distinguish implementation-relevant concepts. This means that any comparison between cases, beyond general comments and conclusions, is left much more difficult.

To summarise the foregoing, research on implementation is of interest and is relatively neglected. Of the research which has been carried out, much is specific to public administration and concerns the execution of policy. This research has tended towards description rather than analysis. What is now required is work which looks at implementation processes in a number of different organisations, and which attempts to derive concepts to aid analysis and comparison.

The study now discussed is an effort in this direction and, although it concentrates on British organisations – and within Britain, English companies only – it is, in fact, one component in an international study of decision-making and implementation. More will be said about the wider aspects of this research in due course.

THE PRESENT STUDY – CASES AND CONCEPT FORMATION

The research carried out for this study was centred on eleven cases of implementation in six organisations. Cases and organisations are given below to indicate the diversity and range of the project. Names of organisations are fictitious.

1 Easyshop Mail Order Company: The installation of a new computer system.
2 Great Northern Mail Order Company: The installation of a new computer system; the building of a new, multi-million pound warehouse.
3 Vale University: The building of the university and campus; boiler house modifications and installation of energy management system.
4 Central Water Authority: The introduction of a CAD system into development sections; the building of a water-treatment works.
5 S & D Chemical Company: Centralisation of transport and distribution systems; the installation of a new computer system.

6 Wharf Chemical Company: The formation of Wharf Chemicals; merger of two divisions within Wharf Chemicals.

The research was carried out using case study methods and interviewing a wide range of respondents in each organisation. Interviewing began with those managers who were most closely concerned with the decision and then spread in a 'snowballing' fashion to as many significant others at all levels who were mentioned during the course of interviews. In all 113 respondents were interviewed and in this way an overall picture was gradually built up.

The objectives of the study were to provide some conceptualisation of the factors which make implementation more or less 'successful'. In other words what causes problems during implementation, and under what circumstances, and what makes things go more smoothly.

It is recognised that 'success' is this context is a vague and value-laden term, open to differing interpretations. For the purposes of this project three dependent variables were distinguished to operationalise successful implementation. These were 'Completion', which refers to whether the decision was fully implemented within the expected time period; 'Achievement', whether it achieved all the objectives which were intended; and 'Acceptability', which refers to how people in the organisation viewed both the process and the outcomes of implementation.

To examine the reasons why some strategic decisions may be implemented with more or less success than others, the cases of Easyshop and Great Northern Mail Order are now briefly recounted. Both companies operate in the mail order industry and, to further control for comparison, both decisions selected for this paper concern the installation of mainframe computer systems. These decisions and their implementation were crucial to both companies. In the mail order business, survival and success depend upon the speedy and accurate handling of customer orders. Computerisation here is not merely a matter of changing a managerial support system. It is changing the core technology of the entire organisation.

Easyshop Mail Order

Easyshop Mail Order company was established in the 1890s in the north of England and today employs some 3,000 people. From the 1960s to the mid-1970s, Easyshop, in common with other mail order companies, was enjoying expansion and financial success. However, the business depended on extensive administrative arrangements in order to run its empire, which consisted of a large number of 'agents' – usually housewives – who were sent the Easyshop catalogue, ordered goods for themselves and friends and generally ran the paperwork side of things from home. Since the company employed numerous clerks to receive and process the agents' orders, the whole business was extremely labour-intensive. By the 1970s labour-costs were rising and it was decided to install computerised systems to try and cut costs and increase efficiency.

In taking this step the company was one of the first in the industry. But such an initiative also meant that Easyshop had little experience on which to plan such an exercise, and this, coupled with the fact that the computer industry itself was still in a learning stage, resulted in many unknowns with which the company had to cope. For reasons of safety and low risk, managers decided to simply transfer all the manual routines straight on to the computer without re-organising or rationalising them. This eventually was to mean that they were burdened with over-complicated, over-detailed systems, which took up vast computer capacity and yet did not provide information in a readily accessible or usable form. As the chief executive remarked, they had a 'Rolls Royce system for a Ford operation', and they were becoming bogged down in the minutiae of their activities.

In the early 1980s the company was in a very serious financial condition, debt recovery procedures were ineffective and profits were falling. Even though financial resources were scarce, a decision was made to start again and attempt to re-computerise.

This was not a popular decision as much time and effort had already been invested in the existing system. Several members of senior management were averse to spending more money in this way and the general climate at the top of the organisation was conservative and wary of risk.

A feature of this decision was the intense conflict between interests at a senior level which began during decision-making and continued into the implementation phase. Indeed, the antagonism was so damaging that implementation ceased almost completely at one point. This conflict centred around the computer director and the development staff who had spearheaded the existing system and were not in favour of another radical change. The job of re-writing the systems was taken out of the development section and put under the auspices of the sales administration director, who was therefore left with the unenviable task of trying to implement one department's decision while working in another. In spite of this (or perhaps because of it), the computer director was able to delay implementation for nearly a year by withholding necessary information and resources.

Implementation was especially complex since all the different parts of the computer operation (the order-processing section, stock control, agency administration systems etc.) interlinked with each other, which made it very awkward to try and separate one from another in order to upgrade an area at a time. Matters were made particularly difficult because the current system had to be kept running while the new one was being developed.

Implementation was initially anticipated to take a year (although the sales systems manager, who was writing the software, privately forecast twice this time). The internal conflict, and also the possibility of a takeover by another large company (whose computer systems were already running smoothly and would therefore be installing these into Easyshop in the event of a successful bid) caused long delays. In the event, the decision was still not fully implemented seven years later, although the arrival of a new managing director and the subsequent enforced departure of the contentious computer director provided new impetus to implementation.

What are the features of this particular implementation process? It was certainly not an easy, straightforward one. Disagreements during the pre-decision process continued even when the decision had been taken by the board to go ahead. There were delays due to internal conflicts, and to external eventualities. There were also the problems resulting from the complexity of an unfamiliar technology, and the inexperience and lack of expertise of organisational members. Political behaviour impeded progress, and because the disruption emanated from the top of the organisation, it both absorbed senior management's attention, and filtered downwards to hold up the work of those beneath. Conservative senior management seemed unable or unwilling to rectify the difficulties and provide a suitable climate for change.

In short, the process encountered impediments both from conflict and from the occurrence of unforeseen events. The complexity and unfamiliarity of the new technology also caused problems, while the culture and structural arrangements of the organisation only served to aggravate matters.

All the above combined to ensure that the decision was not implemented completely, it did not achieve what it was supposed to, and neither the process of implementation nor its outcome were acceptable to most organisational members. In these terms, implementation was unsuccessful.

The second case described below, another computer installation in another mail order company, presents a vivid contrast to Easyshop, being a much smoother process with a much more successful outcome.

Great Northern Mail Order Company

In many ways the history of Great Northern is similar to that of Easyshop. Both did well in the 1960s while the industry was enjoying growth and expansion, and both suffered the consequences of a check in growth during the 1970s. Like Easyshop, the early 1980s saw Great Northern in a serious financial position. Lulled into comparative inertia by past successes, management had failed to anticipate, and subsequently respond to, changes in the retailing world. There was increased competition from other mail order companies and from high street shops. Tentative attempts at introducing some computerisation had resulted in limited, uncoordinated systems which performed poorly. Debt recovery procedures in particular were inadequate and the company was losing money.

The need for a thorough up-dating of the company's systems, was just as urgent as in Easyshop, the technical difficulties just as complex and interrelated. The problems which each company faced stemmed from similar causes, the same solution was chosen, and both companies made the decision to develop major new computer systems in the early 1980s. But while Easyshop was still battling to fully implement its decision at the end of the 1980s, Great Northern had its systems up and running at the beginning of the decade. The implementation in Easyshop took more than seven years, in Great Northern it took six months. Why was this?

One of the essential features of Great Northern's success story is the fact that the decision was made and implemented by a management team which already had first-hand experience of implementing a similar decision in another company. In 1981 the chairman of Great Northern brought in a new managing director, who although young, had considerable experience in a larger, rival, mail order company. He attracted with him a huge number of senior staff from his old company, in all over twenty people, most of whom were computer personnel. Many established Great Northern directors and senior managers lost their jobs as a result, and one department in the computer section was closed completely.

The new managing director immediately recognised that the computer systems required major improvements, and he made this his first priority. In essence, this decision was unopposed. First, because most of the old Great Northern personnel (directors and computing staff who might have been unhappy about such a radical change) were replaced by new people, who included three new directors in the computing area. Secondly, it was accepted by the staff that the company was in a serious position and that radical remedies were necessary.

Because they had already been involved with the successful installation of a new computer system at their previous company, the MD and the computer director already knew which hardware and systems they wanted. Although the software had to be written to accommodate Great Northern's requirements, the fact that senior management were already familiar with a similar operation meant the company could start further along the learning curve, and that fewer mistakes were likely to be made. Unlike Easyshop, they were not struggling with unknowns.

Of course it was not all plain sailing. The decision required a large capital investment, not an easy matter in a flagging company. In addition, there was a shortage of manpower and also time, since a strict deadline was set for completion. Some of the staff who were left in the computer section were demoralised and frightened of losing their jobs. Yet it was these individuals to whom the task was given of compiling the new programs. They had to get used to new equipment and operating systems, had to learn a new, higher-level, computer language and then write programs in it.

Nevertheless, both old and new employees rose to the task. Implementation was rushed along at a frenetic pace which was exhilarating but highly pressured. By working evenings and weekends for six months the deadline was met, implementation was complete and achieved everything which had been intended in a way acceptable to most employees in the organisation.

CONTRASTING CASES – EXPLANATIONS FOR SUCCESS AND FAILURE

What then can be learned from these two contrasting cases? What concepts can be derived to enable them to be compared, and to enable further comparisons? Is it possible to begin to deduce some of the reasons why one was more successful than the other, reasons that may be generalised and applied to other cases?

The first point of interest is the fact that the implementation processes in the two companies differed so sharply. Easyshop and

Great Northern are companies in the same industry, mail order, implementing the same kind of decision, to computerise. Yet implementation in each followed a very different path. So there is no evidence whatever to suggest that if the same decisions are taken in two similar organisations, even at about the same time, they will be carried out in the same way.

Great Northern's story is one of the most successful of the eleven cases studied, scoring highly on each of the three dependent variables of Completion, Achievement and Acceptability. Easyshop is the least successful case with a low score on each of these variables. What factors (or *independent* variables) may contribute to success and failure in implementation?

From the cases it is clear that Easyshop suffered from internal conflict and opposition, while Great Northern enjoyed relatively high commitment from organisational members. The concept of *backing* emerges from this, operationalised as the degree to which influence patterns favour implementation. At Easyshop the lack of backing impeded implementation, and though at Great Northern some backing was the result of desperation and fear, it was sufficient to ensure success.

Another variable to emerge is that of *propitiousness*; the degree to which any unforeseen occurrences favour implementation. This refers to those unforeseen events which may help or hinder implementation. Not everything can be predicted or foreseen beforehand and there is always the possibility that some chance event may occur. As in everything, a bit of 'luck' may play a part in organisational activities. In Easyshop, this chance event was the unexpected takeover bid by a rival company and it proved to be unfavourable for implementation, delaying matters for a considerable time. In contrast, Great Northern suffered no such event – nothing happened to impede implementation.

The *complexity* of the matter for decision was significant for both organisations. Both were faced with implementation tasks of great intricacy which affected many parts of the organisation. This idea of complexity complements the findings of the Bradford Studies (Hickson *et al*. 1986), where it is argued that it is a major determinant of the decision-making process.

However, the present study suggests an important qualifier to this. It has been shown that even highly complex implementations can be made easier if those involved have relevant experience. This is clearly demonstrated by Great Northern's computer installation. The fact that a substantial number of managers had already implemented a similar decision helped a great deal in this organisation. In contrast, Easyshop's lack of experience exposed them to error. Thus *familiarity* is a crucial concept here. Complexity can make implementation harder but only if there is low familiarity. High familiarity can render complexity less harmful.

Further independent variables are concerned with the climate and the structure of the organisation. In Great Northern the culture was ripe for change. A new management team could make radical changes – an instance of a 'new broom sweeping clean' perhaps. At Easyshop implementation was hampered by senior management very much 'stuck in their ways' and wary of risk, who failed to provide the right impetus for change. It is interesting to note that when Easyshop's 'new broom' eventually arrived in the form of a new managing director, things moved forward much more speedily.

In Great Northern the structure of the organisation was suitable for implementation. Although decision-making was centralised, bureaucracy was minimised in order to allow the implementors to get on with the job with as much autonomy as possible. This allowed implementation to proceed at speed and helped to alleviate problems of morale. At Easyshop, the structure was actually a hindrance, since the main implementor had to attempt implementation from the wrong place in the hierarchy. Therefore, *cultural* and *structural appropriateness* are also variables which may affect implementation.

The final issue illustrated by these two cases is that of *resource availability*. The view that resources – such as manpower, finance and time – which are necessary for implementation need to be made available is a truism which is often cited as a precondition of implementation success. In the present study it must be said that no cases were unsuccessful solely because they lacked resources. Many cases had fewer resources than was ideally desirable, but none failed completely because of this. But it does not then follow that the more successful implementations were the ones with the greatest abundance of resources. Indeed, Great Northern was one of the most successful cases, but had the least resources available to it, being short of everything – people, money and time. So limited resources do not necessarily impede implementation – as long as there is a sufficiency, implementation can be highly successful.

In summary, the cases have highlighted a number of factors which may affect implementation. Backing, propitiousness, complexity, familiarity, cultural and structural appropriateness and resource availability have all been suggested as influential features of the implementation process. The formation of concepts such as these is a useful aid in providing a more analytical framework with which to carry out research in this area.

CONCLUSIONS

The cases described above have suggested seven independent and three dependent variables which may be helpful in analysing the implementation of strategic decisions in organisations. Other cases in the study corroborate these findings and also suggest other variables not discussed here. While these may not be exhaustive, they do provide a partial explanation of implementation processes. At this stage specific associations are not made between independent and dependent variables. Such relationships await the result of further analysis and research. What is clear is that no one variable can explain success, or the lack of it. The fostering of success in implementation is multi-variate in nature.

What is also clear is that post-decision processes, unlike pre-decision processes, can follow very different paths even if the matter for implementation is substantially the same. It is not solely what has to be implemented that causes problems – if there are problems – the particular features of the organisation and its personnel must also be taken into account.

The research presented here is an attempt to go beyond mere description and attempt an analytical framework with which to conceptualise implementation processes. The investigation of eleven cases is a first step in this and obviously more work needs to be carried out to broaden the enquiry.

With this in mind further research is currently being undertaken which will not only evaluate and refine concepts, but also seeks to compare and contrast how managers in other countries make and implement decisions. 1992 sees an expansion in more direct contact between managers in Europe and it will be important to understand how these central organisational activities are carried out in different nations. The cultural attributes of individual organisations have already been shown to play a part in post-decision processes; it may be that wider cultural components play a significant part in making decisions and putting them into effect. This has still to be explored.

Nevertheless, it is hoped that this study is a beginning in that it provides a guide to the factors which are influential during the implementation process. Research of this kind may highlight the reasons why implementation problems do sometimes occur. More importantly perhaps, it may indicate the areas in which it is fruitful to search for potential solutions.

REFERENCES

Bardach, E. (1977) *The Implementation Game – What Happens After a Bill Becomes Law*, Cambridge, Mass., MIT Press.

Barrett, S. and Fudge, C. (1981) *Policy and Action*, London, Methuen.

Barrett, S. and Hill, M. (1984) 'Policy, bargaining and structure in implementation theory – towards an integrated perspective', *Policy and Politics* 12(3), 219–40.

Cohen, M. D., March, J. C. and Olsen, J. P. (1972) 'A garbage can model of organizational choice', *Administrative Science Quarterly* 17, 1–25.

Heller, F., Drenth, P., Koopman, P. and Rus, V. (1988) *Decisions in Organizations – A Three-country Comparative Study*, London, Sage.

Hickson, D. J. and Miller, S. (1991) 'Concepts of decision: Making and implementing strategic decisions in organizations', in F. Heller (ed.) *Leadership and Organizational Decision-making*, Cambridge, Cambridge University Press.

Hickson, D. J., Butler, R. J., Cray, D. Mallory, G. R. and Wilson, D. C. (1986) *Top Decisions: Strategic Decision Making in Organizations*, Oxford, Blackwell; San Francisco, Jossey-Bass.

Hjern, B. and Porter, D. O. (1981) 'Implementation structures: a new unit of administrative analysis', *Organization Studies* 2(3), 211–27.

Mintzberg, H., Raisinghani, D. and Theoret, A. (1976) 'The structure of "unstructured" decision proceses', *Administrative Science Quarterly* 21, 246–75.

Nutt, P. (1984) 'Types of organizational decision processes', *Administrative Science Quarterly* 29(3), 414–50.

Pressman, J. L. and Wildavsky, A. B. (1973) *Implementation: How Great Expectations in Washington are Dashed in Oakland*, Berkeley, California, University of California Press.

Simon, H. A. (1960) *The New Science of Management Decision*, New York, Harper & Row.

15 Values and decisions

Roy Wilkie

Perhaps a word or two of academic autobiography might help to introduce this chapter. For over twenty years now I have been involved in the teaching of management, and, in particular, the teaching of organisation behaviour, to undergraduates, postgraduates and post-experience students, as well as to managers working in many different kinds of organisations. Throughout this period I have many times pointed to the conceptual poverty of much that passes under the rubric of management theory; to the thin, insubstantial people who are described in the hundreds of textbooks that have been pouring out – mainly from the United States of America. As a corollary of this, I have had to draw upon other resources of our culture – movies, plays, novels and short stories – to compensate for this deficiency.

In a book published in 1974, *The Concept of Organization*, which I co-authored with David Bradley, we advocated that, for understanding organisational life:

> We should recognize that we need all the help we can obtain. This means not only being alert to work being done in related social sciences, but also being sensitive to the insights and descriptions of the artists of our society. Just as we lose much of the information content of speech by printing it, so we often lose much of our organizational life in the records of academics. . . . We would strongly urge the importance of those aspects of our minority and popular culture that deal with organizational affairs, for there we have provided for us an abundance of serious and comic comment on the problems, foibles and rewards of life in organizations. It must surely be one of the most suspect features of contemporary social science that it has neither the inclination nor the structure to relate to and draw upon the culture of our time.
>
> (Bradley and Wilkie 1974: 111)

In the mid-1980s, my attention was drawn to the work of Sanford Lottor and his colleagues at Brandeis University who had also been involved in using literature for similar purposes. The origins of their interest lay in an invitation by the Chief Justice of the Massachusetts District Court system to develop a continuing education programme for his judges who were, in his judgement, overworked, understaffed, constantly faced with difficult decisions and insoluble problems, and generally exposed to the most troubling examples of human conflict and distress. They were suffering, he thought, extraordinary stress and were liable to 'burn-out'. Lottor's response was to design a pilot programme in which literary texts would be used in seminars to help the judges explore some of their dilemmas. In this pilot programme the texts used were Melville's *Billy Budd* and Brecht's *The Caucasian Chalk Circle*. After his success with the judges, Lottor became involved with physicians:

> We soon found that physicians were affected by the same tensions and issues that surfaced in our judges' programmes: the tension between public expectations and the ability to fulfill them; the asymmetry of power between those exercising judgements and those affected by it; the inordinate pressures and the debilitating exposure to humanity in travail; the disparity between professional ideas – what they were educated for – and the environment of work; the commonly felt conflict between the public demands and private conscience; in short, all the stresses that lead to 'burn-out'. We also found that themes of judgement and justice were not unique to judges but were shared by physicians. Difficult decision-making (often with 'cost-benefit' considerations at odds with fundamental rights or obligations) was surely an attribute of both groups, and one had to ask whether those making the decisions had done justice not only to the people affected . . . but, indeed, to themselves and their families. Each profession clearly had to reflect on difficult issues of how its power was exercised in whose interests, with what results.
>
> (Brandeis University 1986: 2–3)

Lottor offered two primary justifications for his approach: first, 'great literature alone was able to stimulate and sustain the kind of discussion that was wanted. It was only literature that could touch universal notes which resonated in the lives of our participants'; second, 'by providing fictional plots and characters as the crux material for discussion, usually about situations analogous to that of the professionals involved, literature gave the participants a kind of neutral frame on which to project their thoughts and feelings'. (Brandeis University 1986: 4–5).

This chapter represents an attempt to examine these claims by consideration of examples from my own teaching experience with various kinds of students and of the standard material offered to them. In particular, I shall be concerned to demonstrate how these students' understanding of the nature of their own and others' methods of decision-making, as a central aspect of the organisational environments in which they are involved, may be augmented by techniques drawn upon works of literature. The chapter begins with an acknowledgement of the importance of the notion of decision-making in the discipline of organisational behaviour. Secondly, some reservations about the concept of decision-making derived from other disciplines will be discussed. Thirdly, the usefulness of films and novels in education and management will be examined. Then, in the final section, there will be a brief case description and analysis of one session where managers met to discuss Tolstoy's *The Death of Ivan Ilyich*. The argument will be presented, in John Wisdom's phrase, (1953: 157), not as links of a chain, more like legs of a chair.

DECISION-MAKING AND ORGANISATIONAL BEHAVIOUR

Our culture has, for some time, polarised our knowledge into two – the way of the sciences and the way of the humanities. The characteristics of science are generally accepted as verbal or mathematical conceptualisations of people's public experiences, of correlating these conceptualisations into a coherent system and of trying to prove, by observation and experiment, that the findings square with certain aspects of events taking place 'out there' (Huxley 1963:8). The thrust of the discipline of organisation behaviour and management theory in general is in this direction. Many textbooks in organisational behaviour – there may well have been over a hundred published in the last ten to fifteen years – have appeared, usually simply with the title 'Organisational Behaviour' and usually distilling the findings of social psychology, sometimes industrial sociology, into attractive packages of easily assimilated pieces of knowledge. With the arrival of the textbooks, a discipline has emerged. As Kuhn (1970: 10) pointed out, they are the recognised expression of normal science.

The textbooks on the discipline of organisational behaviour demonstrate the 'normal science' aspects of the subject, most obviously with respect to matters of motivation – but also, and this is one of the main planks of this chapter, with respect to matters of decision-making. Research done elsewhere in other disciplines has been redescribed and honed down into comments, suggestions and prescriptions about decision-making whereby the processes by which decisions are made are perceived by management specialists to be the consequence of the logical operation of deductive reasoning and counterintuitive thought. Successful decision-making techniques are supposed to represent procedures applied to the deliberate, conscious, rational evaluation of alternative choices (see, for example, George 1964: 19; Michael and Jones 1973: 255; Dessler 1976: 328; Glueck 1977: 382; Brown and Moberg 1980: 544; Weinshall and Raveh 1983: 58; Miner 1985: 404; Harrison 1987: 1, 487).

What these texts demonstrate is that decision-making is a central concept in organisational behaviour and management theory. But what does it add up to? Why is it important? There seem to be two main reasons for its importance, according to the aforementioned commentators and theorists. One reason is that, because managers spend a great deal of their time making decisions, they need to learn how to make effective decisions. In the final analysis, it seems, managers are paid for doing only one thing: making decisions. The job of managing is the job of making decisions. Another reason is that managers are judged (and hence, rewarded or punished) on their success or failure rate in making these decisions. Hence, many chapters are written about decisions and decision-making, the object of which is to help managers make better decisions.

There is general agreement in the literature about the process of decision-making. The common ingredients are usually described as a search process to discover goals, the formulation of objectives after search, the selection of alternatives (strategies) to accomplish objectives and the evaluation of outcomes (see, for example, Scott 1971: 19; Moore and Thomas 1976: 41; Vecchio 1988: 321). To some, this process of learned rationality will ultimately result in a better world (Kaufman 1968: 245). The process of learned rationality, deductive reasoning and conscious decision-making is the direct antithesis of unconscious motivation, unstable intuition and the murky imprecision of non-rational processes of intellection. According to Simon (1977: 69), for example, we can abandon consideration of unconscious psychological influences on decision-making because these human processes can be explained without postulating mechanisms at subconscious levels that are different from those that are partly conscious and partly verbalised.

There doesn't seem to be a lot of harm in all of this. In fact, the whole tenor of these comments has a 'motherhood' look about it. They are warm and cuddly, and seem almost as informative as maintaining that a niece must have an uncle or an aunt. And, if a manager, or whoever, wants to read such books and wants to facilitate making decisions, then it isn't obvious that reading such texts would be bad for one. One might add that reading about decision-making can be an effective way of postponing the making of decisions. At best, it is harmless; at worst, merely time-wasting.

But, of course, this naive faith in the 'science' of decision-making does not predominate just in organisational behaviour and management theory. It also appears in other social sciences. In sociology, some work has been done on the relation of decision-making to organisations and their environments. Meyer and Scott, (1983: 143) for example, identify three types of decisions which they term programmatic, instrumental and funding which they use 'to capture variation in the distribution of decision-making rights' within an industrial sector. In anthropology, also, there has been some work done on the importance of decision-making processes. Heath (1976), for example, has pointed out the relevance of such work for exchange theory but, to his credit, has gone on to question the assumptions upon which this work is based.

A moment's reflection suggests that this concentration upon the nature and significance of visible, legible decision-making as a key theme within the social sciences is unsurprising, for, as an object of inquiry, it appears peculiarly amenable to the methods which Huxley perceives as characteristic of the scientific approach to social life – encouraging, as it does, an emphasis upon the significance of observable behaviour, the analytical primacy of general explanatory and taxonomical categories, and the logical interrelationship of the various components within the explanatory framework thus produced.

SOME RESERVATIONS ABOUT DECISION-MAKING

We should note that, throughout this emphasis and development of the notion of decision-making, there have been reservations. In the first place, the proposed model is over-rationalistic. As Mintzberg (1977) convincingly argued, Simon's *The New Science of Management Decision* celebrated the effects of technology, analysis as well as automation, and that all modes of thinking can be represented in sequential form, that what we call judgement or intuition can be simulated in the computer, and that the modern techniques of analysis must be applied to that judgement if society is to solve its problems. Mintzberg (1977: 350) himself considered that we should question the extent to which we can trust analysis untempered by intuition. Furthermore, Robert Miewald, writing from the perspective of public administration, and acknowledging Simon's influence on decision-making theory, considered that the revolution he wrought did not seem such a big deal since decision-making is a human function almost as natural as breathing. In his eyes, Simon was only updating Weber's bureaucratic model as a structure for denying the irrationality of life: decision theory was the heir to all the traditions of rationalistic approaches to administration (Miewald 1978: 168).

But it is not just among Simon's critics that reservations about our current thinking about decision-making in organisations has arisen. For example, work being done in the field of artificial intelligence has forced philosophers to try and clarify the notion. In general, it is recognised that it is difficult to give an account of how we reach decisions. What we can safely assert is that decisions are not arbitrary and that, in deciding what to do, we are autonomous agents. Lucas (1976: 14), for example, has pointed out that there is a tension between these two truths and that thinkers have often been so much at pains to emphasise one that they have been led to ignore or even deny the other. David Pears (1968: 98) has observed that deciding and acting may be almost simultaneous, and even when they are not, deciding need not be a definite event.

There has also been the quite different charge that such a model is all-inclusive, in particular, collapsing the distinction between decisions made on the basis of factual evidence and decisions made on the basis of evaluative premises. This confusion of logics is observed by Oldenquist (1967: 98): decisions that something is the case are either true or false but decisions to do something are neither true nor false. Rescher, (1969) by expounding upon the situational logic of evaluative decision-making, further underlined the over-general use of the term, and demonstrated how the rationalistic model is inappropriate to the context of practical decision-making. Practical reasoning, for him, has to do with rational deliberation regarding the 'things to be done' by us or others in the circumstances in which we find ourselves. Where a situation arises which demands a comparative assessment of alternative courses of action, then there has to be a recourse to values as the requisite means for affecting the necessary choice among mutually incompatible alternatives. Values are key to arbitration (Rescher 1969: 48).

The implications of these dangers – a misplaced confidence amongst powerfully placed decision-makers and decision-brokers as to the generic suitability of a prospective, rationalistic method of choice, led by experts claiming privileged and exclusive knowledge mandates – is well expressed by Miewald (1978: 174). To him, the main danger was the assurance from otherwise intelligent men and women that they are not in fact impinging upon the political process. There would be only one standard of truth. Analysis would be value-free. And decision-takers would use the approved methods for organising information to make better decisions.

Now all of us want better allocative decisions. But, to Miewald, there are countless definitions of these and they cannot be settled within the confines of contemporary decision theory. The insidious dangers of a particular rationalistic methodology do not, however, rule out the value of a more general conception of rationality as an aid to the decision-making process. Lucas (1976: 19) quite reasonably, pointed out that there is no method of always reaching right decisions or avoiding wrong ones, but we can reason about them and check one another's reasoning. In other words, the rejection of a particular rationalistic method does not also involve the rejection of a more general intellectual process of rational reflection as a means of improving decisions. In this more modest sense, the rational method involves asking the right sorts of retrospective questions in order to render accessible and to be able to subject to informed evaluation, the contextual basis of past decisions, and then attempting to feed the results of this process of reflection into the particular context of future decisions.

THE RELEVANCE OF CULTURE

Let us turn now to a consideration of culture. What are novels and short stories, films and plays supposed to do? How, if at all, do they help us with our management and decision-making? To be useful for our purposes, first of all, these novels, short stories, plays, films and the like must all have a specific shape and structure. As Tolstoy put it,

The most important thing in a work of art is that it should have a kind of focus, i.e. there should be some place where all the rays meet or from where they issue. And this focus must not be able to be completely explained in words. This indeed is one of the significant facts about a true work of art – that its content in its entirety can be expressed only by itself.

(Tolstoy 1948: 147)

Art, unlike life, has shape, a boundary line which encloses what is being expressed. Art, in other words, is a lot tidier than life. One can grasp it for it is there to be grasped. Conrad (1984: 107) said that the form of imagined life in a novel can be 'clearer than reality' and it can 'put to shame the pride of documentary history'. This is true in the contrast between the contingency of life and the order of art. In real life events are fragmentary and what we come to know of them is often disjointed. It is we who have to make sense of them. A novel or short story, as we have pointed out, is a construction designed to say something. By shaping what is shapeless in real life, the novelist and the film director make us see things in a new light and with more clarity.

Secondly, not only must these artefacts have shape and structure, they must also be 'saying something' worth listening to. As Thomas Hardy noted,

a story *must* be striking enough to be worth telling. Therein lies the problem – to reconcile the average with that uncommonness which alone makes it natural that a tale or experience would dwell in the memory and induce repetition.

(Hardy 1948: 152)

Camus said that Dostoevsky has revealed to him 'la nature humaine'. Nietzsche said that Dostoevsky was the only psychologist from whom he had anything to learn about the psychology of the criminal, the slave mentality and the nature of resentment (Wellek 1962: 74). In the words of George Eliot:

[M]y strongest effort is . . . to give a faithful account of men and things as they mirrored themselves in my mind. The mirror is doubtless defective; the outlines will sometimes be disturbed, the reflection faint or confused; but I feel as much bound to tell you as precisely as I can what that reflection is, as if I were in the witness-box narrating my experience on oath.

(Eliot 1948: 239)

That fictional literature is a reliable source of knowledge about the world has long been held as a good reason for reading it. David Novitz, for example, has recently argued that the beliefs which people acquire about the fictional world presented to them in literature include both descriptive beliefs (that pride breeds self-deception as suggested in the world of Jane Austen's *Emma*) and empathic beliefs (what it is like to be in Anna Karenina's desperate situation). Novitz contends that, when some of these beliefs strike the reader as doubtful, he or she tests these beliefs by tentatively projecting them on to the real world. If the beliefs enable the reader 'to negotiate the world more successfully', then he or she can properly be said to have acquired knowledge from a source in fiction (Novitz 1988: 132).

It is a fact of life that we get 'caught up' in films, plays, novels, short stories and the like. All these artefacts are made by human beings. They create self-contained worlds into which we are invited to enter and make-believe. They are worlds of the imagination which we enter through our own imagination. It is in the world of the imagination that we are afraid of King Kong, the devil in Quatermass's pit, or the gunfighter Wilson in Shane. In Mary Mothersill's phrase, 'the muzzles of the battleship *Potemkin* are positively menacing' (Mothersill 1984: 52). It is a different world from that of our knowledge which tells us we are at the cinema or watching television or reading a book. We, in Kendall Walton's phrase, 'play along with fictions' (Walton 1979: 206–7). It is this make-believe character of art which, as Dilman (1984: 107) put it, 'we can respond to it without the fear that we might have to follow our responses through'. We bleed but we are not injured.

Novels, stories, films, and other artefacts of human creativity provide an important adjunct to overly rational evaluations of human behaviour. Creative works have a definable shape and structure. They 'say something' about the human condition. And they demand a particular form of perception. But it is not the job of art to reveal any characteristics of things at all – it would then compete ineffectually with science and, apparently, decision-making – but rather to do something valuable to the psyche of the person experiencing art.

A BRIEF ACCOUNT OF A CASE STUDY

How were these thoughts about the utility and desired effect of art employed in the management training sessions? First of all, the students who have been practising managers in different kinds of industrial organisations, in educational organisations and in police forces were invited to see a film or read a story. The choice of film or story was dictated by the themes to be raised in subsequent discussions. Secondly, the issues raised by the films and stories were explored in small groups, the largest consisting of eighteen persons. The stories were chosen to dramatise and localise fundamental existential dilemmas. They depicted situations and people, and characterised these situations with forms of understanding and action. The texts, as representations of troublesome aspects of human existence, demanded a critical engagement and usually evoked unexpected emotional responses. Thirdly, the texts became a means of accessing those poorly understood, frequently misunderstood, sub-texts – our own lives. Reading the texts compelled us to re-read – and re-evaluate – those sub-texts.

We grapple with the author's or director's construct on the basis of a certain experience and our own understanding. Because we perceive imperfectly, we are bound to a finite point of view and the gap between this point of view and our fullest capacity to understand – and to act on that understanding – can be closed in imagination. If it cannot be closed, the nature of the gap can be investigated. The best fiction invites us to consider and reconsider, explore and test our current attitudes and beliefs. Reading and viewing, in a supportive group setting, become an exploration of resonance between literary and cinematic themes and personal experiences. An opportunity is offered for recuperation and revision of a fragile sense of meaning and personal worth. In one session, for example, a senior teacher suggested that he might fit the role of Big Nurse in *One Flew Over The Cuckoo's Nest*.

As a consequence of aesthetic interpretation, respect can be rebestowed on a sense of self which locates the possibility of personal growth in a restricted but revisable point of view. The whole show gives priority to the formation of a personal viewpoint and the cultivation of a sympathetic understanding of alternative points of view. The formula for the programme alludes to a search for creativity in organisational settings and the recovery of an imaginative dimension of thinking and living. The search is delicately balanced. 'If people talk too much about their lives', writes Touster of Brandeis University, 'we lose the meaning that literature can give to life. If they talk too much about the meaning of the literature, they lose the life of the experience' (Touster 1987: 3).

There is, of course, a long tradition of this method of exploration in learning. In a quite different context, Peter Winch makes an intriguing point about Jesus Christ's response to the abstract questions, what shall I do to inherit eternal life? Who is my neighbour? Jesus, he italicises, *tells a story*. Moreover, Jesus does not tell the lawyer which of those who encountered the wounded traveller was his neighbour.

He asks him. The suggestion is that each of us has within him or herself the resources for answering the question (Winch 1987: 156–7).

One time, with a group of senior educationalists, we read, as a group, Tolstoy's story, *The Death of Ivan Ilyich*. We began the discussion with the question, why does the story begin with an affirmation of the recent demise of its eponymous hero? Someone wanted to assess the meaning and quality of Ivan Ilyich's life in the light of his inexorable mortality. Participants found it difficult not to accept the representativeness of Ivan Ilyich, or to move towards identification with him on the grounds of his emphatic mortality. Or, alternatively, we could ask, what kind of a man had Ivan Ilyich been? Was he likeable? But what about his ambition? Tolstoy tells us he was 'a capable, cheerful, good-natured and social fellow' but did his appetite for status and power overshadow the subsequent assessment of his professional conduct and of the quality of his life? Was he not really self-centred? Corrupt in discharging his official duties and public responsibilities? And what would we make of Tolstoy's claim that 'the story of Ivan Ilyich's life was of the simplest, most ordinary and therefore most terrible'? Was this simply an expression of Tolstoy's own intense and extreme puritanism? Was Tolstoy not simply giving vent to his own moral prejudices and naive religious ideology through some parable which denigrated the bureaucrat, Ivan Ilyich, and idolised the peasant, Gerassim? By degrees, this interpretation was supplanted by another. Ivan Ilyich's life has been 'simple, ordinary and therefore terrible' because he had failed in his private life (most obviously in his marriage) and in his professional life to make himself available to others. He derived pleasure in his private life from his accumulated possessions. He drew pleasure in his official capacity from a pusillanimous withholding of the power to punish. In both spheres of his life, Ivan Ilyich had denied his common humanity. Tolstoy's parable stressed that the bureaucrat had suppressed the evidence of his own humanity while the peasant embraced his own mortality and the suffering of his fellows.

Then the discussion came to a climax with regard to the notion of professional detachment. Like an uninvited ghost, professional ethics were on the agenda. The demeanour and attitudes of Ivan Ilyich's doctors dramatised the chasm that can open up between professional values and a humanitarian ethic. The doctors treated organic disease, not suffering. They attended patients, not human beings. They fostered their reputations as diagnosticians; they refined their knowledge of physiological pathologies; they congratulated themselves on their dispassionate bedside manners; and they abandoned the dying man to his fate. Had the doctors and Ivan Ilyich fallen victim to some generic professional disease? Was this why Tolstoy made Gerassim the custodian of a more spontaneous and generous response to misfortune? The discussion shifted now to the question, would businessmen recognise the symptoms of this disease? Was there a place for professional detachment? And so the discussion went on. Some themes were touched on but underdeveloped – the abuse of power and betrayal of responsibility as career options in large-scale organisations, the segregation of public and private domains as an institutional sickness, the divergence between professional ethics and any guarantee of humane action as a fundamental contemporary problem.

For most of us, we were witnessing an unfamiliar pedagogy. Traditional teaching methods were being overhauled. Managers' personal problems engendered by organisational milieux were being looked at quite afresh. Their organisational or vocational needs were being put to one side. But underlying the customised, client-centred and low-key learning programme was a coherent and robust liberal-progressive philosophy of education. This philosophical undercurrent made its mark in various ways. There was an avoidance of formality in address and a disavowal of authority in the pedagogic style. The presentation of material was paced by the group as a whole, although, by default, as a result sometimes of diffidence in the learning group, the experts were frequently required to take the initiative. Moreover, the presentation did not have a schematic core; the leaders (instructors, teachers?) neither offered typologies and primary conceptual categories nor did they labour to inculcate an analytical method.

This further departure from standard educational practice reflected, in turn, a principled commitment not to define learning in terms of reparation of cognitive deficits. By the same token, the method had broken loose of the rampant delusion that knowledge is 'out there', waiting to be harvested and ingested or annexed and colonised. This alternative pedagogy was adapted to the supposition that the key element in education is the transformation of the learner. The seminar steered clear of certainties and provided no hard data. Spontaneity was prized above deliberation, and disconcerting insights were valued over intellectual commentary. At one extreme, the programme whose principle was self-development was geared to promote imagination;

at the other extreme, the emphasis was on participation. What was being sought were collectively mediated and individually focussed remedies for collectively orchestrated and individually expressed pathologies of organisational life – for the numbing effects of routinisation and standardisation in organisational milieux and for the personal isolation caused by the fragmentation of organisational responsibilities. Wouldn't you think that, given such a programme, dedicated to the development of a self-awareness informed by factors typically excluded from and dissonant with the cultural environment within which organisational choices are made, decision-making would improve?

CONCLUSIONS

To try and conclude: I think my chapter, at best, belongs to what Peter Strawson (1970: 31) called the species 'loosely ruminative' and 'comparative-historical' rather than to the species 'strictly argumentative' or 'systematic analytical'. First of all, I am registering an uneasiness about the use of the words 'decision' and 'decision-making' as corner-stones in helping us to understand the processes of management and the behaviour of managers. When Simon asked himself what part does decision-making play in managing, he maintained that he found it convenient to take mild liberties with the English language by using 'decision-making' as though it were synonymous with 'managing' (Simon 1965: 53). Now, of course, this is more than a mild liberty. It borders on downright highjacking. For a start, certainly the set of activities normally described as 'decision-making' would be far greater than the set of activities normally described as 'managing'. (And not only does 'decision-making' cover a great many human activities, there is also evidence that the notion can account for bits of the behaviour of many different kinds of animals, fish, baboons and apes (Blackmore and Greenfield 1987: 191–2, 399–400).[1]

But there seems to be a great deal of conceptual muddle going on. And not just in the distilled textbooks on organizational behaviour, which I picked on, partly because they are appearing, apparently unchecked, in large numbers, and partly because they are solidfying a discipline into something quite unreal. But there is apparent confusion elsewhere (see, for example, Lindley 1971:v, 1, 3, 13). We're in pretty slippery conceptual country alright. Adjectives and adverbs like 'main', 'essentially', 'sensibly', 'coherent', 'simpler', 'basic' carry a persuasive – as against a descriptive –

power. And the notion of logical processes that need to be used in arriving at a decision presupposed that this need can be identified. By whom? Everyone, obviously, who wants 'to reach a decision sensibly'. And what is the logical status of these 'logical processes' – are they somehow logically necessary or are they contingent? Are they guidelines or basic structures or what? And what about all these 'sensible' decisions? Who owns them? As Miewald (1978: 22) put it about the American decision-making over the Vietnam War, if George Washington had been a system analyst, he might have concluded that he was finished at Valley Forge. The Vietcong, in Miewald's view, persevered the same way the American rebels had.

So the load the notions of 'decision' and 'decision-making' have to bear (and the dangerous conceit with which organisational behaviourists and management theorists are prepared to accept this burden on behalf of their favoured concepts, in turn arrogating to themselves an exclusive explanatory and political prerogative in the relevant field) is too heavy. [Compare, at the time of writing this chapter (July 1989), Castello cigar's advertisement announcing 'there's no decision that couldn't wait half an hour' with the notion in Giovannitti and Freed's (1967) *The Decision to Drop the Bomb* and Ian Kennedy's (1988) *What is a Medical Decision?*, and all of these with General Stroop's decision to destroy the entire Jewish area in Warsaw (Shirer 1972: 977). Are all these 'decisions' the same? Are they all, as Von Wright (1983: 7) put it, normally the outcome of deliberation?]

Secondly, I am recommending an alternative route for decision-making, signposted in the earlier part where Miewald and Lucas are referenced. It is another world of discourse captured in David Wiggins' reflections on choice and deliberation in Aristotle. In a bureaucracy, he rightly observes, the acute theoretical and practical problem is to make room for some such stepping back, and for the constant remaking and re-evaluation of concerns (Wiggins 1980: 233–4).

Now, thirdly, to make such room, I am recommending the engagement of managers and administrators and what-you-will in some imaginative exercises, most immediately provided by novels and films, short stories and plays, but also, of course, provided by the more formal deliberations of philosophising. In practical terms, business schools should establish units or centres or departments primarily concerned with such activities. [They can even, if you wish, be given appropriate 'sexy' titles of Centres of Imaginative

Excellence, Departments of Postmodernist Decision-Making, and
Chairs in Organizational Resolutions.] As Passmore recently pointed
out:

> Careful reading, the critical examination of texts, close reasoning
> are inherent in the humanities, not just possible outcomes of
> studying them. It would be monstrous to say that the whole
> point of studying history or literature or philosophy is to be
> trained in such skills. But it is not merely philistine to see in the
> possession of them the possibility of exhibiting a different kind of
> good citizenship, peculiar to democratic societies.
>
> (Passmore 1989: 567)

Business schools, then, should be advocating the claims of literature and films as ideal vehicles for furthering our understanding of
ourselves and the situations we are, or may be, facing as organisational participants. If they are to be modelled on something more
substantial than driving schools for progress chasers, then it is in
the direction of culture, of the humanities, of philosophy that they
should be going.

I think I am also indirectly questioning the whole so-called discipline of organisational behaviour which is now generally accepted
as a core discipline in business schools. As I said in my introductory remarks, the people who occupy the pages of the textbooks in organisational behaviour rarely, if ever, resemble the
human beings one encounters in tutorials or at senate meetings
or at football games or jazz concerts. At the moment, decision-
making is one topic within the discipline which shows some of the
cracks. Motivation is another. But that's perhaps another story
and probably, unfortunately, another paper. In the meantime, a
better approach would be to return to Hume and retitle these
various departments of human resource management or organisational behaviour or whatever is the current fashion and call
them departments of moral sciences. Then we would be getting
somewhere.

NOTE

1 See, for example, the comment: 'The complexity of decision-making in
  the societies of baboons and apes may mark a step nearer the human
  condition. Decisions regarding choice in the formation of alliances
  (which have considerable effects on individuals' formation in repro-
  duction) depend on assessments of relations between two other animals
  (say) and each of these with self. Such a calculus must involve some

conceptualisation, at least implicit, of self's involvement in the process' (Blackmore and Greenfield 1987: 191–2, 399–400).

REFERENCES

Blackmore, Colin and Greenfield, Susan (eds) (1987) *Mindwaves*, Oxford, Blackwell.
Borge, Jorge Luis (1979) quoted by Kendall L. Walton, 'Fearing Fictions', in David L. Boyer, Patrick Grim and John T. Sanders (eds) *The Philosopher's Annual*, Oxford, Blackwell.
Bradley, David and Wilkie, Roy (1974) The Concept of Organization, Glasgow, Blackie.
Brandeis University (1986) *Humanities and the Professions Program*: A six year report, 1980–1986.
Brown, Warren B. and Moberg, Dennis J. (1980) *Organization Theory and Management*, New York, John Wiley & Sons.
Conrad, Joseph (1984) quoted by Ilham Dilman, 'Dostoyevsky: psychology and the novelist', in A. Phillips Griffiths (ed.) *Philosophy and Literature*, Royal Institute of Philosophy Lecture Series 16, Cambridge, Cambridge University Press.
Dessler, Gary (1976) *Organization and Management*, Englewood Cliffs, NJ, Prentice-Hall.
Dilman, Ilham (1984) 'Dostoyevsky: psychology and the novelist', in A. Phillips Griffiths (ed.) *Philosophy and Literature*, Royal Institute of Philosophy Lecture Series 16, Cambridge, Cambridge University Press.
Eliot, George (1948) quoted in *Writers on Writing*, selected and introduced by Walter Allen, London, Phoenix House.
George, Claude Jr. (1964) *Management in Industry*, Englewood Cliffs, NJ, Prentice-Hall.
Glueck, William F. (1977) *Management*, Hinsdale, IL, Dryden Press.
Giovannitti, L. and Freed, F. (1967) *The Decision to Drop the Bomb*, London, Methuen.
Hardy, Thomas (1948) quoted in *Writers on Writing*, selected and introduced by Walter Allen, London, Phoenix House.
Harrison, Frank (1987) *The Managerial Decision-Making Process*, Boston, Houghton-Mifflin.
Heath, A. F. (1976) 'Decision making and transactional theory', in *Transaction and Meaning*, Institute for the Study of Human Issues.
Huxley, Aldous (1963) *Literature and Science*, London, Chatto & Windus.
Kaufman, Arnold (1968) *The Science of Decision-Making*, London, Weidenfeld & Nicolson.
Kennedy, Ian (1988) 'What is a medical decision?', in *Treat Me Right*, Oxford, Clarendon Press.
Kuhn, Thomas S. (1970) *The Structure of Scientific Revolutions*, 2nd edn, Chicago, University of Chicago Press.
Lindley, Dennis (1971) *Making Decisions*, New York, John Wiley & Sons.
Lucas, J. R. (1976) *Democracy and Participation*, Harmondsworth, Penguin Books.
Meyer, John W. and Scott, W. Richard (1983) *Organizational Environments*, London, Sage.

Michael, Stephen R. and Jones, Halsey R. (1973) *Organizational Management: Concepts and Practice*, New York, Intext Educational.

Miewald, Robert D. (1978) *Public Administration*, New York, McGraw-Hill.

Miner, John B. (1985) *The Practice of Management*, Toronto, Charles E. Merrill.

Mintzberg, Henry (1977) 'Review', *Administrative Science Quarterly* 22 (2), 350.

Moore, P. G. and Thomas, H. (1976) *The Anatomy of Decisions*, Harmondsworth, Penguin.

Mothersill, Mary (1984) *Beauty Restored*, Oxford, Clarendon Press.

Novitz, David (1988) *Knowledge, Fiction and Imagination*, Philadelphia, Temple University Press.

Oldenquist, Andrew (1967) 'Choosing, Deciding, and Doing', in Paul Edwards (ed.) *The Encyclopaedia of Philosophy*, Vol. 2, London, Macmillan.

Passmore, John (1989) *The Times Literary Supplement*, 26 May–1 June.

Pears, David (1968) 'Predicting and Deciding', in P. F. Strawson (ed.) *Studies in the Philosophy of Thought and Action*, Oxford, Oxford University Press.

Rescher, Andrew (1969) *Introduction to Value Theory*, Englewood Cliffs, NJ, Prentice-Hall.

Scott, W. G. (1971) 'Decision Concepts', in F. G. Castles, D. J. Murphy and D. C. Potter (eds) *Decisions, Organizations and Society*, Harmondsworth, Penguin.

Shirer, William L. (1972) *The Rise and Fall of the Third Reich*, London, Book Club Associates.

Simon, Herbert (1965) *The Shape of Automation*, New York, Harper & Row.

Simon, Herbert A. (1977) *The New Science of Management Decision*, Englewood Cliffs, NJ, Prentice-Hall.

Strawson, P. F. (1970) 'Imagination and Perception', in Lawrence Foster and J. W. Swanson (eds) *Experience and Theory*, London, Duckworth.

Tolstoy, Leo (1948) quoted in *Writers on Writing*, selected and introduced by Walter Allen, London, Phoenix House.

Touster, Saul (1987) *The Chronicle of Higher Learning*, 28 January.

Vecchio, Robert P. (1988) *Organizational Behaviour*, Hinsdale, IL, Dryden Press.

Von Wright, Georg Henrik (1983) *Practical Reason*, Oxford, Blackwell.

Walton, Kendall L. (1979) 'Fearing Fictions', in David L. Boyer, Patrick Grim and John T. Sanders (eds) *The Philosopher's Annual*, Oxford, Blackwell.

Weinshall, Theodore D. and Raveh, Yael-Anna (1983) *Managing Growing Organizations*, New York, John Wiley & Sons.

Wellek, Rene (1962) *Dostoevsky*, Englewood Cliffs, NJ, Prentice-Hall.

Wiggins, David (1980) 'Deliberation and practical reason', in Amelia Oksenberg Rorty (ed.) *Essays on Aristotle's Ethics*, Berkeley, California, University of California Press.

Winch, Peter (1987) *Trying to Make Sense*, Oxford, Blackwell.

Wisdom, John (1953) *Philosophy and Psychoanalysis*, Oxford, Blackwell.

Index